M000279065

（英文版）日本語で読もう エッセイ編

Read Real Japanese Essays
Contemporary Writings by Popular Authors

2008 年 2 月　第 1 刷発行
2009 年 5 月　第 3 刷発行

編　者　ジャネット・アシュビー
朗　読　松永玲子

発行者　富田 充

発行所　講談社インターナショナル株式会社
　　　　〒112-8652　東京都文京区音羽 1-17-14
　　　　電話　03-3944-6493（編集部）
　　　　　　　03-3944-6492（営業部・業務部）
　　　　ホームページ　www.kodansha-intl.com

印刷・製本所　大日本印刷株式会社

Japanese-English Dictionary

Essays

あ

あ　oh

ああ　oh; well

あい【愛】love　—愛する to love

あいさつ【挨拶】greeting

あいじん【愛人】lover

あいそ【愛想】amiability　—愛想笑い diplomatic smile

あいだ【間】① while…; during…, over … ② among… —AとBとの間に between A and B

あいちゃく【愛着】attachment; love

あいつ　that guy [fellow]

あいて【相手】the other party

アイデンティティー　identity

あいま【合間】interval　—AとBの合間に between A and B

あいまい（な）【曖昧（な）】obscure, vague —曖昧さ ambiguity, vagueness

アイライン　—アイラインを引く to apply eyeliner

あう【遭う】to experience, to have

あおぐ【仰ぐ】to look up, to raise one's eyes

あおじろい【青白い】pale

あかい【赤い】red

あかじ【赤字】—赤字で in red

あかてん【赤点】failing grade

あがる【上がる】to go up

あきらめる【諦める】to give up; to abandon　—あきらめた resigned

あくしつ（な）【悪質（な）】wicked, malicious

あくしゅみ【悪趣味】bad taste　—悪趣味である to be in bad taste

あくまで　only

あげる【挙げる】① to name, to mention ② ➢ れい（例）

あこがれ【憧れ】aspiration; longing

あこがれる【憧れる】to aspire; to long [thirst] for

あさ【朝】morning

あざやか（な）【鮮やか（な）】brilliant; vivid　—鮮やかに vividly

あじ【味】taste, flavor　—味が薄い bland; to have a weak flavor

あしもと【足元】—足元で [に] at one's feet

あじわう【味わう】to experience, to taste

あせ【汗】sweat

あたいする【値する】to deserve, to be worthy of

あたま【頭】head; brain　—頭にくる to get angry　—頭の固い thickskulled, rigid in one's thinking　—頭のいい smart; sharp

あたらしい【新しい】new; another

あたりまえ（の）【当たり前（の）】① ordinary, usual, common ② natural

あたる【当たる】to be tantamount (to) ➢ しつれい（失礼）

あちこち　—あちこちで・あちこちに here and there; all over (the place)

あっ　oh, ah

あっというま（に）【あっという間（に）】in an instant, instantly

アップ　up

あつまり【集まり】gathering, party

あと【後】—…の後（に）after　—後は after that

アナーキー　anarchy　—アナーキーな anarchist(ic)　—アナーキーである to be an anarchist

アナーキスト　anarchist

あなた　—あなたは・あなたが you　—あなたの your　—あなたに・あなたを you

あの　that

あの（う）　um, uh

あのとき【あの時】that time

5

あ

か

さ

た

な

は

ま

や

ら

わ

あのように【あの様に】like that

アハハハハ ha-ha-ha

アピール appeal　—アピールする to appeal; to tout the fact that...

あぶらあせ【脂汗】greasy sweat　—脂汗を流す to break out in a greasy sweat

あふれる【溢れる】—...であふれている to be filled with..., to be full of...

あまり【余り】—あまり...ない not very..., not much

あまりに(も)【余りに(も)】very, so; too...　—あまりに(も)...すぎて so...that

あまりの【余りの】too much, excessive

アメリカ America　—アメリカ人 American　—アメリカ文学 American literature

あら oh

あらげる【荒げる】to raise (one's voice)

あらゆる all (sorts of); every (possible)...

あらわす【表(わ)す】to express　—表される to be expressed

あらわれでる【表(わ)れ出る】to come [show] up

あらわれる【表(わ)れる・現(わ)れる】① to appear, to show ② to be disclosed, to be revealed　—効果が現れる to take effect, to (start to) work

ありうる【有り得る】possible; it can [could] be...

ありとあらゆる every (single)...

ある¹【或る】a..., a certain...

ある²【有る】① to be; there is [are]... ② to have

あるいは【或いは】or

あるがまま【有るが儘】as it is, the way it is

あるく【歩く】to walk, to come [go] on foot

あるひ【或る日】one day

あれ　—あれは that

あれだけ that [so] much; like that

あれほうだい(の)【荒れ放題(の)】to be left unattended

あれほど(の)【あれ程(の)】like that　—あれほどの量[数]の that much [many]

あわせる【合わせる】① to put...together ② to adjust, to go along with

あんい(な)【安易(な)】easy

アンガールズ the Ungirls (a comedy duo)

あんがい【案外】contrary to one's expectation

あんじ【暗示】suggestion　—暗示する to suggest

あんない【案内】guidance, directions; knowledge　—案内する to lead... (to a place)　—御案内の通り as you know

あんないず【案内図】guide map

い

いい【良い・好い】① good, nice ➤ かんじ(感じ), みなり(身なり) ② wealthy ③ favorable ④ [as a response] Okay, All right. ⑤ ➤ おとな(大人)　—いいほうに in a favorable way

いいかげん(な)【いい加減(な)】irresponsible

いいかた【言い方】way of saying; expression　—言い方を変えれば to put it differently; in other words

いいよう【言い様】way of saying [speaking]　—...としか言いようのない there's no other way to put it but...

いう【言う】to say, to tell ➤ でたらめ(出鱈目), もんく(文句)　—言われる to be said

いうまでもなく【言うまでもなく】needless to say

いえ【家】house

いえる【言える】it can [could] be said
　that...

−いか【−以下】below

いがい（な）【意外（な）】unexpected

−いがい（の）【−以外（の）】except (for),
　but, other than...

いかにも【如何にも】quite; certainly

いかん¹【遺憾】—遺憾なく fully, satisfac-
　torily; to the fullest

いかん²【如何】—...の如何にかかわらず
　irrespective [regardless] of...

いきた【生きた】living

いきつづける【生き続ける】to live on

いきどおる【憤る】to be indignant (at)

いきる【生きる】① to live; to be alive ②
　to earn one's living

いく【行く】① to go; to visit ② ➤ なっ
　とく（納得）、よめ（嫁）

いくつか【幾つか】some, a few, several

いくらでも【幾らでも】as many [much]
　as one likes; however much...

イケメン　good-looking [handsome]
　man　—イケメンの good-looking,
　handsome

いけん【意見】opinion; comment

イコール　to mean...; to be equal to...

いごこち【居心地】—居心地悪く un-
　comfortably

いささか　rather

いじいじ　—いじいじする to be hesitant,
　to hesitate to do

いしづくり【石造り】—石造りの stone-
　built

−いじょう【−以上】more than...

いぜん【以前】once; before　—以前の
　previous　—以前よりも... ...than be-
　fore　—...以前に before...

いそがしい【忙しい】busy　—忙しく

busily

いそぐ【急ぐ】to hurry

いたい【痛い】painful

いだい（な）【偉大（な）】great

いたいたしい【痛々しい】pathetic, shame-
　ful; embarrassing

いだく【抱く】to have (in mind)

−いただく【−頂く】[humble way of say-
　ing that one receives a favor from
　someone of higher status than one-
　self]　—...していただきたい I'd like you
　to...

いちおう【一応】—一応の ...of sorts;
　...to a certain extent

いちど【一度】—一度（は）once, one time
　—一度として...ない never

いちばん【一番】(the) most

いつか【何時か】someday, sometime

いっかしょ【一箇所】one spot [place]

いっき（に）【一気（に）】at a burst

いっけん【一見】seemingly, apparently

いっこうに【一向に】—一向に ...ない not
　...at all

いっこく【一刻】—一刻も早く as soon as
　possible

いつごろ【何時頃】when

いっさい【一切】—一切...ない not...at
　all

いっしゅ【一種】—一種の a kind of

いっしゅん【一瞬】(for) a moment

いっしょ（に）【一緒（に）】together　—
　...と一緒に together with...

いっしょうけんめい【一生懸命】hard; with
　great effort

いっせだい【一世代】one generation

いったい¹【一体】(what / how / who) on
　earth

いったい²【一帯】area, district

いつだって【何時だって】always

あ

か

さ

た

な

は

ま

や

ら

わ

いったりきたり【行ったり来たり】―行ったり来たりする to go back and forth

いっち【一致】unification

いっつう【一通】a letter

いってん【一点】one point

いっぱん(に)【一般(に)】generally, in general

いっぴん¹【一品】one dish

いっぴん²【逸品】masterpiece

いっぽ【一歩】a step　一一歩一歩 step by step

いっぽう【一方】on the other hand

いっぽん【一本】one (line)

いつまで【何時迄】―いつまでたっても…ない never

いつも　always

いどう【移動】move ―移動する to move

いなかざむらい【田舎侍】rustic samurai

イベント　event

いま【今】now; nowadays　一今の of today　一今と[に]なって now　一今現在 now in the present　一今に始まったことではない This is nothing new.

いまだに【未だに】still

いまでも【今でも】even now, still

いみ【意味】meaning; implication　一意味する to mean

いみあい【意味合い】sense, meaning; connotation

いみづけ【意味付け】attaching significance (to something)

イメージ　image

いや【否】no

いや(な)【嫌(な)】disagreeable, disgusting, nasty　一嫌な気分で in a bad mood

いやがる【嫌がる】to be reluctant (to do)　一嫌がって reluctantly, unwillingly

いやけ【嫌気】―嫌気がさす to get tired of; to be fed up

イヤホン　earphone(s)

いよう(な)【異様(な)】strange, weird

いる¹【入る】＞き(気)

いる²【居る】① to be, to exist ② there is [are]…

いれる【入れる】＞て(手)

いろいろ【色々】in many ways　一いろいろな・いろいろの various

いろけ【色気】sex appeal; allure, sexiness

いろんな　[colloquial form of いろいろな] various

いわば【言わば】so to speak

インターネット　the Internet

インタビュー　interview　一インタビューする to interview

インパクト　impact

う

ウインク　wink ―ウインクする to wink

ウェブサイト　Web site

うかがいしる【窺い知る】to figure out; to get an idea of…

うかがえる【窺える】can be seen; to be evident

うかびあがる【浮(か)び上(が)る】to come up, to emerge

うかぶ【浮かぶ】to come up

うかべる【浮かべる】to have (a smile) on one's face　一…を浮かべて with (a smile) on one's face

うけいれる【受け容れる】to accept

うける【受ける】to suffer

うさん(な)【胡散(な)】dubious　一胡散らしさ dubiousness

うしろ【後ろ】―後ろから (from) behind

うすい【薄い】weak (describing flavor)

うそ【嘘】lie, fib; falsity　一嘘をつく to lie, to tell a lie

うた【歌】song

うたう【歌う】to sing

うたがう【疑う】to suspect; to doubt —疑わせる to make (a person) suspect

うたれる【打たれる】➤ たき（滝）

うち —…するうち as one does…

うちあわせ【打ち合わせ】meeting

うちまくる【打ちまくる】to bang away

うつ【打つ】① to strike ② ➤ タイプライター —…に打たれる to be struck by…

うつくしい【美しい】beautiful

うつくしさ【美しさ】beauty

うつりかわる【移り変わる】to change; to undergo changes

うで【腕】arm —腕によりをかける to put all one's skills into…

うまれかわる【生まれ変わる】to be born again, to be reborn

うまれる【生まれる】① to be born ② to happen, to occur

うみだす【生み出す】to create; to make happen

うようよ —うようよしている to be swarming with

うら【裏】back; reverse (side) —裏に in the back —…の裏に behind…

うらむ【恨む】to think ill of (a person), to bear a grudge (against a person)

うるさい noisy; annoying

うれしい【嬉しい】happy

うろうろ —うろうろする to walk [wander] around

うんざり —うんざりする to get tired of; to be sick of

うんちく【蘊蓄】a fount of knowledge

うんと much, a lot

うんどう【運動】movement

え

えいえん【永遠】eternity —永遠に forever

えいが【映画】movie

えいご【英語】English (language)

えいこく【英国】the U.K., Britain

えいやく【英訳】translation into English —英訳する to translate…into English

えいよう【栄養】nutrition —栄養バランス nutritional balance

ええ [form of affirmative reply] yes

えがお【笑顔】smiling face; smile

えき【駅】station

エゴイスティック（な）egoistic

エネルギー energy

エピソード episode

えみ【笑み】smile —満面の笑みを湛えて with a big [broad] smile on one's face

えらい【偉い】important, big, great —偉そうに with an air of importance

えらびぬく【選び抜く】to choose carefully

えらぶ【選ぶ】to choose

える【得る】to get, to obtain

えん【円】yen

エンゲルけいすう【エンゲル係数】Engel's coefficient

えんしゅうりつ【円周率】pi, the circle ratio

えんじん【円陣】circle —円陣を組んで in a circle

えんぴつけずり【鉛筆削り】pencil sharpener

お

お-【御-】[prefix added for politeness or to show respect]

おいしい【美味しい】delicious; good

オイラー Euler —オイラーの公式 Euler's formula

あ
か
さ
た
な
は
ま
や
ら
わ

オイル　oil

おうへい（な）【横柄（な）】arrogant

おうらい【往来】―往来する to come and go

おえる【終える】to finish; to end [終える is generally a transitive verb, but it is used intransitively in「無常ということ」]

おおい【多い】many, a lot of

おおかた（の）【大方（の）】most

おおかみ【狼】wolf

おおきい・おおきな【大きい・大きな】big, large; great ―大きくなる to increase (in number)

おおく【多く】―多くの a lot of

おおけが【大怪我】serious injury ―大怪我をする to be seriously [gravely] injured

おおげさ（な）【大袈裟（な）】exaggerated ―大げさに with exaggeration

おおさ【多さ】plentifulness, extensiveness

おおぜい（の）【大勢（の）】a lot of, a large number of

おおにもつ【大荷物】a lot of stuff [baggage]

おおらか（に）【大らか（に）】broadmindedly, generously

おおわらい【大笑い】good [hearty] laugh, a roar of laughter ―大笑いする to have a good laugh, to laugh heartily

おかね【お金】＞かね（金）

おく¹【置く】to put, to place

おく²【奥】the depth(s), the back; the recesses

おくゆかしい【奥床しい】modest, reserved, restrained

おくる【送る】＞ねん（念）

おこす【起こす】＞けいさんまちがい（計算間違い）, めまい（眩暈）

おこなう【行う】to do; to hold (a ceremony)

おこる【怒る】to get angry [mad], to lose one's temper

おさない【幼い】young, small

おさめる【収める】to put...into; to enshrine

おしえる【教える】to teach

おじさん【小父さん】middle-aged man

おしつける【押し付ける】to impose

おしゃべり　chat, chitchat ―おしゃべり（を）する to chat, to chatter

おそらく（は）【恐らく（は）】probably, perhaps, maybe, likely

おそろしい【恐ろしい】fearful, scary

おちこむ【落ち込む】to get discouraged, to get depressed

おちゃ【お茶】＞ちゃ（茶）

おっしゃる【仰る】[honorific form of いう] to say

おと【音】sound　―音を出す to make a sound　―音を小さくする to turn the volume down

おとこ【男】man

おとこのこ【男の子】boy

おとな【大人】adult　―いい大人 a full-grown adult

おどろき【驚き】surprise

おなじ【同じ】[irregular adjective of neither the -i nor -na type] the same ―同じような similar, alike ―同じように likewise; in the same way ―...と同じ（ように）(just) like...

おねがいだから【お願いだから】for God's [goodness', heaven's] sake

おのおの【各々】each

おび【帯】wrapper band (of a book)

おぼえる【覚える】① to remember ② to learn, to memorize

おまえ【お前】 [second-person pronoun; used when addressing a friend or person of lower status] you

おまけに in addition

おもい【思い】 ① thought, feeling; thinking ② experience ―(...な) 思いをする ① to feel... ② to have a (good, bad, etc.) time [experience] ―思いを巡らす to think over ―思いも寄らない unexpected; inconceivable ―思いのほか unexpectedly

おもいきって【思い切って】 ―思い切って...する to gather the courage to do, to venture to do

おもいこむ【思い込む】 ① to be under the impression (that...) ② to assume

おもいだす【思い出す】 to remember, to recall, to recollect

おもいつく【思い付く】 to hit on; to think of, to come up with

おもいで【思い出】 memory

おもう【思う】 ① to think, to feel ② to regard (a person) as...

おもえる【思える】 to seem, to look, to appear

おもしろい【面白い】 interesting ―面白いことに interestingly enough

おもわしむる【思わしむる】 [same as 思わしめる, 思わせる; rather formal or old-fashioned] to make (a person) think

おもわず【思わず】 in spite of oneself; involuntarily

おもわれる【思われる】 to seem, to look, to appear

およがせる【泳がせる】 to let...wander

おりる【降りる】 to get off (a train)

おろか(な)【愚か(な)】 stupid, silly

-オロジスト -ologist

おわる【終(わ)る】 to finish, to end

-おん【-音】 the sound (of...)

おん-【御-】 [polite or honorific prefix; different form of お-]

オン・ザ・ロード *On the Road*

おんがく【音楽】 music

おんな【女】 woman

おんなだいがく【女大学】 *Onna-daigaku* (a book on etiquette for women in feudal Japan)

か

が but

-が though, although

ガーッ [harsh noise from a TV]

がい【害】 harm ―害のない harmless

かいぎゃく【諧謔】 wit, humor

かいけつ【解決】 solution

かいけつさく【解決策】 solution

がいこくご【外国語】 foreign language

がいこくさん(の)【外国産(の)】 foreign-made

がいこくじん【外国人】 people of other nationalities

かいこむ【買い込む】 to buy up (in large quantities)

かいさつぐち【改札口】 ticket gate

かいじょう【会場】 conference room; hall

がいねん【概念】 concept

かいもの【買いもの・買(い)物】 shopping

かう【買う】 to buy

ガウス Gauss

かえって【却って】 (all the) more

-がえり(に)【-帰り(に)】 on the [one's] way home from...

かえる【変える】 to change; to alter ➣ いいかた(言い方)

かお【顔】 ① face ② look, expression ③ aspect

かおく【家屋】 house

かかえる【抱える】to hold [carry]… (in one's arms) ―…を抱えて with…in one's hands [arms]

かかる ➤ コスト, じかん (時間)

かかわらず ➤ いかん² (如何)

かかわり【関わり】relation ―…に関わりのある related to…

かかわりかた【関わり方】relationship

かかわる【関わる】 to take part (in a movement)

かかん(に)【果敢(に)】bravely; with courage, courageously

かきて【書き手】writer

かぎらない【限らない】―…とは限らない not always, not necessarily

かぎり【限り】―…する限り as long as … ―…(し)ない限り unless…

かく¹【書く】to write ―書いてある to say, to read ―書くこと act of writing ―書く人 a person who writes

かく²【描く・書く】to draw

かく³【欠く】to lack, to want

かく−【各−】each… ➤ かくしゃ (各社)

かくう(の)【架空(の)】fictitious

がくえんさい【学園祭】school festival

かくご【覚悟】―覚悟する to get prepared, to prepare oneself

かくしゃ【各社】each company; various companies

がくしゃ【学者】scholar

かくしん【核心】point, core ―核心に触れる to get at the heart of…

かくす【隠す】to hide, to conceal ―隠された hidden

がくせい【学生】(college) student ―学生の町 college town

がくぜん【愕然】―愕然とする to be astonished [astounded]

かくも such

かくれる【隠れる】to hide ―隠れた hidden

がけ【崖】cliff

かける¹ ➤ うで (腕) ―時間をかける to take (the) time

かける²【欠ける】to lack; to want ―欠けている to be lacking [wanting]

かける³【掛ける・×】times; multiplied by

かさなる【重なる】to overlap

かし【歌詞】lyrics (of a song)

かじ【火事】fire ―火事になる to catch fire; to be burnt in a fire

かじる【齧る】to know a bit of (literature); to dip into

かじん【歌人】tanka poet

かず【数】number, figure

かぜ【風】wind ―風に乗って on the wind

かた【肩】shoulder

かたい【固い】hard, stiff ➤ あたま (頭)

かたがた【方々】[polite or honorific expression] people

カタカナ katakana; one of the two Japanese syllabaries

かたづける【片付ける】to dismiss; to do away with…

かたりかける【語りかける】to talk [speak] to (a person)

かたりくち【語り口】way of speaking

かたる【語る】to talk (about…)

かたわら【傍ら】side ―かたわらで by…, next to…

かち【価値】value

−がち【−勝ち】―…がちである to tend [be apt] to do

かちこち(に) stiffly

かちゅう【渦中】―…の渦中にある to be in the midst of…

かつ【且つ】besides, plus

がっかい【学会】academic society; academic conference

かっきてき(な)【画期的(な)】epoch-making, revolutionary

がっこう【学校】school

かつじ【活字】printed letters [words]

かつて【嘗て】previously; once

かつぼう【渇望】—渇望する to be eager [anxious] to do

かてい【過程】process

カテゴリー category

−かどうか if, whether

かなえられたいのり【かなえられた祈り】*Answered Prayers*

かなしい【悲しい・哀しい】sad

かなしみ【悲しみ・哀しみ】sadness

かなしむ【悲しむ・哀しむ】to lament (over)

かならず【必ず】always

かならずしも【必ずしも】—必ずしも…ない not always…, not necessarily…

かね【金】money

かねもち【金持ち】the rich, rich people

かのう(な)【可能(な)】possible

かのうせい【可能性】possibility

かのじょ【彼女】 —彼女は・彼女が she —彼女の her —彼女を[に] her

カポーティ Capote

かまわない【構わない】one doesn't care [mind]

がまん【我慢】—我慢する to stand, to bear

かみ【紙】paper

かみさま【神様】God

かみしめる【噛み締める】to ponder the meaning of

カメラ camera; video camera

−かもしれない may, might, could; it might be that…

−から ① from; since ② because, as, since

ガラスケース glass showcase

からだ【身体】body

かりに【仮に】—仮に…としても even if

かりる【借りる】to borrow

かるい【軽い】light ➤ き(気)

かれ【彼】 —彼は・彼が he —彼の his —彼に・彼を him

カレー curry; curry and rice

かれら【彼等】—彼らは・彼らが they —彼らの their —彼らに them

かわ【革】leather

−がわ【−側】side; part

かわいげ【可愛げ】amiability; the charm of innocence —可愛げがない to lack the charm of innocence

かわらない【変わらない】unchanged

かわらぬ【変わらぬ】➤ かわらない(変わらない)

かわり【変わり】change —変わりはない to remain unchanged

かわりつづける【変わり続ける】to keep on changing

かわりゆく【変わりゆく】changing —無常に変わりゆく ever-changing

かわる【変わる】to change —(ずっと)変わらず constantly, always

−かん【−感】sense, feeling ➤ しあわせ(幸せ)

かんがえ【考え】idea, thought

かんがえかた【考え方】concept, idea

かんがえだす【考え出す】to think up

かんがえなおす【考え直す】to rethink, to think over

かんがえる【考える】to think, to ponder —考えさせる to make (a person) think

かんかく【感覚】feeling

かんけい【関係】relation, relationship

—…に関係している to be related to…

かんこう【観光】 tourism; sightseeing —観光都市 tourist city, city of tourism

かんこうきゃく【観光客】tourist

かんこく【韓国】South Korea

かんこくご【韓国語】Korean (language)

かんさい【関西】the Kansai area

かんじ【感じ】feeling; impression —感じのいい nice, agreeable —…という感じの like…

かんじる【感じる】to feel, to notice

かんしん【感心】—感心する to admire; to be very impressed

かんずる【感ずる】[same as 感じる] to feel

かんせい¹【完成】—完成させる to complete

かんせい²【感性】sensitivity

かんぜん（な）【完全（な）】complete, absolute

がんぜん【眼前】—眼前に before one's eyes

かんたん（な）【簡単（な）】easy, simple

かんちがい【勘違い】misunderstanding —勘違い（を）する to misunderstand, to be mistaken

かんづく【感付く】to find (out), to notice

かんどう【感動】—感動的な moving, touching

かんとく【監督】director

き

き【気】feeling —気がする to feel like …, to feel (that)…, to have a feeling (that)… —気が軽くなる to feel relieved —気が抜ける to feel relieved (that)… —気に入る to like; to be happy with… —気に食わない to not like [care for] … —気にする to worry,

to care, to mind —気になる to be interested in…

キー key

きえる【消える】to disappear

きおく【記憶】memory

きがかり【気掛かり】concern, worry —気がかりである to be concerned for, to be worried about

ききゅう【気球】(hot-air) balloon

きく【聞く】1 to hear 2 to ask

ぎこちない clumsy —ぎこちなく awkwardly, stiffly

きざみつける【刻み付ける】to carve

きず【傷】wound; scratch —傷だらけになる to get covered with wounds [scratches]

ぎすぎす —ぎすぎすした unsociable

きずく【築く】to build, to construct

きずつく【傷つく】to be hurt —傷つきやすい vulnerable, sensitive

きずつける【傷つける】to hurt

きせい【既成】—既成の established, existing

きせき【奇跡】miracle —奇跡的に miraculously

きせつ【季節】season

きそく【規則】rule —規則的な regular

きぞく【帰属】—帰属する to belong

きたい【期待】expectation, hope —期待する to expect, to hope

きちんと regularly

きづかい【気遣い】care

きづく【気付く】to realize, to be aware of —気づき始める to begin noticing…

きっさてん【喫茶店】coffee shop, café

きっすい（の）【生粋（の）】pure; born and bred

きてん【起点】starting point

きのどく（な）【気の毒（な）】pitiable —

…は気の毒である to feel sorry for…

きひん【気品】dignity, grace —気品が漂う to exude dignity

きぶん【気分】mood, feeling —(…な)気分である to feel…, to be in a… mood

きほん【基本】basics, fundamentals —基本中の基本 the most basic of basics

きみょう(な)【奇妙(な)】strange, odd

きもち【気持・気持ち】feeling; mood

ぎゃく【逆】the opposite —逆の opposite —逆に on the contrary; conversely

ぎゃくギレ【逆ギレ】counterblast —逆ギレする to snap back (as when the party arguably in the wrong goes on the attack)

ぎゃくてん【逆転】—逆転する to be reversed

キャリア career

きゅうきょく【究極】the ultimate —究極的な ultimate

きょうぞん【共存】coexistence —共存する to coexist

きょうちょう【強調】emphasis —強調する to emphasize

きょうつう(の)【共通(の)】common —共通点 point in common

きょうとじん【京都人】Kyotoite

きょうみ【興味】interest —興味深い interesting —興味をもつ to be interested

きょうゆう【共有】—共有する to have in common

きょくど(に)【極度(に)】extremely

きょじゅうく【居住区】living quarters, dwelling place

きょすう【虚数】imaginary (number)

きょねん【去年】last year

きょむ【虚無】nothingness, emptiness

きょり【距離】distance

きらい【嫌い】➤ だいきらい(大嫌い)—

嫌いである・嫌いになる to dislike, to hate —…のきらいがある to have a touch of…, to smack of…

きり【霧】fog

キリスト Christ —キリスト主義 Christianity —キリスト主義者 Christian

きる【切る】➤ でんげん(電源)

ぎれい【儀礼】courtesy —儀礼的な courteous

キレる to blow one's top, to lose it

ぎろん【議論】argument; discussion —議論する to argue, to talk about —議論になる to be discussed

きわめて【極めて】very; extremely

きんだい【近代】modern age —近代の modern

きんだいご【近代語】modern language —近代語化 modernization of the language

きんだいこっか【近代国家】modern state [nation]

きんちょう【緊張】tension —緊張した nervous

◀

く【九】nine

くうふく【空腹】hunger —空腹の hungry

くさる【腐る】to rot, to go rotten, to be spoiled —腐った rotten, spoiled

くしょう【苦笑】—苦笑する to smile wryly

くじょう【苦情】complaint

−くせに【−癖に】despite [in spite of] the fact that …

ぐたいてき(に)【具体的(に)】specifically —具体的に言うと to be specific

−くださる【−下さる】—…して下さる [honorific form of…してくれる ; used

15

when the subject is of a higher status than the speaker] ➤ －くれる

くだらない【下らない】 worthless

くち【口】 mouth ―口にする to say, to mention ―口を開く to open one's mouth, to speak

くちばしる【口走る】 to say before one can stop oneself; to burst out

くちょう【口調】 tone

くったく【屈託】 ―屈託のない carefree

くに【国】 nation, country

くべつ【区別】 distinction

くみあわせ【組み合わせ】 combination

くむ【組む】 to form (a circle) ➤ えんじん (円陣), ざぜん (座禅)

－くらい【－位】 ① about…, approximately ② …or so; something like that ③ at least…

くらう【喰らう】 [rather brusque] to eat

グラフ graph

くらべる【比べる】 to compare… (with/to) ―…に比べれば compared with [to]…

くらやみ【暗闇】 darkness, the dark

くりかえし【繰り返し】 repetition

くりかえす【繰り返す】 to repeat ➤ へんせん (変遷)

くりひろげる【繰り広げる】 ―繰り広げられる to unfold

くる【来る】 to come ➤ ピン, よぶ (呼ぶ)

グルメ gourmet

クレーン crane

－くれる [added to verbs as an acknowledgement by the speaker that the subject's action benefits the speaker] ―…してくれる to be nice and do, to be kind enough to do

くろう【苦労】 difficulty, trouble ―苦労がない easy; to have no trouble (doing)

くわしい【詳しい】 detailed ―詳しく in detail

け

けいか【経過】 ―経過する to experience

けいかん【景観】 scenery, sight(s) ―景観破壊 destruction of the scenery ―景観保護 scenic preservation

けいこう【傾向】 tendency ―…する傾向にある to tend to do, to be inclined to do

けいざい【経済】 economy ―経済の economic

けいざいたいこく【経済大国】 a major economic power

けいさん【計算】 calculation ―計算式 calculating formula

けいさんまちがい【計算間違い】 miscalculation ―計算間違いを起こす to make a mistake in calculation

けいたい【携帯】 ―携帯用の portable; mobile

けいたいでんわ【携帯電話】 cell(ular) phone, mobile (phone)

けいばつ【刑罰】 punishment

けいべつ【軽蔑】 contempt ―軽蔑する to despise, to look down on

けしからぬ【怪しからぬ】 [rather old-fashioned] improper, shameful

けしき【景色】 sight, view

けしょう【化粧】 makeup ―化粧をする to put on (one's) makeup, to make (oneself) up

けたはずれ (に)【桁外れ (に)】 extremely

けちらす【蹴散らす】 to conquer

けっか【結果】 result; effect ―(…の) 結果 (として) as a result (of…)

けっかん【欠陥】 defect

げっかんし【月刊誌】 monthly magazine

けっきょく（は）【結局（は）】 after all, in the end; ultimately　—結局のところ after all, in the end

けっこう（な）【結構（な）】 ① fairly, pretty ② rather, quite ③ fine, okay

けっさく【傑作】 masterpiece

けっして【決して】 —決して…ない never

けってい【決定】 —決定する to decide on —決定的な decisive

けつまつ【結末】 ending; end

-けど　though, although

けなす　to run down, to abuse

けはい【気配】 ① sign, hint, suggestion ② atmosphere

ケルアック　Kerouac

けれど　though, although

けれども　but, however

-けれども　① though, although ② and

けん【県】 prefecture

けんきゅう【研究】 —研究する to study

けんきゅうか【研究家】 researcher

げんざい【現在】 the present

げんじつ【現実】 reality　—現実の real —現実に（は）in reality

けんせつ【建設】 construction

けんぞうぶつ【建造物】 structure, building

げんそく【原則】 principle

げんだいご【現代語】 current language

けんちく【建築】 architecture

げんど【限度】 limit

けんとう【見当】 guess　—見当がつく to guess (at), to be able to imagine

げんぶんいっち【言文一致】 unification of spoken and written languages　—言文一致運動 the movement to unify the written and spoken styles of the Japanese language (during the Meiji era)

けんろう（な）【堅牢（な）】 durable, strong

こ

-こ【-個】 [general-purpose counter]

ご【五】 five

ご-【御-】 [polite or honorific prefix; different form of お-]

こい【濃い】 strong

こいつ　this guy

こうい【行為】 act, action(s); behavior　—行為（を）する to act

こういう　like this, this way

こうえん【講演】 speech, talk; lecture

ごうおん【轟音】 roar　—轟音を鳴り響かせる to roar

こうか【効果】 effect

ごうがんふそん（な）【傲岸不遜（な）】 arrogant, haughty

こうきゅう（な）【高級（な）】 high-class, high-grade; exclusive　—高級車 luxury car　—高級スーパー fancy supermarket

こうきょう（の）【公共（の）】 public

こうけい【光景】 scene, sight

こうげき【攻撃】 attack

こうこ【江湖】 the world

こうこう【高校】 high school　—高校時代（に）in one's high school days

こうこうせい【高校生】 high school student

こうさてん【交差点】 intersection, crossing

こうしき【公式】 formula

こうして　in this way, thus

こうしゃ【校舎】 campus

こうじょうしん【向上心】 a desire for self-improvement

こうじょりょうぞく【公序良俗】 public morals

こうせい【恒星】(fixed) star

こうせん【光線】beam (of light); ray

ごうぜん（と）【傲然（と）】haughtily

こうそうビル【高層ビル】high-rise building

こうだい（な）【広大（な）】vast, extensive

こうふん【興奮】excitement ―興奮さめやらず still being excited

こうへい【公平】fairness ―公平な fair

こうりゅう【交流】communications

こうりょ【考慮】consideration ―考慮する to consider; to take into consideration [account]

こえ【声】voice ―声を荒げる to raise one's voice

コーヒーカップ　coffee cup

ごかい【誤解】misunderstanding

こがす【焦がす】to burn

こきつかう【こき使う】to work (a person) hard, to push [boss] (a person) around

こくせき【国籍】nationality

ここ（で）【此処（で）】here

ごご【午後】afternoon

ここう（の）【孤高（の）】proudly independent

こころ【心】heart, mind

こころいき【心意気】spirit; determination

こざいく【小細工】petty tricks

こしかける【腰掛ける】to sit down, to take a seat

こじんてき（な）【個人的（な）】personal; individual ―個人的に personally

コスト　cost ―コストがかかる to cost (much)

-こそ　(the) very...

こたえ【答え】answer ―答えを出す to give [find] an answer

こたえる【答える】to answer, to reply

こだわる　to stick to; to be particular about

こちょうらん【胡蝶蘭】phalaenopsis [a kind of flower]

こちら　①this ②here ③me; us

こぢんまり　―こぢんまりとした small

コツ　the secret(s), the trick

こっけい（な）【滑稽（な）】funny, comical; ridiculous, absurd

こっち　[casual form of こちら]

こてん【古典】classics

こと【事】thing(s); events ―...したことがある to have done...

-ごとき【-如き】[indicates the speaker thinks lightly of the subject] something like..., something so trivial as

-ごとく【-如く】like...

ことさら（に）【殊更（に）】particularly

ことし【今年】this year

ことば【言葉】①word; phrase ②language ③remark

こども【子供】child, kid; children

こな【粉】powder; flour ―粉っぽい mealy

この　this; these

このたび【この度】recently

このむ【好む】to like, to be fond of

このような【この様な】like this

ごひゃく【五百】five hundred

ごまかす【誤魔化す】to fake (it)

こまやか（な）【細やか（な）】tender, delicate, thoughtful

こまる【困る】①to be at a loss, to be embarrassed ②to have trouble; to not like...

ゴミ　garbage ―ゴミ収集 garbage collection ―ゴミ集積所 garbage collection site

コメント　comment　—コメントする　to comment

ごめんなさい【御免なさい】I'm sorry.

こゆう（の）【固有（の）】distinctive, peculiar

こりる【懲りる】to have enough of...; to learn one's lesson (from)

こる【凝る】to be particular about... —凝りに凝って　elaborately

これ　this; these

これまで【これ迄】until now

これら　these

-ころ【-頃】when...

ころす【殺す】to kill

ころもがえ【衣替え】renovation

こわい【恐い・怖い】① to be afraid ② scary

こわす【壊す】to break (down), to destroy

こわれる【壊れる】to break (down); to become broken　—壊れた　broken

コンヴィニエンス・ストア　convenience store

こんき【根気】patience

こんとん【混沌】chaos　—混沌とした　chaotic

こんな　(like) this; such...

こんなにも　so (much)

こんにち【今日】—今日の　of today

コンマ　comma

こんらん【混乱】—混乱させる　to throw ...into confusion [disorder]

さ

さーっと　[mimetic word describing a swift motion]

-さい【-際】when...

さいうよく【最右翼】the dominant person [party]

さいきん【最近】—最近（は）recently, lately, these days　—最近の　recent

さいげん【再現】reproduction　—再現する　to reproduce

さいご（の）【最後（の）】(the) last

さいこう（の）【最高（の）】(the) best　—最高傑作　masterpiece

さいこうほう【最高峰】the pinnacle, the highest peak

さいしゅう【最終】(the) last　—最終的に（は）① finally, in the end ② ultimately

さいじょう（の）【最上（の）】the best

さいちゅう【最中】—...の最中に　in the middle of...; during

さいのう【才能】talent

さがしだす【探し出す】to find, to search for

さがす【探す】to look for

さかな【魚】fish

さかみち【坂道】slope

-ざかり【-盛り】the peak, the height　—...の盛りに　at the height of...

さがる【下がる】➢ ちのけ（血の気）

さき【先に】first　—先の ① first ② above-mentioned

さぎ【詐欺】swindle, fraud, scam

さぎょう【作業】work

さくしゃ【作者】author

さくせん【作戦】strategy

さくひん【作品】work(s)

さくら【桜】cherry (blossoms)

さげる【下げる】to lower, to turn down ➢ ボリューム

ささやか（な）small　—ささやかさ　smallness, insignificance

さしだす【差し出す】to present, to hand out

さす【射す】to come in

さすが【流石】—さすがは［に］indeed; as

あ

か

さ

た

な

は

ま

や

ら

わ

may be expected

ざせき【座席】seat

-させる to make [have, let] (a person) do

ざぜん【座禅】Zen meditation ―座禅を組む to sit in meditation; to practice Zen meditation in the lotus position

さそう【誘う】to provoke ➤ びんしょう（憫笑）

ざだんかい【座談会】roundtable talk

-さつ【-冊】[counter for books, magazines, etc.]

さつえい【撮影】filming, shooting

ざつおん【雑音】noise, static

さっか【作家】writer

さっき some time ago; just now ―さっきから for some time ―さっきまで until a little while ago

さっこん（の）【昨今（の）】recent

さびしげ（な）【寂しげ（な）】sad, lonely

さびしさ【寂しさ】sadness

ざひょうじく【座標軸】coordinate axes

さほど【左程】―さほど…ない not… much, not particularly ―…さほど（に）[same as それほど] that much

さめる【冷める】to cool down [off], to subside

さもしい mean, base, sordid

さら【皿】plate, dish

さらさら（と） readily ―さらさらと書く to reel off

さらす【晒す・曝す】to expose

さらなる【更なる】further; another

サラリーマン a salaried worker, a company employee

さる¹【去る】to leave; to go away

さる²【猿】ape

さわぐ【騒ぐ】to make a fuss; to fuss

ざわざわ ―ざわざわした noisy

-さん [suffix added to personal and occupational names]

さんかくすう【三角数】triangular numbers

さんぎょうこく【産業国】industrial(ized) country

ざんこく（な）【残酷（な）】cruel, harsh

さんじゅう【三十】thirty

し

し【死】death

-じ【-時】① when… ➤ ようしょう（幼少）② …o'clock

しあわせ【幸せ】happiness ―しあわせ感 a sense of happiness

シーッ Shh!

しいて【強いて】―強いて…すれば if I had to (do…) ―強いていえば… if I had to, I'd say…

しいてき（な）【恣意的（な）】arbitrary

しいる【強いる】to force (to do)

しおあじ【塩味】salty taste ―塩味が濃い salty

-しか [followed by a negative] only, just ―…するしかない to have no (other) choice but to do…

しかい【視界】(one's) view, visibility

じかい（は）【次回（は）】the next time

しかく【資格】qualification

じかく【自覚】awareness, consciousness ―自覚する to be aware of

しかし but

しかた【仕方】―仕方ない it cannot be helped; there's no choice but to… ―…して仕方がない one can't help doing…

しかも and, besides; moreover; in addition

しかるべき【然るべき】proper, right

じかん【時間】time　―時間がかかる to take (a lot of) time

しき【式】ceremony

じき【時期】period, time

じく【軸】axis ➤ たて（縦）, よこ（横）

しくみ【仕組み】mechanism

しげきてき（な）【刺激的（な）】stimulating

じけん【事件】incident

じこけいはつ【自己啓発】self-development, self-enlightenment

じこしゅちょう【自己主張】self-assertion ―自己主張の激しい very (self-) assertive

しごと【仕事】work, job

ししつ【資質】quality

じじつ【事実】fact

じしゅう【自習】self-study ―自習（を）する to study by oneself

じじょう【事情】reasons; circumstances ―事情があって for some reason

–じしん【自身】oneself

–シスト　-ist

しせん【視線】one's gaze [eyes]

しぜん【自然】―自然な natural ―自然に naturally ―自然対数 natural logarithm

したい　to want to do

–じたい【-自体】itself

じだい【時代】period, era; days ➤ こうこう（高校）, だいがく（大学）―あの時代（では）in those days ―…していた時代に when one was doing…

しだいに【次第に】gradually, little by little

したうち【舌打ち】―舌打ちをする to click one's tongue

したしらべ【下調べ】preliminary study; research ―下調べをする to prepare (for one's work)

したまち【下町】the old traditional districts (of Tokyo)

しつ【質】quality

じつがい【実害】real damage [harm]

しっかく【失格】disqualification ―失格宣言 declaration of disqualification

じっさい（の）【実際（の）】actual, real ―実際に（は）actually; in fact

じつざい【実在】―実在する to exist

じっち【実地】practice ―実地に試す to put…into practice

じつは【実は】actually; in fact

しっぱいさく【失敗作】failure

しっぴつ【執筆】writing

じっぽん【十本】ten (tulips)

しつもん【質問】question

しつれい【失礼】a breach of etiquette ―失礼に当たる to be discourteous

してき【指摘】―指摘する to point out

じてん【時点】point in time ―…の時点で at the point (that)…

じどうしゃ【自動車】car, vehicle

しなぞろえ【品揃え】assortment of articles, variety of items

しぬ【死ぬ】to die

しばしば　often

しバス【市バス】city bus

しばらく【暫く】for a while

じぶん【自分】oneself ―自分の one's

しまつ【始末】―始末に悪い difficult to deal with

しみこむ【染み込む】to soak [sink] in [into]

しみじみ　deeply, seriously

じゃあ　well, then

シャーッ　[harsh noise from a TV]

ジャーナリスト　journalist

しゃかいじん【社会人】a working adult

シャカシャカ [noise leaking from the headphones of a personal audio player]

しゃこう【社交】—社交する to speak up; to associate with…

しゃしょう【車掌】conductor

シャット shut

ジャパニーズ Japanese

しゃべる【喋る】① to chat, to chatter ② to speak, to tell

シャラップ Shut up!

しゃりょう【車両】car, carriage —女性専用車両 a car for women only

じゆう【自由】freedom —自由な free

じゅう【十】ten

しゅうい【周囲】(one's) surroundings —周囲の surrounding; …around one —周囲の人 those around one

しゅうかんし【週刊誌】weekly magazine

しゅうしゅう【収集】collection

しゅうせき【集積】accumulation —集積する to accumulate, to pile up

しゅうせきじょ【集積所】➤ ゴミ

しゅうちゅう【集中】concentration —集中する to concentrate —集中力 concentration, the ability to concentrate

じゅうぶん（に）【十分（に）】enough, sufficiently

じゅうみん【住民】inhabitants, people

しゅぎ【主義】principle ➤ キリスト

しゅくめい【宿命】fate

しゅご【主語】the subject (in a sentence)

じゅしょう¹【受賞】—受賞する to win [receive, get] an award

じゅしょう²【授賞】—授賞式 award ceremony

じゅしょうしゃ【受賞者】prizewinner

しゅちょう【主張】claim, assertion —主張する to claim, to assert

しゅつげん【出現】appearance —出現する to appear

しゅっせき【出席】attendance —出席する to attend

しゅつだい【出題】—出題する to give (a person) a problem

しゅっぱん【出版】publication —出版する to publish

しゅみ【趣味】hobby

しゅるい【種類】kind

じゅん【順】—順に in order —大きい [小さい] 順に in decreasing [increasing] order

じゅんか【純化】purification —純化する to purify

しゅんかん【瞬間】instant, moment —…の瞬間に the moment (that)…

じゅんかん【循環】circulation —循環する to circulate

じゅんすい（に）【純粋（に）】genuinely

じゅんぜん【純然】—純然たる pure

じゅんばん【順番】① order ② (one's) turn —順番に in order

じゅんび【準備】preparation —準備が整う to be ready

しよう【使用】use —使用する to use

しょう【賞】award, prize

–じょう¹【–上】on…; from the standpoint of…

–じょう²【–乗】power —2乗 square —3乗 cube —2乗 [3乗] する to raise …to the power of two [three], to square [cube]

じょうきゃく【乗客】passenger

じょうきょう【状況】situation, circumstances

じょうげ【上下】—上下に one above the other

しょうげきてき（な）【衝撃的（な）】shocking, dramatic

じょうけん【条件】condition(s), criteria ―条件がつく Conditions are set.

しょうこ【証拠】proof, evidence

じょうし【上梓】―上梓する to publish

しょうじき【正直】to be honest, honestly speaking

じょうしき【常識】common sense [knowledge]

しょうしょう【少々】a little

しょうしん（な）【正真（な）】honest; true

じょうせい【醸成】―醸成する to create, to bring about

しょうせつ【小説】novel, work of fiction

じょうたい【状態】condition, state

じょうだん【冗談】joke ―冗談を言う to crack [make] a joke

しょうちょう【象徴】symbol ―象徴する to symbolize

しょうてんがい【商店街】shopping street

しょうとつ【衝突】―衝突する to conflict; to bump heads

しょうねん【少年】boy ―…少年 the young…

しょうめい【照明】light(s)

しょうめつ【消滅】extinction

しょうめん【正面】front

しょき【初期】the beginning ―初期の early; in the early days (of)

しょくざい【食材】foodstuff; ingredient(s)

しょくじ【食事】meal ―食事をとる to have a meal, to eat

しょくたく【食卓】table

しょくよく【食欲】appetite

しょさい【書斎】(one's) study, library

じょし【女子】girl, woman

じょしこうせい【女子高生】a high school girl, a female high school student

じょじょうてき（な）【抒情的（な）】lyrical

じょせい【女性】woman; girl ➤ しゃりょう（車両）

しょせん（は）【所詮（は）】after all, in the end, ultimately

しょたいめん【初対面】meeting for the first time

しょだな【書棚】bookshelf

しょひょう【書評】book review

しらせ【知らせ】news

しらべる【調べる】to look up, to check

しりょう【資料】materials; reference book(s)

しる【知る】to know

-じん【-人】[suffix for indicating a person's nationality]

じんかく【人格】personality

しんかんせん【新幹線】Shinkansen, bullet train

しんけん（に）【真剣（に）】earnestly; seriously

しんこく（な）【深刻（な）】serious, grave

じんじゃ【神社】shrine

しんじる【信じる】to believe ―信じられない incredible; unbelievable ―信じられないほど incredibly, unbelievably

しんせい【新星】new star

じんせい【人生】(one's) life

しんだ【死んだ】dead

しんぱい【心配】worry ―心配する to worry

しんぴ【神秘】mystery ―神秘的な mysterious

しんぶんきしゃ【新聞記者】newspaper reporter, journalist

シンポジウム symposium

ず

ず【図】graph, diagram

すいこむ【吸い込む】to draw in

スイスイ(と) swiftly; easily

ずいひつ【随筆】essay

ずいぶん(と)【随分(と)】quite, very

すいません ➤ すみません

すうがく【数学】mathematics

すうがくしゃ【数学者】mathematician

すうじ【数字】figure, number

すうしき【数式】numerical expression

すうじゅうねん【数十年】a few [several] decades

ずーっと [emphatic form of ずっと] all the time

すうねんかん【数年間】(for) several years

スーパー supermarket

すがた【姿】form; figure; sight ―…の姿で in the form of...

すき【好き】―好きである to like, to be fond of ―好きになる to come to like ... ―好きなことをさせる to let one do as one pleases

-すぎない【-過ぎない】just, only; no better [more] than...

すきほうだい(に)【好き放題(に)】(just) as one pleases

-すぎ(る)【-過ぎ(る)】too...

すぐ(に) at once, instantly; soon, in no time

すくう【救う】to help

すぐさま ➤ すぐ

すくない【少ない】few ―少なくない not a few; many

ずけい【図形】figure ―図形化する to be expressed as a figure

すこし【少し】a little, a bit

すこしずつ【少しずつ】gradually, little by little

すごす【過ごす】to spend (time)

すごみ【凄み】gravity, severity

すさまじい tremendous

すさむ to get disgusted ―すさませる to disgust

すすむ【進む】to go; to make one's way

スチュワード steward, male flight attendant

ずっと ① the whole time, all the time, (all) through...; always ② much, (by) far ―ずっと...する to keep (on) doing...

すでに【既に】already

ステレオ stereo

すなお(に)【素直(に)】straightforwardly, simply

すばらしい【素晴らしい】wonderful

すべて【全て】all; everything

スポンジ sponge

すませる【済ませる】to do; to get done with

すみずみ【隅々】every corner ―隅々にまで into every corner

すみはじめる【住み始める】 to begin [start] living (in)

すみません ① Excuse me. ② I'm sorry.

すむ【住む】to live (in)

-すら even

ずらずら [mimetic word indicating the quality of verbosity]

すらすら(と) easily, with ease

すりきれる【擦り切れる】to wear out ―擦り切れた worn-out

する ① to do ② ➤ き(気), コメント

ずるい unfair

すると (and) then

すれすれ(に) just barely

すわる【座る】to sit (down)

せ

せい【生】life; living

−せい¹【−性】[suffix added to indicate the state of having a particular quality] −ty, −ness

−せい²【−製】made in...

せいかく【性格】character, personality, nature

せいかく(に)【正確(に)】precisely, accurately

せいかつ【生活】life　—生活する to live

せいさん【生産】production

せいさんせい【生産性】productivity

せいじゃく【静寂】silence, quiet(ness)

せいしょ【聖所】holy place

せいしん【精神】spirit

せいしんてき(な)【精神的(な)】mental, spiritual

せいせい【生成】formation; creation

せいぶつがくしゃ【生物学者】biologist

せいようご【西洋語】Western language(s)

せかい【世界】(the) world

せき【席】seat

セクシー(な) sexy

せけん【世間】the world; people

−せずにはいられない one cannot help doing

せだい【世代】generation

セックス・ピストルズ the Sex Pistols

せっしょく【接触】touch, contact　—接触する to touch, to contact

ぜったい(に)【絶対(に)】—絶対(に)...ない never

せっちょ【拙著】my book

ぜっちょうき【絶頂期】one's prime [peak]

せっとくりょく【説得力】powers of persuasion　—説得力がある to be persuasive, to be convincing

せつない【切ない】sad, wistful

ぜつぼうてき(な)【絶望的(な)】desperate

せつめい【説明】explanation　—説明する to explain

せつやく【節約】—節約する to save [conserve] (time)

せまい【狭い】small; limited

セミナー seminar

ゼロ zero

せん【線】line　—線グラフ line graph

ぜん−【前−】pre-　—前近代 premodern age [times]

せんげん【宣言】declaration　—宣言する to declare

ぜんこく【全国】the whole country　—全国に all over the country

せんじつ【先日】the other day

ぜんしん【全身】the whole body

せんせい【先生】teacher; professor　—...先生 Mr. [Ms., Mrs.]...; Professor...

ぜんぜん【全然】—全然...ない not...at all

ぜんたい【全体】the whole　—全体的に on the whole

せんにひゃく【千二百】twelve hundred

せんねん【専念】—専念する to concentrate

せんぱく(な)【浅薄(な)】shallow, superficial

せんぱくさ【浅薄さ】shallowness, superficiality

せんひゃくなんじゅうねんめ【千百何十年目】eleven hundred and some years later

ぜんぶ【全部】all　—全部で in all, in total, all together

ぜんめん【全面】all-out, overall

ぜんめんひてい【全面否定】complete denial

せんもんか【専門家】expert

せんよう【専用】—...専用の for...only;

exclusively for... ➣ しゃりょう（車両）

せんれん【洗練】―洗練された refined, sophisticated

そ

そう　①so; it, that　②in that way　③ [followed by a negative] not very..., not...much　④yes

-そう　①it looks like...; it seems that ...　②to be likely [about] to do　―... しそうになる to be about to do, to come near to doing; almost do　―...しそう にない to be not likely to do

そういう　such, ...like that

そういえば【そう言えば】come to think of it

そうおん【騒音】noise

そうさく【創作】―創作する to create

そうした　that, those; such

そうとう【相当】―...に相当する to correspond to [with]

そくざ（に）【即座（に）】at once, instantly

そこ¹【其処】there　―そこに・そこで there

そこ²【底】bottom　―底知れない impenetrable

そこしれぬ【底知れぬ】bottomless, fathomless

そこで　(and) so, therefore; then

そこまで【そこ迄】to that extent; that much

そざい【素材】ingredient(s)

そして　and, (and) then

そすう【素数】prime number

-そだち【-育ち】(born and) bred in...

そと【外】―外へ・外の out

そなえる【備える】to have, to possess

その　that　―その日 that day

そのて【その手】―その手の that kind

of...; ...like that

そのとおり【その通り】It's true; That's right.

そのとき【その時】then, at that time

そのまま【その儘】as it is

そのもの　itself

そのような【その様な】such...; like that

ソフト（に）　softly; calmly, gently

そもそも　in the first place

それ　―それは it, that　―それを it, that

それから　and, (and) then

それだけ　that much

それでは　then

それでも　and yet, even so, nonetheless

それとも　or

それなら（ば）　then

それに　and, besides

それほど【それ程】―それほど...ない not ...that [very] much

それまで【それ迄】until then

それも　(and) ...at that

それら　―それらは[が] they; those　― それらの their; those　―それらを[に] them

そろう【揃う】to get together, to assemble

そろそろ　before long, soon　―そろそ ろ...する it's about time to...

そんざい【存在】existence　―存在する to exist

そんな　such; like that

た

だ・であるちょう【だ・である調】da/de aru style

-たい　―...したい to want to do

たいおん【体温】body heat

だいがく【大学】university, college　―大 学時代に in one's college days

だいきらい【大嫌い】―大嫌いである to hate

たいけん【体験】experience ―体験する to experience

たいしょう【大将】boss

たいすう【対数】logarithm

だいすき(な)【大好き(な)】favorite

たいせい【体勢】posture, position

たいせつ(な)【大切(な)】important

だいたい【大体】roughly

たいだん【対談】conversation, interview; talk ―対談集 collection of conversations

たいど【態度】attitude; manner

だいどころ【台所】kitchen

たいひ【対比】contrast

だいひょう【代表】representative ―代表する to represent ―代表的な typical

タイピング typing

タイプ type

だいふくもち【大福餅】*daifuku-mochi*, sweetened *mochi* stuffed with bean paste

タイプライター typewriter ―タイプライターを打つ to type, to pound a typewriter

たいへん【大変】very, very much, a lot

たえざる【絶えざる】unceasing, incessant, constant

たえまなく【絶え間なく】constantly

たえる【耐える】to stand, to bear, to tolerate ―耐え切れない unbearable, intolerable; one cannot stand

たおれる【倒れる】to fall down

たかい【高い】high; expensive

たかだか【高々】at most

たかまる【高まる】to rise

だから so, therefore

―だから because; since, as

たき【滝】waterfall ―滝に打たれる to stand under a waterfall (as spiritual training)

―たぐい(の)【―類い(の)】like…

―だけ ① [often in the pattern ただ…だけ] only, just ② as much as…; enough to… ―…Aだけではなく(Bもまた) not only A, (but B)

だけど but

たしざん【足し算】addition ―足し算する to add (up)

たしなみ【嗜み】modesty, etiquette

たしょう【多少】somewhat

たす【足す】to add

だす【出す】① to give off (a beam) ② to serve ③ ➤ おと(音), こたえ(答え), ムード, もんだい(問題)

―だす【―出す】to start [begin] to do

たずさわる【携わる】to be engaged [involved] in

たずねる【訪ねる】to visit, to call on

たた【多々】a lot

ただ ① only, just ② but

たたえる【湛える】➤ えみ(笑み)

たたく【叩く】to hit; to tap

ただしい【正しい】correct ―正しくは to be correct [precise]

ただの【只の】ordinary, common; just (a)…

ただよう【漂う】to hang (in the air) ➤ きひん(気品), ニュアンス

―たち【―達】[suffix added to form plurals]

たちあがる【立ち上がる】to take action

たちきる【断ち切る】to break, to cut off

たちこめる【立ち込める】to envelop, to be filled with

たちつづける【立ち続ける】to keep [continue] standing

あ

か

さ

た

な

は

ま

や

ら

わ

あ

か

さ

た

な

は

ま

や

ら

わ

たちはたらく【立ち働く】to work dili-
gently

たちまち【忽ち】instantly, immediately,
right away

たつ¹【経つ】to pass (by), to go by

たつ²【立つ・建つ】to stand

たった　[often used in the pattern たっ
た…だけ] just, only

だって　because, since

−だって　① [used when reporting something; shows one's disapproval or sur-
prise] ② [same as − も, emphatic ex-
pression] too, also

たて【縦】—縦の vertical —縦軸 vertical axis

たてかえる【建て替える】to rebuild　—
建て替わる to be rebuilt

たてる【建てる】to build　—建てられる
to be built

たとえ　—たとえ…でも even if…, —
たとえ…としても even were [had]…

たとえば【例えば】for example, for instance; (let's) say; such as…, like…

たにん【他人】others, other people

たのしい【楽しい】fun, enjoyable, pleasant

たのむ【頼む】to ask, to request

たはつ【多発】—多発する to occur frequently

たび【旅】trip

−たび(に)【−度(に)】—…するたびに
every time one does…

たびだつ【旅立つ】to set off, to start
out (on a journey)

たびたび【度々】often

たぶん【多分】probably

たべる【食べる】to eat

たまたま　by chance　—たまたま…する
to happen to do

たまに　occasionally, once in a while,
sometimes

たまらない【堪らない】unbearable, intolerable

だまる【黙る】to keep quiet, to be silent
—黙って without saying anything

−ため(に)【−為(に)】for the purpose
of, in order to, so as to…

だめ【駄目】no good

ダメージ　damage

ためす【試す】to try ≻ じっち(実地)

たもつ【保つ】to keep

−たら　if; when; in the case (that)

−だらけ　≻ きず(傷)

だらだら　—汗をだらだら流す to sweat
profusely

だれ【誰】—誰が…しようと whoever

だれか【誰か】somebody, someone

だれでも【誰でも】anyone

だれの【誰の】—誰の…ない nobody's
…, no one's…

だれも【誰も】—誰も…ない nobody

−だろうか　I wonder…

たんい【単位】unit

たんじゅん(な)【単純(な)】simple —単
純に simply

たんじゅんか【単純化】simplification —
単純化する to simplify

たんじゅんさ【単純さ】simplicity

たんじる【嘆じる】[formal or old-
fashioned] to lament (over)

だんせい【男性】man

たんなる【単なる】mere

たんに【単に】simply

ち

ち【地】place

ちいさい・ちいさな【小さい・小さな】①
small, little; small-minded ② low

(describing sound) ―小さくなる to decrease (in number) ―小さくする to reduce, to turn down

チーズ　cheese

チェック　check

ちかい【近い】close, near

ちがい【違い】difference

ちがいない【違いない】―…に違いない must be…; no doubt that…

ちがう【違う】to be different, to differ ―…と違って unlike

ちかく【近く】―近くに nearby, close by

ちかづく【近づく】to get close to

ちから【力】ability; power, strength

ちじん【知人】acquaintance

ちず【地図】map

ちぢ(に)【千々(に)】➤ みだれる（乱れる）

ちつじょ【秩序】order

ちっそく【窒息】suffocation ―窒息死させる to choke… (to death)

ちっぽけ(な)　tiny, insignificant

ちのけ【血の気】―血の気が下がる the blood drains (from a person's face); to turn pale

ちへい【地平】surface of the earth; horizon

ちゃ【茶】tea

ちゃくもく【着目】―…に着目する to pay attention to

ちゅう【宙】air ―宙に in the air

-ちゅう【-中】① in, among ② in the middle of…

ちゅうい【注意】caution, warning ―注意する to caution, to warn, to give a warning ―注意される to be given a warning, to be warned

ちゅうごく【中国】China

ちゅうごくご【中国語】Chinese (language)

ちゅうしん【中心】the center

ちゅうねん【中年】middle age ―中年の middle-aged

ちゅうへん【中編】novella

チューリップ　tulip

ちょう-【超-】super-; really, extremely

-ちょう【-調】―…調で (in) the…style

ちょうえつ【超越】―超越する to go beyond; to transcend

ちょうき【長期】―長期的な long-term

ちょうど【丁度】just

ちょうり【調理】cooking ―調理する to cook

チョコレート　chocolate

ちょしゃ【著者】author

ちょっと　a little, a bit ―ちょっとした little, small; a little, pretty

ちる【散る】to fall; to scatter

ちんもく【沈黙】silence

つ

ついつい　one cannot help doing…

ついに　at last, in the end, finally

つうじょう(の)【通常(の)】ordinary; general

つうじる【通じる】―…に通じている to be familiar with; to be well versed in

つうしん【通信】communication, correspondence

つうせつ(な)【痛切(な)】vigorous, furious

つうよう【通用】―通用する ① to be communicated ② to be accepted

つうろ【通路】aisle

つかいわけ【使い分け】the (proper) use (of…)

つかいわける【使い分ける】to use… properly

つかう【使う】to use

つかえる【使える】can be used

あ

か

さ

た

な

は

ま

や

ら

わ

つかみとる【摑み取る】 to catch, to grab

つかむ【摑む】 to get, to grasp

つき【月】 moon

－つき【－付き】 with...

つきあい【付き合い】 relationship

つきあう【付き合う】 ―買い物に付き合う to go along shopping (with...)

つきとばす【突き飛ばす】 to push (a person) down

つく ➤ うそ（嘘）, けんとう（見当）, じょうけん（条件）, よそく（予測）

つくりえがお【作り笑顔】 artificial smile

つくりだす【作り出す】 to start making [cooking]

つくりもの【作り物】 artificial thing

つくる【作る・造る】 ① to make, to prepare ② to build

つける【付ける】 ➤ み（身）

つたわる【伝わる】 ① to be handed down ② to be conveyed, to come across ③ to be felt

－つつ with...; while doing...

つづく【続く】 to continue, to last

－つづける【－続ける】 to continue doing, to keep (on) doing

つつむ【包む】 to wrap, to envelop ―...に包まれる to be wrapped in...; to be covered with...

つね【常】 ―...するのが常である one usually does...; it is customary for a person to...

つねに【常に】 always

つまらない worthless; dull

つまり in other words; that is to say; in short ―つまりは after all

つみ【罪】 sin, guilt ―罪のない harmless ―罪のないうそ white lie

つめこむ【詰め込む】 to stuff...into

－つもり ―...のつもりでいる to fancy

that..., to be of the conviction [belief, thinking] that...

つよい【強い】 strong

つよく【強く】 deeply

つらなり【連なり】 sequence

－づれ【－連れ】 a party of (two people)

て

て【手】 ① hand ② kind, type ➤ そのて（その手）―手が離せない to be tied up with work, to be busy ―手に入る available ―手を[が]つけられない out of control ―手を振る to wave ―...を手に入れている to have... in one's possession

であう【出会う】 to meet; to run across [into]

てあたりしだい（に）【手当たり次第（に）】 at random

ていぎ【定義】 definition

－ていど【－程度】 about

ていねい（に）【丁寧（に）】 politely

ていひょう【定評】 accepted opinion

でいり【出入り】 ―出入り自由 free entry [access]

デート date; dating

テーブル table

てがみ【手紙】 letter

－てき【－的】 (from) the viewpoint of...

できあがる【出来上がる】 to be created

テキスト text

てきせつ（な）【適切（な）】 suitable

できる【出来る】 ① can do, to be able to do ② to open ③ ➤ よゆう（余裕）―...のできる to be good at... ―注意ができる to be able to give a warning (to someone)

－できる【－出来る】 can, be able to

できれば【出来れば】 if possible

あ か さ た な は ま や ら わ

です・ますちょう【です・ます調】desu/
-masu style

でたらめ【出鱈目】nonsense; lie ―出鱈
目を言う to talk nonsense

てぢか(に)【手近(に)】near at hand

てつだい【手伝い】helper, assistant

でっちあげ【でっち上げ】fiction, story
―でっちあげる to make [cook] up (a
story)

てっていてき(に)【徹底的(に)】com-
pletely, exhaustively

でてくる【出てくる】to appear, to come
up, to emerge

でなおす【出直す】to come again

てにをは usage of particles

では well; now; then

デビュー debut ―デビューする to make
one's debut

でまかせ【出任せ】irresponsible remark
―でまかせを言う to talk irresponsibly
[without thinking], to say whatever
pops into one's head

てまわし【手回し】―手回しの hand-
turned, hand-cranked

でも but

-でも even, only ➤ たとえ

てらしあわせる【照らし合わせる】to com-
pare ... (with ...)

てりょうり【手料理】home cooking

でる【出る】to appear, to show ➤ テレビ

テレビ television, TV ―テレビに出る
to appear [be] on TV

テレビたいだん【テレビ対談】TV talk
show

てん¹【点】point

てん²【天】sky; heaven

てんいん【店員】salesclerk

でんき【伝記】biography

でんげん【電源】power supply [source]

―電源を切る to turn off (a TV)

てんさい【天才】genius

でんじは【電磁波】electromagnetic
waves

でんしゃ【電車】train

でんたつ【伝達】communication ―伝
達する to communicate, to convey

テント tent

てんとう【転倒】overturn ―転倒する to
upset, to overturn

てんない【店内】the inside of the shop
[store]

でんぱ【電波】radio waves

と

-と and; with

どあい【度合い】degree, extent

といあわせ【問い合わせ】inquiry ―問
い合わせが来る to receive an inquiry

-という(ふうに)【-という(風に)】like
..., as...

-というもの what is called

-というより【-と言うより】or rather ―
...と言うよりは rather than...; not so
much...as

-といった such as

とう【問う】to ask, to question

どう how; what

どういう what (kind [sort] of)

どういつ(な)【同一(な)】the same

どうくつ【洞窟】cave

とうし【投資】investment ―投資する to
invest, to put money into...

とうじ【当時】at that [the] time

-どうし【-同士】[indicates that two or
more nouns belong to a single cate-
gory] ――同士で between, among

どうしたって ➤ どうしても

どうして why; how

どうしても　① no matter how... ② [followed by a negative] by no means; despite all one's efforts

とうじょう【登場】appearance ―登場する to appear, to show up

とうせい【統制】control ―統制する to control

とうぜん【当然】naturally, of course ― 当然の[な] natural

どうぜん【同然】―...も同然で almost, practically, as good as...

どうたら　this and that, something or other

とうちゃく【到着】arrival ―到着する to arrive at, to get to

どうでもいい　➤ どうでもよい

どうでもよい　unimportant

とうとう　at last

どうどう（と）【堂々（と）】unashamedly

どうとく【道徳】morals, morality ―道徳感 a moral sense, a sense of morality

どうにゅう【導入】introduction, adoption ―導入する to introduce, to adopt

どうめいし【動名詞】gerund

どうも　① somehow　② apparently

どうやって　how

とおい【遠い】far ➤ むかし（昔）―はるか遠い far away

―とおり【―通り】➤ あんない（案内）―...の通りに　as

とおりかかる【通りかかる】to pass by...

―とか　or, like

とがめる【咎める】to reprove, to reproach

―とき【―時】when

とく【解く】to solve

とくい【得意】―(...が) 得意である to be good at...

どくじ（の）【独自（の）】unique, original

どくしゃ【読者】reader

とくしゅ（な）【特殊（な）】peculiar, unique

とくせい【特性】characteristic

どくぜつ【毒舌】words of abuse; sharp tongue

とくに【特に】especially

とくべつ（の）【特別（の）】special

とける【解ける】to be able to solve

どこ【何処】where

どこか　① somewhere　② somehow, somewhat

どこから　from where

どことなく　somehow, in some way

どこまで　how far, to what extent

どこまでも　endlessly

ところ【所】① place; point; part　② family [used in いいところに嫁に行く]

―ところ　when　➤ けっきょく（結局）

ところが　but, however

―ところで　even if [though]

とし【都市】city

―として（の）　as

―としても　even if...; however

―とすれば　assuming that

とたん【途端】―途端に　at once

とちゅう（で）【途中（で）】halfway, along the way

どちらの　either

とつぜん【突然】suddenly, all of a sudden, abruptly

どっち　[colloquial form of どちら] which ―どっちの which ―どっちかというと rather

―とって　for; to

とっても　[emphatic form of とても] very, so, truly

とても　very, so

とどく【届く】to arrive; to come in

ととのう【整う】to be completed

とどまる【留まる】 to stay, to remain

となり【隣】 —…の隣で[に] next to…

とにかく   anyway; at any rate

どのような   what kind of…

どのように   how

–とはいえ【–とは言え】 though, although; however

とばす【飛ばす】 ① to fly ② to skip (over), to omit

とびこむ【飛び込む】➢ め（目）

ともだち【友達】 friend

どようび【土曜日】 Saturday

トラック   truck

とらわれる【囚われる】 to be snagged on; to be hung up on

とりあげる【取り上げる】 to take up, to feature

とりだす【取り出す】 to take out

とる¹【取る】 ① to take…(in one's hand), to pick up ② to eat, to have (a meal)

とる²【採る】 to adopt, to take (a measure)

トルーマン・カポーティ   Truman Capote

どれほど（の）【どれ程（の）】 how much

とんでもない   terrible, awful, ridiculous, outrageous —とんでもなく terribly, awfully

どんどん ① one after another, continuously ② increasingly —どんどん…する to continue doing

どんな   how; what (kind of), which —どんな…でも however…, no matter how…

どんなに   however…, no matter how…

な

ない¹【無い】 there isn't [aren't]… —…がなければ   without…

ない²【内】 —…内   inside…, in…

–ない【–無い】 not, no

ないし（は）【乃至（は）】 or

ないそう【内装】 interior decor

ないぶ【内部】 inside

ないよう【内容】 content, substance; meaning

なおす【直す】 to improve (one's humanity)

なか【中】 inside —…の中で in, inside; on; among

ながい【長い】 long

ながき【長き】 long time

ながす【流す】➢ あぶらあせ（脂汗）

なかなか ① pretty, quite; very ② [followed by a negative] will not…; not … easily, it is difficult to…

ながめる【眺める】 to see, to look at

–ながら   though; while

なぐさめる【慰める】 to comfort

なくなる —…することがなくなる to stop doing

なぐりかかる【殴り掛かる】 to make as if to strike [hit] (a person)

なす【成す】 to do, to make

なぜ【何故】 why

なぜか   somehow; for some reason

なぜなら   (that is) because

なぞ【謎】 mystery

なっとく【納得】 —納得のいく satisfactory

–など【–等】 and the like, and all that

なな【七】 seven

なに【何】 what

なにか【何か】 something; some (kind of)

なにごと【何事】 everything, anything —何事においても in everything [anything]

なにも【何も】 —何も言わずに without saying anything —何も…ない nothing

あ   か   さ   た   な   は   ま   や   ら   わ

あ

か

さ

た

な

は

ま

や

ら

わ

なにもかも【何もかも】everything

なべ【鍋】pan, pot

なまいき(な)【生意気(な)】cocky, saucy, impudent ─生意気盛りである to be at that cocky age ➤ –ざかり(–盛り)

なやむ【悩む】to worry, to be troubled

–ならない ─…してはならない must not do, should not do ─…しなければならない must do, have to do

–ならぬ ➤ –ならない

ならべたてる【並べ立てる】to tell (a pack of lies), to spout off (a load of crap)

ならべる【並べる】① to lay [put] side by side ② to put in the same category; to compare…side by side

–なり [archaic form of –である] to be

なりたつ【成り立つ】to consist of, to be made up of

なりひびく【鳴り響く】to resound ➤ ごうおん(轟音)

なる ① to be, to become, to get, to come to… ② ➤ かじ(火事), ぎろん(議論)

なるほど【成程】indeed

なれしたしむ【慣れ親しむ】to become familiar with and fond of

なん–【何–】how many…

–なんて   and the like

なんでも【何でも】anything, everything

なんと【何と】how, what ─何と言っても no matter what one says

なんとか【何とか】somehow ─…とか何とか… or something ─何とかする to do something about it; to take care of it

なんとなく【何となく】somehow, in some way; for some reason or another

なんとも【何とも】quite; very, really ─なんともいえぬ indescribable

なんども【何度も】many times

なんもん【難問】difficult question [problem]

なんら【何ら】─何ら…(も)ない not at all

に

に【二】two

–に   to

においたつ【匂い立つ】to be enveloped (in fragrance); to be radiant

–において【–に於いて】in (the field of)…, at…; on…

–における【–に於ける】with, in, at

にがて(な)【苦手(な)】─(…が)苦手である ① to be bad [poor] (at…) ② to dislike

にがにがしい【苦々しい】bitter

–にかんする【–に関する】about, on, concerning

にぎやか(な)【賑やか(な)】lively, noisy

にく【肉】meat

–にくい【–難い】─…しにくい to be hard to do

にくたい【肉体】body ─肉体的な physical

にくづきめん【肉付き面】undetachable (face) mask [from a Japanese folk tale]

にこにこ ─にこにこする to smile

にじっぷん【二十分】(for) twenty minutes

にじむ【滲む】to ooze

にじゅう【二十】twenty

にせ(の)【偽(の)】false, fake

にせん【二千】two thousand

にせんまん【二千万】twenty million

にた【似た】─…に似た similar to…

–にたいして【–に対して】to, toward

–にたいする【–に対する】to, toward

にちじょう【日常】every day (routine)

—日常の everyday, daily　—日常生活（せいかつ）
everyday life

にちべい【日米】Japan and America

-について　about, on　—…については
as for [to]…

にっこり　—にっこり笑（わら）う to smile sweetly

-につれ　as…

-にとって　for; to

にひゃく【二百】two hundred

にひゃくねん【二百年】two hundred years

にほん【日本】Japan　—日本の Japanese
—日本文学（ぶんがく）Japanese literature　—日本
民族（みんぞく）Japanese race　—日本列島（れっとう）Japa-
nese islands　—日本数学会（すうがくかい）Mathemat-
ical Society of Japan

にほんご【日本語】Japanese (language)

にほんじん【日本人】the Japanese

-にもかかわらず　however; nevertheless

ニュアンス　nuance, a shade (of meaning)　—（…という）ニュアンスが漂（ただよ）う to
have the nuance (that…)

にゅうもん【入門】introduction; An Introduction to…(in book title)

にょじつ（に）【如実（に）】clearly

-によって　①owing to, due to, thanks
to　②by

にる【似る】to look like…, to resemble

-にわたって【-に亘って】for, over

-にん【-人】[counter for people]

にんい（に）【任意（に）】at random

にんげん【人間】person, people; human
being

にんげんかんけい【人間関係】human re-
lations

にんげんせい【人間性】one's human nature, humanity

ぬ

ぬぐう【拭う】to wipe (off), to mop

ぬけだす【抜け出す】to get out (of…)

ぬまち【沼地】marsh

ね

ねいす【寝椅子】couch, lounge

ねだん【値段】price　—値段の高（たか）い pric-
ey, expensive

ねっしん（に）【熱心（に）】earnestly

ねん¹【念】(strong) desire; wish　—念を
送（おく）る to pray (for), to deeply desire

ねん²【年】①[counter for years]　②[suf-
fix for a specific year]

-ねんかん【-年間】[counter for year-
long periods]

ねんがん【念願】wish　—念願する to wish

ねんげつ【年月】years; (long) time

ねんだい【年代】age, period　—…年代
the…(')s

ねんぱい【年配】—年配の elderly

-ねんめ【-年目】[ordinal counter for
years]

の

ノーマン・メイラー　Norman Mailer

のこす【残す】to leave; to preserve

のっとる【則る】—…に則って accord-
ing to…, following…

-ので　because; since, as

-のに　in spite of, despite; though

のびる【伸びる】to extend, to continue

のまれる【飲まれる】to be overwhelmed

-のみ　only, just; alone

のみほす【飲み干す】to drink up; to
finish

のる¹【乗る】①to take (a train), to get
on [in]　②➢かぜ（風）—…に乗って
in, on

のる²【載る】①to appear (in a magazine)　②to be put on (a table)

ノンフィクション　nonfiction

は

ば【場】place; occasion

ばあい【場合】case; occasion

バイオロジスト　biologist

はいご【背後】the back, the rear

はいじん【俳人】haiku poet

はいたつ【配達】delivery ―配達する to deliver

はいりこむ【入り込む】to find one's way into…; to be introduced

はいる【入る】① to enter, to go into ② ➤ て(手), ほんだい(本題), みみ(耳) ―入ってゆく to go [walk] into

はかい【破壊】destruction ―破壊する to destroy

はかせ【博士】doctor, PhD ―…博士 Dr.…, Professor…

はかない【儚さ】transient

はかなさ【儚さ】fragility; transience

ばかばかしい【馬鹿馬鹿しい】foolish, stupid, ridiculous

バカヤロー【馬鹿野郎】Idiot!

-ばかり　only ―…ばかりか not only…

ばくは【爆破】blowing up; blast ―爆破する to blow up, to blast

はくぶつかん【博物館】museum

はくりょく【迫力】appeal; power, punch ―迫力がある appealing; powerful

はげしい【激しい】strong, intense ➤ じこしゅちょう(自己主張)

はさむ【挟む】to put…between ―…を挟んだ across…from

はじまる【始まる】to start, to begin ➤ いま(今)

はじめて【初めて】for the first time ―…して初めて…する it's not until… that (one) does…

はじめる【始める】to start, to begin

-はじめる【-始める】to begin to do

ばしょ【場所】place

はしる【走る】to run

はず【筈】should be, ought to be, must be ―…のはずである it should be… ―…するはずがない it cannot [can't] be…; it is highly unlikely that…

はずかしい【恥ずかしい】shameful, embarrassing; ashamed, embarrassed ―恥ずかしながら I'm ashamed to say that…

パスタ　pasta

バスターミナル　bus terminal

はち¹【八】eight

はち²【鉢】pot, flowerpot

パチンコてん【パチンコ店】pachinko parlor

バツ　× mark

はっき【発揮】―発揮する to show, to display

はっきり　―はっきりした clear ―はっきりする to become clear

はっけん【発見】discovery ―発見する to discover

はっそう【発想】idea

はっぴょう【発表】―発表する to publish (a book)

ばとう【罵倒】―罵倒する to abuse, to denounce

はな【花】flower; blossom

はなし【話】story

-(っ)ぱなし【-放し】[emphatic expression indicating that a current (undesirable) state is allowed to continue]

はなす¹【話す】to talk

はなす²【放す】to let…go

はなつ【放つ】to spit out

はなはだしい【甚だしい】enormous, extreme, gross

はなや【花屋】flower shop

はなれる【離れる】to leave ―離れにくい difficult to leave (the place)

ははおや【母親】mother

ハムレット Hamlet

ばめん【場面】scene

はもの【刃物】knife; sharp-edged instruments

はやい【早い】early

はやく【早く】quickly, soon ➤ いっこく（一刻）

はら【腹】stomach ―腹が減る to become hungry

バランス balance

パリ Paris

はる¹【貼る】to put (up), to stick

はる²【張る】➤ ラベル

はる³【春】spring

はるか【遥か】very; far (back)

はれる【晴れる】to lift

ハワイ Hawaii

はん-【反-】anti- ―反キリスト主義者（しゅぎしゃ）anti-Christian

パン [mimetic word indicating decisive action]

ばんぐみ【番組】(TV) program

パンクロック punk rock

ばんこう【蛮行】act of barbarism

はんしんタイガース【阪神タイガース】the Hanshin Tigers (a baseball team)

はんせい【反省】reflection ―反省（を）する to reflect on (one's behavior), to search one's soul; to regret

はんたい【反対】the opposite, the contrary ―反対の opposite ―反対に on the contrary

はんだん【判断】judgment

パンテオン pantheon

ばんねん【晩年】―晩年に in one's last years

パンフレット pamphlet

はんろん【反論】counterargument, refutation

ひ

ひ【日】day

びがく【美学】aesthetics

ひかり【光】light; sunlight

ひきうける【引き受ける】to accept, to take (a job)

ひく【引く】to draw (a line) ➤ アイライン

ビクッと with a start ―ビクッとする to be startled (at)

ひこうき【飛行機】plane

ひさしぶり（に）【久しぶり（に）】after a long time

ひする¹【比する】to compare…(with/to) ―…に比して compared with [to]…

ひする²【秘する】to conceal, to keep…secret

ひたすら ―ひたすら…する to concentrate on doing

ひだりどなり【左隣】―左隣の on one's left

ひつぜんてき（な）【必然的（な）】inevitable, unavoidable

ひっぱる【引っ張る】to draw; to pull

ひつよう【必要】necessity; need ―…する必要がある to need to do ―必要以上（いじょう）に more than necessary

ひてい【否定】negation, denial ―否定する to negate; to deny

ひていけい【否定形】negative ―否定形の negative

ひと【人】person; people; human being

ひどい hard, terrible

ひとこと【一言】a (single) word ―一言

あ
か
さ
た
な
は
ま
や
ら
わ

注意する　to say something (to...)

ひとしきり　for a while

ひとたち【人達】people

ひとつ【一つ】① one　② [followed by a negative] not a single...　―一つの one..., a certain...; alone

ひととおり【一通り】all

ひとびと【人々】people

ひとまえ【人前】―人前で　in public

ひとり【一人】one (person)　―...の一人 one of...

ビバ　Viva!

ひはん【批判】criticism

ひび【日々】every day

ひびき【響き】tone

ひびきあう【響き合う】to match

ひひょう【批評】criticism　―批評する to criticize

ひふんこうがい【悲憤慷慨】―悲憤慷慨 する to be indignant (over); to deplore

ひみつ【秘密】secret

びみょう(な)【微妙(な)】subtle　―微妙 に a little; slightly, subtly

ひゃく【百】hundred

ひゃくねん【百年】a hundred years

ひゃくまんねん【百万年】a million years

ピューリタン　puritan

ひょういつ【飄逸】unconventionality, freedom from convention

ひょうげん【表現】expression　―表現 (を)する to express

ひょうげんしゃ【表現者】writer, word-smith

ひょうじょう【表情】expression, look

ひょうそう【表層】surface

ひょうろん【評論】review; critique　―評 論する to review; to critique

ひょうろんか【評論家】critic

ひらく【開く】to open

ひらける【開ける】to open

ピリオド　period

ビル　(tall) building

ひれい【比例】proportion　―比例する to be proportional

ひろい【広い】large, big; vast

ピン　―ピンとくる to click in one's mind

ひんしゅつ【頻出】―頻出する to appear frequently

びんしょう【憫笑】―憫笑を誘う to make a person smile with pity

びんびん　[mimetic word indicating a powerful, pulsating quality]

びんぼう【貧乏】poverty　―貧乏くさ さ shabbiness

ふ

ふあん【不安】uncertainty

ふいに【不意に】suddenly

ふうあい【風合い】texture; atmosphere

ふうけい【風景】scene; scenery

ふかい【深い】① deep　② serious　―深 く deeply

ぶかつどう【部活動】club activity

ふかのう(な)【不可能(な)】impossible

ふくざつ(な)【複雑(な)】complicated 　―複雑さ　complexity

ふくむ【含む】to include

ふしぎ(な)【不思議(な)】mysterious; wonderful　―不思議に strangely, in-explicably

ふたつ【二つ】two (things)　―二つの two

ふたり【二人】two (people)

ぶちこわす【ぶち壊す】to destroy

ふつう(の)【普通(の)】normal, ordi-nary, usual　―普通に　normally, ordi-narily

ぶっかく【仏閣】temple

ぶつかる　to face (a problem)

ぶつぶつ ―ぶつぶつ文句を言う to mutter, to grumble

ぶべつ【侮蔑】insult

ふへん（の）【不変（の）】unchangeable

プラス plus ―プラスする to add

フランスご【フランス語】French (language)

ふる【振る】to shake; to wave ＞て（手）

ふるい【古い】old

ふるえる【震える】to shake, to tremble

プレゼント present, gift

ふれる【触れる】① to touch ② to touch on (a subject) ＞かくしん（核心）

プロセス process

プロデューサー producer

ふろば【風呂場】bathroom

フン Ha!, Huh!

ぶん【文】writing ＞ぶんしょう（文章）

－ふん・ぷん【－分】[counter for minutes]

－ぶん【－分】insofar as...

ふんいき【雰囲気】atmosphere, mood, air

ぶんか【文化】culture

ふんがい【憤慨】―憤慨する to be outraged

ぶんがく【文学】literature ―文学をする to work on literature

ぶんがくしゃ【文学者】*bungakusha*; litterateur; literary person

ぶんげいし【文芸誌】literary magazine

ぶんしょう【文章】(a piece of) writing; sentence(s)

ぶんじん【文人】literatus

ぶんたい【文体】(writing) style

ふんぱつ【奮発】―奮発する to be generous (with money), to splurge

ぶんまつ【文末】the end of a sentence

ぶんみゃく【文脈】context

へ

へいあんじだい【平安時代】Heian period

へいき【平気】―平気である one doesn't care [mind]

べいご【米語】American English

べいこく【米国】the United States

へいせつ【併設】annex ―併設する to establish...as an annex (to...)

へいほうこん【平方根】square root

－べき should do, ought to do

べつ（の）【別（の）】other, another ―別に...ない not particularly, not...in particular

ベッドカバー bedspread

べつべつ（の）【別々（の）】different; each

ヘドロ sludge, colloidal sediment

へりくだる to be humble ―へりくだった humble ―へりくだって humbly

へる【減る】＞はら（腹）

へん（な）【変（な）】strange, weird

へんか【変化】change ―変化する to change

べんきょうづくえ【勉強机】(study) desk

へんせん【変遷】transition ―変遷を繰り返す to keep changing

ほ

－（っ）ぽい -ish, -like

ほう【方】direction ―...のほうへ toward, in the direction of...

－ほう【－方】① rather than ② [indicates that the speaker is referring to something in comparison or contrast to another] the one

ほうかい【崩壊】collapse ―崩壊する to collapse

ぼうげん【暴言】scathing remark, abusive words

ほうこうづけ【方向付け】orientation

あ
か
さ
た
な
は
ま
や
ら
わ

ほうそう【包装】wrapping 　—包装（を）する to gift wrap

ぼうだい（な）【膨大（な）】enormous

ほうっておく【放っておく】to ignore; to let...alone

ほうべん【方便】means, expedient —方便の expedient

ほうほう【方法】way, method

ほうほうろん【方法論】methodology

ほうめん【方面】way, direction

ホーム　platform (at a station)

ほかの【他の】other

ほがらか（な）【朗らか（な）】cheerful, merry, bright

ぼく【僕】—僕は・僕が I —僕の my —僕に・僕を me

ポケット　pocket

ほご【保護】preservation

-ほしい【-欲しい】—...してほしい to want (a person) to do

ポスター　poster

ほそい【細い】narrow

ほぞん【保存】preservation 　—保存する to preserve 　—保存状態 state of preservation 　—保存状態の良い well-preserved

ほっと【ほっと・ホッと】—ほっとする to be [feel] relieved

ほど【程】limit 　—...にも程がある ...to the extreme, there is a limit to...

-ほど【-程】≻あれほど（の）（あれ程（の）），しんじる（信じる）—AほどBだ　so B that A

ほとけばな【仏花】flowers for offering at a Buddhist altar or grave

ほとんど【殆ど】almost —ほとんどの most

ボリューム　volume —ボリュームを下げる to turn the volume down

ほろびる【滅びる】to go to ruin, to be ruined

ほん【本】book

-ほん・ぽん【-本】[counter for long objects]

ほんしつ【本質】essence

ほんしつてき（な）【本質的（な）】essential

ぼんじん【凡人】ordinary person [people], layman

ほんだい【本題】the main issue [subject] 　—本題に入る to get to the point

ほんと　[colloquial form of ほんとう] the truth —ほんとの true

ほんとう（の）【本当（の）】true 　—本当に[は] actually, really, indeed

ほんぶ【本部】headquarters

ほんもの（の）【本物（の）】true, genuine

ほんやく【翻訳】translation 　—翻訳する to translate 　—翻訳可能な translatable 　—翻訳不可能な untranslatable

ほんらい（の）【本来（の）】① natural, innate ② true; proper

ま【間】time; interval 　—間がもたない Time hangs heavy on one's hands. 　—間をもたせる to fill in the time

まあ　oh; well; Oh dear!

-まい【-枚】[counter for thin, flat objects]

ま

マイナー（な）minor, less famous

マイナス（の）negative

マイノリティ　minority

まえ【前】① (the) front ② ≻もっと —...の前の in front of... —...する前に before doing... —前に before, once —少し前 a little while ago

まぎれもなく【紛れもなく】unmistakably, undoubtedly

まさに　indeed

まし better

まじめ(に)【真面目(に)】 seriously, earnestly

まじめさ【真面目さ】 seriousness

まじる【混じる】 to mix, to mingle

まず first, first of all

まずい Oh no!; Oops!

また【又】 and, moreover, besides

まだ【未だ】 still, too... ―まだ...ない not yet; never

またしても【又しても】 once again

まだまだ ―まだまだ...ある much, even, still

まち【町】 town, city

まちがい【間違い】 mistake, error ➤ けいさんまちがい(計算間違い)

まちがう【間違う】 to make a mistake ―間違った wrong

まちなみ【町並】 (houses on) the street

まちや【町屋】 traditional houses (in town)

まつ【待つ】 to wait (for)

まっか(な)【真っ赤(な)】 (deep) red, crimson ―真っ赤な嘘 outright lie, absolute lie

まっしろ(な)【真っ白(な)】 completely white, snow-white

まっすぐ(な)【真っ直ぐ(な)】 straight

まったく【全く】 ―全く...ない not...at all

-まで【-迄】 ① till, until ② to, into ―今まで (up) until now

-までも even

まど【窓】 window

まどわす【惑わす】 to confuse, to mislead

まぶしい bright ―まぶしいほどの dazzling

まぼろし【幻】 illusion

-まま【-儘】 ―...のままで as it is

まもる【守る】 to keep, to follow, to observe

まりょく【魔力】 magic, magical power

まるで ① as if... ② [followed by a negative] not...at all

まわりくどい【回りくどい】 circuitous, roundabout ―回りくどく in circles; beating around the bush

まわりもち【回り持ち】 (performing one's duty) by taking turns ―回り持ちで by turns

まんぞく【満足】 satisfaction ―満足して content, satisfied ―満足する to be satisfied, to be happy

まんぞくかん【満足感】 (feeling of) satisfaction

まんねんひつ【万年筆】 fountain pen

まんめん(の)【満面(の)】 ➤ えみ(笑み)

み

み【身】 body ―身につける to learn, to acquire

ミイラ mummy

みえる【見える】 ① to seem, to look; to appear ② to see, to show ③ to be seen ➤ め(目) ④ it seems (that)..., it looks like... ―見えてくる to come into sight

みおくる【見送る】 to see...off

みぎの【右の】 foregoing, above-mentioned

みぎどなり【右隣】 ―右隣の on one's right

みごと(な)【見事(な)】 marvelous; excellent

みじかい【短い】 short

みせ【店】 store, shop

みせる【見せる】 to show

-みせる ―...してみせる to do...intentionally

あ
か
さ
た
な
は
ま
や
ら
わ

-みたいな　like...

-みたいに　as if

みたす【満たす】to satisfy

みだれる【乱れる】to be disturbed [confused] ―千々に乱れる to be torn [rent] with conflicting emotions

みち【道】① way; road, route ② specialty; something that a person pursues ―...への道 way to... ―道とする to pursue

みちあふれる【満ち溢れる】to be full of, to be filled with

みつかる【見つかる】to be found

みっともない　shameful, disgraceful, unseemly

みとめる【認める】to admit, to accept

みな【皆】all

みなさん【皆さん】all (of them)

みなり【身なり】appearance ―身なりのいい well-dressed

みみ【耳】ear ―耳に入る to hear ―耳にする to hear

みゃくらく【脈絡】rule ―脈絡のない irregular

-みよう　―...してみよう Let's...

みょう【妙】magic; miracle ―組み合わせの妙 a magical combination

みょうに【妙に】strangely

みりょく【魅力】charm, allure, attraction, appeal

みる【見る・観る】to see, to look at, to watch

-みる　―...してみる to try to do, to try doing

みわける【見分ける】to tell the difference (between)

みんぞく【民族】race, nation

みんぞくしゅぎ【民族主義】nationalism

みんな　everyone; all

む

む【無】nothing, nothingness

むいしき【無意識】unconsciousness ―無意識に unconsciously

ムード　mood; air, atmosphere ―...のムードを出す to suggest something in one's attitude

むかう【向かう】to go, to head for...

むかえる【迎える】to welcome

むかし【昔】(in) olden days; long time ago ―昔の of old; former, ex- ―昔から for a long time; since olden times ―遠い昔から since ancient times

むける【向ける】to direct ➤ め（目） ―...に向けた to...; addressed to...

むげん（に）【無限（に）】infinitely

むごい【酷い】cruel, merciless

むこう【向こう】the opposite [other] side ―...の向こうに beyond...

むじょう【無常】impermanence, mutability ―無常に transiently ➤ かわりゆく（変わりゆく）

むしろ【寧ろ】rather

むしん（な）【無心（な）】innocent

むずかしい【難しい】difficult

むすびあう【結び合う】to be bound together

むすびつく【結び付く】to be related

むすびつける【結び付ける】to connect

むだ（な）【無駄（な）】wasteful

むち（な）【無知（な）】ignorant

むなしさ【空しさ】emptiness

むね【胸】breast; heart ―胸ポケット breast pocket

むり【無理】unreasonableness ―無理な unreasonable ―無理（も）なく reasonably, naturally ―無理に...させる to force (a person) to do

むりすう【無理数】irrational number

め

め【目】① eye ② experience ―目が行く to look at ―目に見える visible ―目に飛び込む to burst into view …の目の前に right in front of… ―目を向ける to look at, to turn one's eyes to ―(…な)目に逢う to have a … experience

めいげん【名言】famous quote; witticism

めいし【名詞】noun

めいじる【命じる】to order ―…を命じられる to be told to…

めいめい【命名】naming ―命名する to name, to call

めぐらす【巡らす】➤ おもい(思い)

めぐる【巡る】―…を巡る[巡って] about …, concerning …

めくるめく【目眩く】dazzling

めだつ【目立つ】to be noticeable, to be conspicuous, to stand [stick] out

メッセージ message

めまい【眩暈】dizziness ―めまいを起こす to feel dizzy

めん【面】aspect

メンタリティー mentality

めんどう(な)【面倒(な)】troublesome, tiresome

も

-も also ―Aも(Bもない) neither A nor B

もう ① already ② [followed by a negative] not…any more, no more

もうひとつ【もう一つ】―もう一つの another

もくぞう【木造】―木造の built of wood

もくてき【目的】goal, purpose ―目的地 destination, goal

もし if

もじ【文字】letter; character ―文字どおり literally

もしかすると possibly; maybe, perhaps

もしくは【若しくは】or

もじもじ ―もじもじ(と)した uncomfortable; restless

もちいる【用いる】to use

もちだす【持ち出す】to bring out

もちば【持ち場】(one's) post

もちろん【勿論】of course

もつ【持つ】① to carry ② to have, to hold; to possess ➤ きょうみ(興味) ③ ➤ ま(間)

もったいぶる【勿体ぶる】―もったいぶって pretentiously

もっと more ―もっと前に earlier

もっとも【最も】(the) most

もっぱら【専ら】chiefly, mainly

もと【元】―もとの as it was

もとづく【基づく】―…に基づいた based on…

もとめる【求める】① to look for, to seek ② to ask for, to call upon ―…を求めて in search of…

もともと【元々】by nature, naturally

もどる【戻る】to come back, to return

もの【物】thing, item; stuff

ものかき【物書き】writer

ものすごく【物凄く】very, extremely

-ものの though, although

ものほしげ(な)【物欲しげ(な)】wistful

もはや【最早】now; already

-もまた【-も又】also

もらう to receive, to get

-もらう ―…してもらう to have (a person) do

もり【森】woods

もりあがる【盛り上がる】to get excited

もろい【脆い】fragile

あ

か

さ

た

な

は

ま

や

ら

わ

もろさ【脆さ】fragility

もんきりがた【紋切型】stereotype

もんく【文句】① words ② complaint ―文句を言う to complain ―文句一つ言わずに without a single complaint

もんぜんばらい【門前払い】―門前払いになる to be turned away at the door

もんだい【問題】problem, question; matter, issue ―問題を出す to give (a person) a question [problem] ―問題は…である The problem is that…

や

やがて in (due) time, eventually; some day

-やがる [added to verb stems to show the speaker's disapproval of the subject's action; used mainly by men]

やく-【約-】about, approximately

やくす【訳す】to translate

やさい【野菜】vegetable(s)

やさしい【優しい】kind ―優しく kindly

やたら【矢鱈】really, very; too, terribly

やつ【奴】① fellow, guy ② thing

やってくる to come over [along]

やってのける to accomplish, to succeed in doing

やってみる to try

やはり ① after all, ultimately ② as expected

やむなく ―やむなく…する to be obliged [forced] to do

やめる【止める】to stop, to quit, to give up

ややこしい complicated, bothersome

やりかた【やり方】how [the way] to do it

やりなおし【やり直し】―やり直す to start again from the beginning; to do over

やる to do

やろう【野郎】guy, fellow ―あの野郎 [referring disparagingly to a man] that guy

やわらかい【柔らかい】gentle

ゆ

ゆいいつ(の)【唯一(の)】(one and) only

ゆううつ(な)【憂鬱(な)】gloomy, depressed

ゆうしょく【夕食】dinner

ゆうじん【友人】friend

ゆうする【有する】to have

ゆうせん【優先】priority ―(…を)優先する to give priority (to…)

ゆうはん【夕飯】dinner

ゆうめい(な)【有名(な)】famous

-ゆえ(に)【-故(に)】because (of)

ゆかい(な)【愉快(な)】① enjoyable, fun ② pleasant, cheerful

ゆきわたる【行き渡る】to spread, to go around

ゆく【行く】≻め(目)

-ゆく ―…してゆく to be doing

ゆるす【許す】to overlook, to excuse ―許される to be excused

よ

よ【夜】night; evening ―ある夜 one night [evening]

よい【良い】good, nice, fine; pleasant

よう【用】something (to do)

-よう【-用】for…

ようご【用語】term

ようしょう(の)【幼少(の)】young, little (describing a person) ―幼少時に when one was a little child

ようす【様子】the situation

ようそ【要素】element, aspect

−ようだ　it seems that…; it looks as if [though]…

−ような　like…

−ように　① like…; as if… ② as… ③ in order to…, so (that) one will…

ヨーロッパ　Europe　―ヨーロッパの European　―ヨーロッパ製の made in Europe

よかった【良かった】Good, Great.　―…すればよかった　should have done

よかん【予感】feeling, hunch　―予感する to have a feeling (that…)

よく【良く】① well, fully, quite ② often, a lot

−よく【−欲】desire (for…)　―知識欲 appetite for knowledge

よこ【横】―横の horizontal　―横軸 horizontal axis

よごす【汚す】to dirty

よさ【良さ】(the quality of) being good

よそう【予想】expectation　―予想外の unexpected

よそく【予測】prediction　―予測がつく to (be able to) predict, to imagine

よそもの【余所者】outsider; stranger

よてい【予定】―…する予定である to be going to do

よにも【世にも】extremely

よのなか【世の中】the world

よびかける【呼び掛ける】to appeal for, to call for

よびりん【呼び鈴】doorbell

よぶ【呼ぶ】to call　―呼んで来る to go and get (a clerk)

よほど【余程】greatly

よみて【読み手】reader

よむ【読む】to read

よめ【嫁】wife　―嫁に行く to marry into (a family)

よゆう【余裕】composure; breathing space, elbow room　―余裕ができる to be unconcerned about (money)

より　➣ うで(腕)

−より(も)　(rather) than…; more…

よりそう【寄り添う】to cuddle　―寄り添い合う to cuddle up together

よる【寄る】➣ おもい(思い)

よろこび【歓び・喜び】pleasure, joy

よろこぶ【喜ぶ】to be pleased

よわい【弱い】weak; easily affected

ら

−ら　[suffix added to form plurals]

らいきゃく【来客】guest, visitor

ライター　writer

ライティング　writing

らいねん【来年】next year

−らしい　① to seem, to look (like); to appear ② it seems that [like]…, it looks like… ③ to be like…, to be suitable for… ④ it is said that…, I hear that…

ラディカル(な)　radical

ラベル　label　―ラベルを張る to label

−られる　[added to the **-nai** stems of Group 2 verbs to form the passive voice]

らん【蘭】orchid

らんぼう(な)【乱暴(な)】rough, rude

り

りかい【理解】understanding　―理解する to understand

りくつ【理屈】theory

りこうがくぶ【理工学部】College of Science and Technology

りじちょう【理事長】chief director

りゅうこう【流行】fashion, trend　―流

あ

か

さ

た

な

は

ま

や

ら

わ

行である to be trendy

りょう【量】amount

りょうて【両手】hands ―両手を合わせる to put one's hands together

りょうほう【両方】both sides

りょうり【料理】cooking; dish, food ―料理をする to cook

りんと【凛と】―凛とした valiant, high-spirited

れ

れい【例】example ―例に挙げる to give an example ― 例 に よって typically; true to form

れいがい【例外】exception ―例外なく without exception

れいけつ【冷血】*In Cold Blood*

れいしょう【冷笑】―冷笑する to sneer at, to mock

れいとうほぞん【冷凍保存】―冷凍保存（に）する to keep...frozen

れきし【歴史】history ―歴史 上 in history

れっとう【列島】(a chain of) islands

-れる [added to the **-nai** stems of Group 1 verbs to form the passive voice]

れんぞく【連続】succession

れんぱつ【連発】―連発する to say (complimentary things) repeatedly

ろ

ローカルせん【ローカル線】local line

ローマ Rome

ろくでもない worthless, silly

ロマン one's ideal; one's dream

わ

わ【和】sum, total

-わい [old-fashioned exclamation]

わかい【若い】young

わがくに【我が国】our country [nation]

わがまま（な）【我が儘（な）】selfish, willful

わかもの【若者】young man [woman], young people

わかり【分かり】understanding ―お分かり（である）[honorific expression] one understands that...

わかりきった【分かり切った】obvious, plain

わかりやすい【分かりやすい】easy to understand; clear

わかる【分かる】to know, to understand; to get, to see

わがみ【我が身】one's body

わく【沸く】to occur, to come up

わくわく ―わくわくする to be excited

わけ【訳】―...というわけではない it is not that...

わけいる【分け入る】to go into...

わざ【技】skill; work, act

わざわざ ―わざわざ...してくれる to be kind enough to do...

わずか（な）【僅か（な）】few

わすれる【忘れる】to forget

わだい【話題】topic (of conversation) ―話題になる to be talked about

わたし【私】―私は・私が I ―私の my を・私に me ―私自身 myself

わやく【和訳】translation into Japanese ―和訳する to translate into Japanese

わらい【笑い】smile ➢ あいそ（愛想）

わらう【笑う】to smile ➢ にっこり

わり【割】―割に・割と rather, fairly; relatively ―...の割に for all...; in spite of...

わる【割る・÷】divided by... ―6÷3＝2 Six divided by three is two.

あ　か　さ　た　な　は　ま　や　ら　わ

わるい【悪い】 ① bad, poor ② ＞ しまつ
　（始末）

を

−**をめぐって**【−を巡って】＞ めぐる（巡る）
−**をめぐる**【−を巡る】＞ めぐる（巡る）

あ

か

さ

た

な

は

ま

や

ら

わ

Notes

Essays

真っ白な嘘

1　**嘘をつく<u>のは</u>**　The の here turns what comes before it—嘘をつく—into a noun phrase. The は after の is not a topic-marker; it simply indicates contrast: the implication is that Murakami may be good at other things, but insofar as telling lies is concerned, he is not so skilled.

でも嘘をつくこと自体は　こと, like の above, is a nominalizer: that is, it turns what comes before it into a noun phrase. Unlike の, however, こと is usually used for abstract actions rather than perceptible ones. 自体 is like the English pronoun "itself" as used for emphasis. The は after it is, again, contrastive: "the act of telling a lie itself."

それほど嫌いではない　それほど literally means "to that extent."

変な言い方<u>だけど</u>　けど is a contracted, colloquial form of けれども.

つまり...<u>ということです</u>　ということです is a fixed phrase used for expressing, among other things, the meaning of a word, saying, passage, etc. Here Murakami uses it to explain the meaning of his first two statements, ぼくは嘘をつくのは得意ではない。でも嘘をつくこと自体はそれほど嫌いではない。"I'm not good at telling lies. But I don't abhor the act of telling a lie in itself." Note the change in style from the plain style in the first two sentences, to the **desu/-masu** style in this last one. This type of shift in sentence style is common in written Japanese. One of the differences between the two styles is that **desu/-masu** sounds *subjective* whereas the plain **da/de aru** sounds *objective*.

「深刻な嘘をつくのは...好きだ」　The quotation marks are used to set off the idea.

2　**<u>ある</u>月刊誌<u>で</u>書評を<u>頼まれた</u>ことがある**　ある ("a certain...") is used to refer to something or someone in a nonspecific way: ある日 "one day." 頼まれる is the passive form of 頼む ("to ask"). で in this case shows the "agent," or the person or thing that initiates the action. に or から more commonly performs this role.

僕は本を書く人間<u>で</u>　で is the -**te** form of **desu**.

書評<u>って</u>できればやりたくないんだけど　って has several usages, but here it serves as a kind of colloquial topic-marker. Think of it as meaning は or ということは.

んだ is a colloquial form of のだ. This のだ/んだ is used to offer an explanation or interpretation. Here Murakami uses it to explain his usual policy on writing book reviews, before going on to say there was a time when he accepted book-reviewing jobs.

そのときは事情があって This は is, again, contrastive: "on that occasion (as opposed to others)…" The -**te** form presents 事情がある as a reason for what follows, and corresponds more to "so" than to "and."

「まあいいや、やりましょう」と引き受けた いいや (pronounced with a falling intonation on the second syllable) is colloquial and has the nuance of "Oh, why not"; that is, it corresponds to いいか rather than to いいえ. Listen closely to the CD (0:37).

でも普通どおりにやっても どおり is a suffix. It attaches to nouns and the -**masu** stems of certain verbs to express the meaning "just as," "in the manner of," etc: 普通どおり "the usual way," 文字どおり "literally (i.e., just as the characters say)," 思いどおり "as I thought."

…ことにした "Dictionary form of a verb + ことにした" is a formal pattern that means "I decided to (VERB)."

実在しない人の伝記の書評とかね The particle combination とか indicates that what comes before it is but an example or sampling.

でっちあげをするぶん The pattern "verb (plain form) + ぶん" means roughly "insofar as (SUBJECT) (VERB)," "to the very extent that (SUBJECT) (VERB)."

「あの野郎、ろくでもないことを書きやがって」 The auxiliary verb やがる attaches to the -**masu** stems of certain verbs to convey the speaker's scorn for the person about whose action he or she is speaking.

と個人的に恨まれたりすることもないですしね –たりする has the meaning of "things like…" Here it connects to a passive verb, 恨まれる.

The "dictionary form of a verb + こともない" pattern is an emphatic variation of "dictionary form of a verb + ことはない," meaning "There is no need to (VERB)," "One doesn't have to deal with (VERBing)."

Ending the sentence with し, finally, is a conversational style for added emphasis.

3 **この偽書評を書いたときには** The は after ときに, used in conjunction with けど (later in the sentence), serves to contrast the author's feelings at the time he wrote the fake reviews with those he experienced when no letters from readers turned up.

「ろくでもない嘘<ruby>嘘<rt>うそ</rt></ruby>をつくな」　な attached to the dictionary form of a verb indicates a blunt negative imperative: "Don't (VERB)!"

<u>という</u><ruby>苦情<rt>くじょう</rt></ruby>の<ruby>手紙<rt>てがみ</rt></ruby><u>とか</u>　という (a combination of the quotation particle と and the verb <ruby>言<rt>い</rt></ruby>う) is used after a noun or clause that expresses a quotation. The noun that follows という (in this case, 苦情) defines or summarizes the noun or clause preceding it. It is easy to think of という as meaning "called …" or "that says…," though it doesn't always translate that way.

とか at the end of this phrase suggests that such a letter is one of a number of possible consequences of writing fake book reviews.

「どこに<ruby>行<rt>い</rt></ruby>けばこの<ruby>本<rt>ほん</rt></ruby>が<ruby>手<rt>て</rt></ruby>にはいる<u>のか</u>」<u>といった</u><ruby>問<rt>と</rt></ruby>い<ruby>合<rt>あ</rt></ruby>わせ　Using のか after a verb in one of its plain forms is another way of asking a question.

といった following a noun or quotation presents that word or the content of that quotation as one of many possible examples. In this case,「どこに行けばこの本が手にはいるのか」is one of many possible responses Murakami had anticipated when he wrote the fake reviews.

<ruby>来<rt>く</rt></ruby>る<u>んじゃないか</u>と<ruby>覚悟<rt>かくご</rt></ruby>していた<u>んだ</u>けど　This んじゃないか means the same as のではないですか but is more casual, more colloquial.

The んだ is, again, the same as のだ but more colloquial. It gives the sentence (everything up to けど) the air of an explanation.

<ruby>気<rt>き</rt></ruby>が<ruby>抜<rt>ぬ</rt></ruby>けた<u>というか</u>　というか is used in this way to insert one's impression or characterization of an event. Think of it as meaning "Perhaps you could say…" or "… is one way to describe it." Usually a paraphrase of some kind follows: "Another way to describe it is to say…"

まあ<u>それはそれで</u>ほっとした　それはそれで means, in this case, "as such" or "that being the case…"

<ruby>月刊誌<rt>げっかんし</rt></ruby>の<ruby>書評<rt>しょひょう</rt></ruby><u>なんて</u><ruby>誰<rt>だれ</rt></ruby>も<ruby>真剣<rt>しんけん</rt></ruby>に<ruby>読<rt>よ</rt></ruby>んで<u>ないんだろう</u>　なんて added to a noun makes that noun the topic with a derogatory tone: "something (trifling) like the book reviews in monthlies."

読んでない is a contraction of 読んでいない, while んだろう is colloquial for のだろう. んだろう and だろう both express the speaker's assumption or supposition, but a sentence ending with んだろう suggests that the speaker has made an assessment based on information or evidence he has perceived directly. だろう does not include this nuance, and generally sounds more objective.

という<ruby>気<rt>き</rt></ruby>もしなくはないんだけれど　気がする ("to feel") is the verb, but here it is used in the negative form 気もしない ("not feel…in the slightest"). The phrase is then further negated—気もしな<u>くはない</u>—with は inserted for emphasis. The meaning is "I wasn't without the feeling that…"

4　**それから**　それから is used here to indicate another similar thing rather than in the chronological sense of "and then."

<ruby>今<rt>いま</rt></ruby><u>は</u>わりにまじめに<ruby>答<rt>こた</rt></ruby>えている　は is obviously indicating a contrast here, rather than singling out 今 as the topic: *Now* the writer answers relatively straightforwardly, even if in his young days he didn't.

<ruby>生意気<rt>なまいき</rt></ruby><ruby>盛<rt>さか</rt></ruby>りの<ruby>若<rt>わか</rt></ruby>い<ruby>頃<rt>ころ</rt></ruby><u>は</u>　盛り can be added to give the meaning of "full of"—in this case, "full of cheek." The は here, too, is definitely contrastive.

インタビューでもしばしば<u>いい<ruby>加減<rt>かげん</rt></ruby>なことを<ruby>言<rt>い</rt></ruby>っていた</u>　いい加減な is a fixed phrase meaning anything from "irresponsible" and "halfhearted" to "random" or "groundless." Here the sense of いい加減なこと seems to be "harmless lies." This becomes clear in the next sentence.

<u>どんな<ruby>本<rt>ほん</rt></ruby>を<ruby>読<rt>よ</rt></ruby>んでいるかときかれて</u>　どんな is a colloquial form of どのような ("what kind of"). きかれて is the passive form of <ruby>聞<rt>き</rt></ruby>く ("to ask"). と quotes the question, What sort of books are you reading [these days]?

そうですねえ　ねえ is an elongated form of the emotive sentence-final particle ね, obviously. そうですね is often used as the immediate response to a question as one gathers one's thoughts or in polite hesitation.

<ruby>初期<rt>しょき</rt></ruby><ruby>言文<rt>げんぶん</rt></ruby><ruby>一致<rt>いっち</rt></ruby><ruby>運動<rt>うんどう</rt></ruby>　The "movement to write in the vernacular" refers to the process by which writing employing colloquial language came to replace the classical styles (Chinese and Japanese) that were used in the Meiji period (1868–1912), and which were difficult for laypeople to understand. The first novel to be written in the vernacular (or at least to be recognized as such) was Futabatei Shimei's *Ukigumo* (1887–89).

<u>とか</u><ruby>答<rt>こた</rt></ruby>えたりしてね　Murakami uses とか to give merely one example of how he answered the question, What sort of books are you reading? If he were quoting himself verbatim, he would have used と instead.

5　もちろん<u>どっち</u>の<ruby>作家<rt>さっか</rt></ruby>も<ruby>実在<rt>じつざい</rt></ruby>し<u>ない</u>　どっち is the more colloquial form of どちら ("which"). In the form どっちの…も…ない, it means "neither."

<ruby>完全<rt>かんぜん</rt></ruby>なでっちあげ<u>である</u>　である is a formal, written form of です. It gives the sentence more weight than です would.

そういう口<ruby>口<rt>くち</rt></ruby>からでまかせのことをすらすらと並<ruby>並<rt>なら</rt></ruby>べ立<ruby>立<rt>た</rt></ruby>てるのが　そういう口 is, of course, the kind of 口 that would utter things like "I find the works of Mudaguchi Shōgo or Ōsaka Gohei exciting to read even today." すらすら(と) is a mimetic word—擬態語<ruby>擬態語<rt>ぎたいご</rt></ruby> in Japanese—meaning "smoothly," "without a hitch."

得意<ruby>得意<rt>とくい</rt></ruby>というか、苦労<ruby>苦労<rt>くろう</rt></ruby>がないというか　This is the same というか we saw in paragraph 3, but here Murakami uses it twice in the same sentence to give two slightly different impressions of himself.

6　「真<ruby>真<rt>ま</rt></ruby>っ赤<ruby>赤<rt>か</rt></ruby>な嘘<ruby>嘘<rt>うそ</rt></ruby>」っていうけど　This って is a colloquial equivalent of the quotation particle と. It is different from the topic-marking って we saw in paragraph 2.

悪質<ruby>悪質<rt>あくしつ</rt></ruby>な嘘<ruby>嘘<rt>うそ</rt></ruby>をついて世間<ruby>世間<rt>せけん</rt></ruby>を惑<ruby>惑<rt>まど</rt></ruby>わせた人<ruby>人<rt>ひと</rt></ruby>には　惑わせる is one of two causative forms of 惑う, the other being 惑わす (a word in its own right that, not surprisingly, means "to confuse").

というのは例<ruby>例<rt>れい</rt></ruby>によって嘘<ruby>嘘<rt>うそ</rt></ruby>だ　例によって is a fixed expression meaning "true to form," "as usual," "as is to be expected."

いつか調<ruby>調<rt>しら</rt></ruby>べようと思<ruby>思<rt>おも</rt></ruby>っていたんだけど　The pattern "volitional form of a verb + と思う" indicates intention and usually translates as "plan to (VERB)," "think of (VERBing)," "would (VERB)."

7　これは「罪<ruby>罪<rt>つみ</rt></ruby>のない(方便<ruby>方便<rt>ほうべん</rt></ruby>の、儀礼的<ruby>儀礼的<rt>ぎれいてき</rt></ruby>な)嘘<ruby>嘘<rt>うそ</rt></ruby>」のことです　のこと is often used to explain meanings. Here it clarifies the sense of "white lie."

(これはほんと)　ほんと is a contraction of ほんとう. Note that it is missing です. The copula is often omitted in both speech and writing, for emphasis.

僕<ruby>僕<rt>ぼく</rt></ruby>の嘘<ruby>嘘<rt>うそ</rt></ruby>はどっちかというとこっちに近<ruby>近<rt>ちか</rt></ruby>い　どっちかというと is a colloquial equivalent of どちらかというと, meaning "If I had to say one way or the other..." こっち is colloquial for こちら.

赤<ruby>赤<rt>あか</rt></ruby>い大福餅<ruby>大福餅<rt>だいふくもち</rt></ruby>を12個<ruby>個<rt>こ</rt></ruby>無理<ruby>無理<rt>むり</rt></ruby>に食<ruby>食<rt>た</rt></ruby>べさせられたりしちゃ　食べさせられる is the causative-passive form of 食べる. しちゃ is a contraction of しては, essentially equivalent to "if" but signaling the expression of an unpleasant feeling on the part of the speaker/writer.

たまらないものね　たまらない is a fixed phrase meaning "can't stand." The もの that follows it is used in combination with the だって at the beginning of the sentence. In conversation, people often use this construction in explanation or self-justification for doing or not doing something: だって忙しいんだもの "But I'm busy!" Here, however, it is used more for a lightly humorous emotional touch. Often です (or another form of the copula) follows it, but here it has been omitted, making the sentence sound more "spoken."

真っ白な嘘

電車の中で若者に注意

1　**新幹線に乗っていた時のこと**　Sentences of this type, which end with の
こと（でした）, are often used in writing to introduce an episode. The
subject is "it": "It happened when I was on the bullet train." Note the
omission of the copula after こと. Sometimes writers drop the verb at
the end of the sentence, ending it with a noun, to make it tighter,
lighter, or more rhythmical.

　　若い男性二人連れが座っていたのでした　のでした is the past tense of の
です, which we saw in the previous essay (paragraph 2) in the form ん
だ, and which you will see many, many more times, not only in this
book but in all manner of literature—fiction and nonfiction—that you
go on to read. In English we wouldn't need anything other than the
words "Two young men were sitting in the seats in front of me" to
explain the circumstances, but in Japanese this particle is needed to
make it clear that these circumstances are a reason or cause for what is
about to be related (that is, "it"—the event that inspired this essay).

2　**携帯テレビのようなものを、ずーっと観ていました**　The lengthening of
ずっと is for emphasis. Note that some people use a different kanji for
viewing things deliberately (観る) and for viewing things that fall into
one's sight (見る).

　　イヤホンを使用せずに　ずに is a mostly written form of ないで and means
"without…" The -**nai** stem of the verb is used before ずに, but in the
case of the irregular verb する, せ is used.

　　音は出しっぱなし　っぱなし is added to the -**masu** stem of a verb to indicate something left as is in an undesirable state, such as a door left
open or water left running.

　　「ガーッ、シャーッ」という雑音も混じって　These are 擬音語 (onomato-
poeic words) that describe the hiss and fuzz of static.

　　とてもうるさいのです　のです again indicates an explanation of circumstances. It also has the effect of making the sentence sound more personal, and enables us to connect with the writer. On another note,
notice the tense: it is not the past tense, even though the situation
occurred in the past. Writers will often use the non-past or continuative
(-**te iru**) forms, even when talking about past events, to make us readers
feel as if we are part of the events, experiencing them as they happen.

3 私は、車掌さんが彼等に注意をしてくれるのを待ちました As you have probably learned, さん can attach to occupations, as well as to names, for politeness.

が、なかなか車掌さんは通りかからない It is not so usual to start a sentence with が in this way. Ordinarily one uses だが or でも.

The は after 車掌さん makes for a subtle contrast with the last sentence: "But the conductor [the one I had been counting on] just didn't come by."

通路を挟んだ反対側の席には To understand the structure of this phrase, think of 挟む as a verb meaning "to sandwich," "to have one thing placed between two others." The seat [in the row] opposite theirs [and mine] that sandwiches an aisle between itself and this row of seats [where we are sitting]. That's the idea.

彼が注意してくれないだろうかと期待し This does not—as it might seem to at first glance—indicate the writer's guess that the businessman "might not" admonish the young men for her. Rather, think of it as her thought, her wish that he would. 注意してくれないだろうか is essentially a request (注意してくれないでしょうか "Mightn't you admonish them for me?" in polite, spoken Japanese); と期待し ("I anticipated...") lets us know that what comes before it is a thought.

「お願いだから、こいつらにひとこと注意してくれーっ」 お願いだから is somewhat irritated in tone. こいつ is a rough form used to refer to a person or thing. It is similar to あいつ、やつ、そいつ. All can be used derogatorily or affectionately. ら indicates the plural. くれ is the blunt imperative form of くれる and is lengthened here for emphasis. The small っ is not actually pronounced but gives a feeling of sharpness.

と念を送ってみたものの ものの is much like けれども or のに.

彼は週刊誌をずっと読んでいるのみ のみ is a stronger, more formal equivalent of だけ or ばかり.

4 「では私が注意するしかないのであろうか?」 The pattern "dictionary form of a verb + しかない" means "There is nothing for it but to (VERB)," "There is no choice but to (VERB)," etc. のであろうか is a more formal form of のだろうか and expresses the speaker's/writer's inference and uneasiness.

逆ギレされてひどい目に遭う キレる is a relatively recent buzzword for

describing a person who snaps and attacks or kills someone in a kind of "street rage"; it is customarily written in katakana and hiragana. Here the form is 逆ギレ, a noun roughly meaning "misguided rage" or "uncalled-for anger"; する in the passive form attaches to it. 逆ギレ denotes the kind of absurd situation in which someone who ought to be blamed/scolded for something bursts into anger at precisely the person who ought to be doing the blaming/scolding—that is to say, the innocent victim of the blameworthy person's wrongdoing.

ひどい目に遭う is a fixed phrase meaning "to have a bad experience." Like 会う, with which this expression is sometimes written, 遭う means "encounter," but it usually refers to a *bad* encounter.

駅のホームにおいて　において in this case means the same as で (the particle for indicating a place where an action occurs) but is more literary-sounding.

大怪我をする事件がありましたっけ　っけ is added at the end of a sentence when recollecting something. It can also be used to confirm something with the listener. Here Sakai is almost confirming with us, the reader.

若い女性の側は... の側 means something close to "for ——'s part."

5　**化粧用スポンジで汗をぬぐっていただけ**　用 is a suffix meaning "for use as." Thus, 化粧用スポンジ is a sponge for applying makeup.

6　**とコメントをしていたわけですが**　わけ has many usages, but here it seems to just add emphasis to the statement, "She commented that…" It draws our attention to a fact we did not know. The が at the end of the sentence does not mean "but"; in conversation, a sentence is often ended with this particle, leaving it to the listener to fill in the conclusion.

7　**女大学的女子のたしなみと照らし合わせてみれば**　女大学 was an eighteenth-century primer of rules for proper female deportment. Think of 的 as meaning "-ish" and the phrase should become clearer.

あってはならぬ行為でしょう　ならぬ is a formal, written equivalent of ならない, ぬ being a classical negative form. The phrase あってはならない (=あってはいけない) means "unacceptable" or "will not do."

電車内化粧が当たり前となってきた今では　となる = になる ("to become"). Here なる is used in the -**te** form and followed by the auxiliary verb くる in the -**ta** form. くる used in this way often indicates progression of an action or event up to a point, either in the present or past. Because what it modifies is 今, we know that the point under discussion is in the present. So the meaning of this whole segment is, basically, "In this day and age, when putting on makeup in the train has become commonplace…"

9　**大人が言ったとしても**　言ったとしても is a more emphatic way of saying 言っても.

10　**私は別に平気だしー**　The sentence-final し makes it sound as if the speaker has more to say but isn't saying it. We can almost read her next thought: "What do you say to that!"

11　**ということで話は終ってしまう**　The こと here refers to the remark in the previous line, 私は別に平気だしー. Perhaps you could think of it as meaning 言葉 ("words") in this case.

携帯電話における電磁波とか、携帯ステレオのシャカシャカ音とか　It is widely accepted in Japan that nearby cell phones can affect heart pacemakers and that the sound leaking from the headphones of someone listening to music on the train is a public nuisance.

わかりやすい実害が無い限りは　限り is a conjunction which translates as "So long as…" or "To the extent that…"

12　**とはいえ**　This is a conjunction often used at the beginning of a sentence. Like "But still…" in English, it tells you that the writer has something more to say, usually something to the contrary.

携帯テレビの音っていうのは　っていうのは is colloquial for というのは, a structure Sakai uses to bring up a familiar subject ("the audio of a portable TV") in order to express her opinion on it. It could be replaced with ということは, but not with just は.

たとえ逆ギレして殴りかかってきたとしても　The auxiliary verb かかる can be added to the -**masu** stem of certain verbs to indicate an act starting or moving toward someone or something. The くる (here in the -**ta** form) that attaches to the -**te** form makes it clear that the movement is toward the writer. And としても makes the whole situation hypothetical: "*Even if* they flew into a rage and came over to sock me…"

相手はアンガールズっぽい若者だから　アンガールズ ("the Ungirls") is the name of a popular comedy duo who are known for their skinniness. っぽい is added to nouns (子供っぽい "childish"), or to the stems of verbs (忘れっぽい "forgetful") or adjectives (安っぽい "cheap-look-ing"), to give the meaning of "-ish" or "-like." Physical weakness is implied in the expression アンガールズっぽい.

さほど痛くはないはず　さほど is a formal equivalent of それほど. The は is here for emphasis. The sentence ends without です or one of its variants, a common characteristic of women's speech.

いやでも　This いや is a form of いいえ.

その手の若者の方が　その手の ("that kind of") can have a somewhat negative nuance.

刃物とか持っていたりして　–たり adds the meaning of "doing things like…"

手をつけられなくなるかも……　かも can be completed かもしれない.

13　**あまりの騒音に耐えきれなくなって**　きれない/きれず is added to the **-masu** stem of a verb for something which cannot be fully carried out, e.g., 食べきれない "to be too much to eat." Here it is in the continuative (-**ku**) form, followed by なる in the -**te** form.

満面の笑みを湛えつつ　"-**Masu** stem + つつ" has several usages, but in its basic sense it means "while": while the subject carries out one action, she also carries out another. It can also mean "while" in the sense of "although," "at the same time that…" It is similar to ながら but is used mainly in writing.

14　**あのう**　This interjection is often used to cautiously attract someone's attention.

15　**ソフトに語りかけた**　The auxiliary かける is added to the -**masu** stem of a verb to indicate an action starting or moving toward someone. 語りかける here means "to go up to and speak to."

16　**彼等はビクッとしたらしく**　ビクッとする is a verb of the "adverb + する" pattern, meaning "to be startled." The ビクッ is written in katakana for emphasis. らしく is the adverbial form of らしい.

17　**あ、すすすいません**　すいません is an informal version of すみません.

19　**『ちょーっと音を小さくしていただけますかぁ?』っていうのは**　Like in 「真っ白な嘘」(paragraph 6), the って is colloquial for と.

音を小さくしろってことじゃなくて　Here, and again in the next clause, って is equivalent to という rather than to と. Think of こと in this case as meaning 意味 ("meaning").

その携帯テレビの電源を切れってことなんだよッ　The ending here is colloquial and emphatic. Listen to the CD (3:48) to get a sense of its strength. In polite, textbook Japanese it would be なのですよ.

自分だってうるさいって思っていたクセに　The だって here is an emphatic equivalent of も ("also"). クセに, here written in katakana for effect, has a strongly negative tone.

注意もしないで　も replaces を for emphasis. Here the meaning is "without so much as a word [of warning]…"

ホッとしたような表情だけしているとは　ホッとする is another "adverb + する" verb, this one meaning "to feel relief." Note again the katakana.

小さい奴だなぁ！　小さい can be used for smallness of character as well as physical size. 奴 is a rough-sounding term, similar to "guy," that is applied to people and sometimes things. And な/なあ is an emotive sentence-final particle.

20　私は注意などできなかったことでしょう　Sakai could have ended this sentence with just でしょう instead of ことでしょう, but こと adds a narrative touch that makes it sound less like a report. ことでしょう/ことだろう is in fact a fixed pattern that is more emphatic, more "written" than でしょう/だろう, though both express conjecture/supposition.

注意される側だったはずです　側 literally means "side": "no doubt I would have been on the 側 of being admonished."

21　友人同士でおしゃべりをしていたら　同士 is often used as a suffix that attaches directly to other nouns for the meaning "fellow," e.g., 作家同士 "fellow writers." Here, too, it retains this meaning: "fellow friends."

おじさんが何も言わずに　おじさん can be used to refer to a middle-aged man (often with a dismissive tone) as well as for "uncle." 言わずに means 言わないで ("without saying") but sounds more literary.

「SHUT UP」と書いてある紙を差し出して去っていった　The auxiliary verb いく (here in its -ta form) makes it clear that the old man goes *away* as he leaves or disappears (去る).

22 **シャットアップって何？** This is of course very casual speech. Here we have another example of the topic-marking って. See paragraph 2 of「真っ白な嘘」for the first instance of this particle.

23 **……あっ、シャラップってこと？** This って is equivalent to という.

24 **シャラップだってさ** だって is emphatic here: "What do you mean 'Shaddup'!" It's different from the one in paragraph 19.

26 **ハワイに行った帰りは** This looks a little confusing at first, but when you break it down, it's not. 帰り is a noun meaning "return," so the literal meaning is "on our return from having gone to Hawaii."

楽しかった旅の興奮さめやらず This is almost a fixed phrase in Japanese. The meaning is basically "the excitement not yet worn off."

イケメンのスチュワードさんに イケメン is a fashionable term of recent origin. Meaning "a handsome guy," it comes from another trendy word, イケてる, meaning "to be cool" in the sense of dressing smart and looking good, and from either the noun 面 ("face") or メンズ (a misuse of "men's"?), it is not clear which.

28 **恥ずかしい思いをしたりもしましたっけか** The も retains the sense of "even": Sakai *even* had an embarrassing experience (among other things she had or did, implied by –たり). っけ, meanwhile, expresses recollection, and か turns the entire sentence into a question to oneself.

29 **そんな時代のことを思い出してみると** そんな is colloquial for そのような.

周囲の乗客なんていないも同然 なんて is sometimes used as a disparaging form of など. も同然 is a pattern for indicating that something is "as if," "just as though," "practically," "in effect." What comes before も同然 is not in fact the case, but it is just as though it were. Another way to translate 周囲の乗客なんていないも同然 would be "The passengers around them are as good as nonexistent."

今、自分達がおしゃべりをしている話題こそが 今 here does not mean "now," but "then," i.e., "now" from the point of view of the girls. こそ is a particle that adds strong emphasis to the word that comes before it.

自分達こそが世界の中心、くらいに思っている くらい applies to everything in the sentence coming before it: "It's to the extent that they even think…"

30 同じようなものなのでしょう　This segment could be worded 同じような
　　ものでしょう; both express supposition. The の, however, makes the state-
　　ment sound more like the writer's own evaluation. Note that な precedes
　　の because もの is a noun, and nouns take な before の.

　　アイラインをひく時の顔を見られても　Although no agent is specified, the
　　context makes it clear that this is the passive form of 見る, not the poten-
　　tial or any other.

　　何ら恥ずかしくない　何ら is equivalent to なにも, 少しも, ちっとも, etc.

31 気付いてきます　This is another example of くる showing progression
　　up to a certain point (see also paragraph 7). The Japanese means just
　　what it looks like it means: "*come* to realize."

　　公序良俗を守るようになってくる　One of the usages of "dictionary form
　　of a verb + ようになる" is to express the idea that something which was
　　not previously possible *becomes* possible.

32 いい大人なのに　いい大人 is an idiom indicating that one is old enough
　　to know better; いい年をしているのに is also possible here.

　　電車の中で化粧をする人を見るものです　見るものです means ときどき
　　見ることがある. もの can be used in this way to indicate a tendency.

　　たいへん痛々しいものなのです　Here we have もの *and* のです. The もの
　　is emotive; the のです is somewhere between explanatory and emphatic.

33 この度　この度 is the formal equivalent of 今度; it can refer to something
　　that has just happened, is now happening, or is going to happen soon.

　　女性専用車両　This refers to one car of a train reserved for women dur-
　　ing the morning rush hour so they can avoid male groping.

　　誰の視線も気にせず　気にせず ＝ 気にしないで.

34 恐いような興味深いような気分がいたします　恐いような modifies 気分.
　　Note the deliberate use of いたします (politer form of します) here: it
　　almost sounds cynical.

1 **男の手料理というやつ** やつ is a rough, colloquial term for people or things. It appeared also in paragraph 19 of the last essay, where it was written 奴.

2 **私が好きになれる男の手料理** なれる is the potential form of なる.

存在するにちがいない にちがいない is a fixed expression that comes at the end of a sentence and means "There is no doubt that..."

ただしくは... This is the adverbial (-**ku**) form of the adjective 正しい ("correct"), followed by the topic-marker は. It means "Correctly speaking...," "To be more accurate...," etc.

今まで喰らってきた男の料理を くらう is rougher in tone than 食う or 食べる.

3 **男はいい素材を買おうとする** 素材 is literally "raw ingredients." 食材, or "cooking ingredients," comes up later in the paragraph. 買おうとする is the "volitional form of a verb + とする" pattern. This pattern has at least two usages, but here it is used for the meaning "want to (VERB)."

もしこれがその男の日常ならば結構な話である 日常 is often used adjectivally to mean "everyday," "daily"; here it is a noun meaning "everyday routine." 結構な話である—"that would be all right"—implies it would be nice if one could afford such extravagance.

エンゲル係数 In Engel's law, the lower a family's income, the greater is the percentage spent on food.

4 **私はもう、少々頭にきはじめている** 頭にくる is an idiom meaning "to get angry." きはじめている is the -**masu** stem of くる, followed by the auxiliary verb はじめる ("to begin to [VERB]") in the -**te iru** form. Kakuta uses the -**te iru** form here, and in the previous clause, to give us the feeling of actually being there in her shoes, shopping with her man-friend and beginning to get irritated.

でも買ってみたい "-**Te** form of a verb + みる" is a pattern used for the meaning "try to (VERB) and see what it is like." Here たい is attached to the -**masu** stem of みる for the meaning "want to (VERB)." Kakuta mulls over buying expensive pasta, cheese, etc. on a daily basis: she *wants to try* buying such items *to see what they are like.*

などといじいじしているものを　と marks the content that comes before it as the writer's thoughts. Think of it as an abbreviated form of と思って.

パン！と買う　Also パーン or バン or バーン; used for the sound of a bang or wham and also figuratively for something done with much enthusiasm or vigor.

その横柄な態度。　The sentence ends with a noun. Kakuta is citing the things that cause her to begin to feel irritated. This is one of them; another follows.

素材がよくないと料理はどうたら　どうたら is an abbreviation of the colloquial, slangy, and fairly new expression どうたらこうたら. It implies a negative outcome, and indeed almost sounds like someone grumbling. The men Kakuta has accompanied on food-shopping excursions probably said something specific like 素材がよくないと料理はまずい. And that was probably not all they said; they no doubt went on about the bad results of cooking with less-than-top-notch ingredients. Kakuta abbreviates all of that with どうたら (which stands in for all those grumbles) in a fine example of the efficiency of the Japanese language. どうたらこうたら is interchangeable with どうのこうの.

料理

ただの蘊蓄でないところが始末に悪い　Usually 始末が悪い. Kakuta probably used に—a variation—because two がs one after the other would sound bad.

高いものイコールいい素材　イコール is a noun here, but it functions just like the topic-marker は. Interestingly, as you'll find out when you listen to the audio for「『博士の愛した数式』を巡って」, は is the usual reading for the equal sign.

と、彼らはピューリタンのごとく　と goes with the 信じている at the end of the sentence. ごとく is from the classical ごとし and is a more formal/written equivalent of ように or ようで.

彼らは信じている　信じる is the verb for "to believe." It is used in the **-te iru** form to indicate that their "believing" is a state that is continuously in effect.

5　**栄養バランスだの、しあわせ感だの、心の交流だの**　だの...だの, like とか...とか, is used to list examples of things. It often carries a negative nuance, though it does not in this case.

男はこの一点を忘れがちである　がち is a suffix that attaches to nouns and -**masu** stems of verbs for the meaning "prone to...," "apt to..."

五時に作り出して　出す is an auxiliary verb that attaches to the -**masu** stems of certain verbs for the meaning "to start to (VERB)." See paragraph 15 of「電車の中で若者に注意」for another such auxiliary with the same meaning.

八時になろうとしているのに　This is a different usage of the "plain volitional form of a verb + とする" pattern we saw in paragraph 3. Here the verb—"to become"—has nothing to do with the writer's will. The meaning is "to be about to (VERB)" in the sense of "to be on the verge of (VERBing)," i.e., "even though it is nearing (lit., 'about to become') eight o'clock..."

まだ作業中、ではこまるのだ　では is used to mean "in such a case" and implies a negative outcome. Think of it as meaning, in this case, そんなに長くかかるのでは or そんなに長くかかっては ("In the event it takes such a long time that...").

6　脂汗がにじんできて　The basic verb here is にじむ ("to run," as of a liquid). The auxiliary verb くる (in the -**te** form) attaches to it, indicating the emergence of a condition or phenomenon—in this case, sweat. くる here has nothing to do with movement, direction, or progression up to a point in time.

それでもほうっておくと　The central verb here is ほうる (放る), "to leave...as is." The auxiliary おく, similarly meaning "to let...be as is," attaches to its -**te** form, and the whole clause is turned into an if-statement with the addition of と: "If I am nevertheless left as is..."

まったく無関係　Kakuta could have used で after 無関係, but that would have weakened the statement. The clause sounds strong precisely because で is not there.

私が青白い顔をしていようが、脂汗をだらだら流していようが　This ようが...ようが is a more formal equivalent of ても...ても.

納得のいくものを　納得のいく is basically a set phrase meaning "satisfactory," "convincing," "compelling."

調理時間と食事のおいしさが比例すると　おいしさ is a noun created from the adjective おいしい. (The suffix さ can be added to almost any

-**i** adjective, and to a limited number of -**na** adjectives, to form a noun.) 比例すると, meanwhile, means 比例すると信じている. In other words, the と refers back to 彼_{かれ}らは信じている in the last line.

7　彼_{かれ}らは料理_{りょうり}をつくるというその一点_{いってん}にのみ　As we saw in「電車の中で若者に注意」(paragraph 3), のみ is a more formal equivalent of だけ. It is completely interchangeable with だけ but sounds stiffer, and stronger. The position of the particle に in this case is flexible: you can write either 一点にのみ or 一点のみに.

　　集中_{しゅうちゅう}しているわけで　わけ is used to explain things. わけで makes what comes before it an explanation for what follows. Unlike the usage of わけ we saw in「電車の中で若者に注意」(paragraph 6), this わけ draws our attention to something we already know or at least can readily understand. It can be translated as "as you know."

　　その集中力_{しゅうちゅうりょく}といったら　といったら in this case is interchangeable with は but is more emphatic. It grabs our attention more than は would.

　　鍋_{なべ}は焦_こがす、台所_{だいどころ}は必要_{ひつよう}以上_{いじょう}によごす　は is used in place of を for emphasis: taking up as a topic 鍋 on the one hand and 台所 on the other in quick succession like this, and then saying what men do to them, makes for a more exciting sentence.

8　これだけ騒_{さわ}いで　これだけ means, in other words, こんなにまで and refers to all the things men make such a fuss about when they cook a meal.

　　カレーだったらカレー一品_{いっぴん}だったりする　–たり's basic usage is to give an example. Here it gives "there being just one dish of curry [and nothing else] when curry is what is for dinner that evening" as paradigmatic of men "having no sense of the art of combining dishes."

　　一品_{いっぴん}であることの...貧乏_{びんぼう}くさき　くさい can be added for the meaning of "smelling of," both in a literal sense (汗_{あせ}くさい "smelling of sweat") and in a figurative sense (素人_{しろうと}くさい "amateurish").

　　一品_{いっぴん}であることの...間_まのもたなさは　間がもたない is used for something not proceeding in a regular fashion, like a stalled conversation or time hanging heavy on one's hands. Here it refers to the awkwardness and lack of rhythm in eating from only having one dish and water.

　　なぜならその一品_{いっぴん}は...逸品_{いっぴん}なのだから　Whenever you see なぜなら(ば),

料理

なぜかというと, or なぜかといえば (all of which mean, literally, "If you ask why…"), you can expect to see a からだ or だから (both meaning "it is because") at the end of the sentence.

凝りに凝って This emphatic pattern of repetition can be used with other words as well: 工夫に工夫を重ねる "using much ingenuity," 迷いに迷った末に "after much doubt and indecision."

腕によりをかけて 腕によりをかける is a set phrase meaning "to use one's skill to the fullest," "to do to the best of one's ability."

9 **彼らに、料理にたいする長期的な向上心がない** にたいする/に対する is a set phrase meaning "with respect to" or "toward," and is used to modify a noun (in this case, 向上心). You also see the form にたいしての/に対しての used as a modifier.

マイナス要素の目立つ意見を口にすると Literally, this might translate as "to give voice to an opinion that has conspicuous negative elements."

料理ごときで他人を傷つけたくない私は ごとき is another form of the classical ごとし (see also paragraph 4). Here it means the same as, but is more stiff-sounding than, のようなこと. It is mainly used in writing. When a writer uses it, she considers what comes before it—料理 in this case—to be trivial.

おいしいよ！ とっても！ とっても is a more emphatic とても.

10 **男が料理をせんとするとき** せんとする is a remnant of classical Japanese meaning しようとする (volitional form + とする).

食欲よりも、グルメ欲よりも、イベント性よりデート性より It helps to know the meaning of the kanji that are repeated here: 欲 ("desire") and 性 (the suffix "-ness").

12 **いつだってもろくて** いつだって is a colloquial and emphatic いつでも.

さびしげである げ (気) is a suffix that attaches to the stems of verbs and adjectives for the meaning "with a touch/trace/look of (whatever the stem expresses)."

男の子なんだから、などとおそらく言われ続けてきたであろう彼ら など と…言われ続けてきた makes it clear that 男の子なんだら is somebody's words. んだから is colloquial for のだから, a pattern used to state that some fact plainly obvious to both speaker and listener is a cause or reason for something else (what comes after んだから—in this case, the "ridiculous, proudly independent spirit" exhibited by men).

であろう is a more formal/written equivalent of だろう that here modifies 彼ら.

そのばかばかしくも孤高の精神を も is equivalent to とも/ても in this case, so ばかばかしくも孤高の精神 means something close to "aloof, if ridiculous, spirit."

やはりどうしたって どうしたって is a colloquial and emphatic どうしても.

料理

1　**高級スーパー**　高級 is one of many words in Japanese that functions as both a noun and a -**na** adjective. Often, however, な is not used; 高級 simply combines with the word it modifies, forming a compound, as it does here.

　　ついつい買いこんでしまい　The auxiliary verb こむ (込む) is added to the -**masu** stem to express various meanings such as motion inward (飛び込む "to jump in/into"), being absorbed in or thoroughly doing some action (信じ込む "to be convinced"), or continuing some act (座り込む "to remain seated"). Here the second meaning applies.

2　**店員さんはひとりしかいなくて**　In order to see how this pattern, "noun + しか + negative," translates as "only," it sometimes help to think of しか as meaning "other than": "*Other than* the one clerk, there were none" = "There was only one clerk."

　　高級仏花　仏花 are flowers (mainly chrysanthemums) placed at small home shrines in honor of dead family members.

　　しかるべき包装をして配達してほしい　しかるべき is an example of a 連体詞, a non-conjugating part of speech that modifies a noun. Technically it means "suitable" (as in "suitable packaging"), but I've translated it as "suitably."

　　金持ち光線と金持ちを優先しろ　しろ is the blunt imperative form of する.

　　光線をびんびん出していた　光線を出す, in the sense of a person emitting a ray of light, is a colloquial phrase used by young people. It is similar in both meaning and register to the English "give off vibes." びんびん (also ぴんぴん) is a mimetic adverb that expresses vigor or vitality.

3　**私は「たったこれだけです!」というのをアピールするために**　たった is a colloquial form of ただ ("only") and emphasizes the smallness of an amount.

　　チューリップ十本二千円というの　The day's specials at a Japanese flower shop are often already separated into bunches for customers.

　　風呂場　In Japanese homes, the bathtub (風呂) is in a separate room from the toilet.

　　先にやってくれないかなーというムード　かな(あ) is an emotive sentence-final particle that expresses a question, sometimes a hope, uttered or thought to oneself.

私の前の人が私と同じ作戦で優先されてしまい This is the person who had come after the rich woman and before Yoshimoto. Presumably, the clerk took a moment to wait on her even while attending to the rich woman's order, then realized he or she couldn't do the same for every customer and so decided to focus on the packaging.

これ以上はもうだめ、胡蝶蘭を包むことに専念します The style of speech here clues us in to the fact that this is the clerk thinking. The omitted です after だめ and the use of the -**masu** style for 専念する make the sentence sound "spoken" and therefore like someone's thoughts. という体勢 makes it absolutely clear that this is Yoshimoto's interpretation of the clerk's thoughts based on his or her actions or demeanor.

4   **どんどん人が来ては** どんどん is a mimetic adverb used for things proceeding at a good pace without hindrance. ては is used here to indicate the repetition of an action: "people kept lining up behind me, only to disappear as if feeling…"

あら、時間がかかりそうね あら (sometimes あらまあ) is a mild exclamation used mainly by women. This along with そうね instead of そうですね again sound very "spoken."

という感じで去って行くのが感じられた The auxiliary verb 行く expresses movement away from the writer. The people who kept coming into the flower shop also kept leaving, going away from where Yoshimoto was.

感じられた is the potential form of 感じる ("to feel").

他の店員さんを呼んで来て何とかしてもらうということもできなかった Grammatically, という is not required in this sentence.

店の中に漂う「できればあきらめて出直してほしい」感じが Normally we would expect to see という after the quote, but Yoshimoto omits it. This is a very contemporary technique. By leaving out という, the feeling 「できればあきらめて出直してほしい」hits us head-on as we read.

その人は私と肩が触れるような距離にいるのに That they are "close enough to touch shoulders" suggests that the other person in front of Yoshimoto ("私の前の人" from paragraph 3) has been served and is gone, and now it is just Yoshimoto, the rich woman in front of her, and the clerk focused on packaging the flowers.

下町育ちの私 The 下町 districts of Tokyo, comprising small shops and cheaper dwellings, are known for their warm informality and neighborliness.

5 **強いて似ているタイプをあげれば** 強いて is a fixed expression whose literal meaning is "by force," "forcibly." Often you see it followed by a verb in the **-ba** form (強いて言えば "if forced to say [one way or another]," for example). Here it is used with あげれば for the sense "if forced to name (the person the beautiful woman resembled)..."

篠ひろ子 篠ひろ子 is a now-retired television actress who was born in 1948.

身なりのいい中年女性 身なり refers to one's general appearance, how a person is turned out.

風のようにやってきて やってくる (やって来る) is a fixed expression meaning roughly "to arrive on the scene."

私はまずい! と思い まずい is used for bad-tasting food and more broadly for awkward or undesirable situations. Here Yoshimoto is afraid the newcomer will be waited upon before her.

終わりそうもないのです— The "**-masu** stem of a verb + そうもない" pattern is used to show that the likelihood of something happening is very low.

それではこのぎすぎすしたムードに飲まれてしまうという気がして それでは means what it looks like: "in that case," i.e., "if I had remained silent."

ぎすぎす (here in the adjectival form ぎすぎすした) is a mimetic word used to describe something (such as an attitude or atmosphere) that is cold or unneighborly.

飲まれる is technically the passive form of 飲む but carries other independent meanings such as "to be overwhelmed," "to be crushed," in addition to the literal "to be swallowed up."

Finally, という is grammatically optional in this case.

思い切って社交してみた "思い切って + **-te** form of a verb + みる" is a more-or-less fixed pattern meaning "to take the plunge and (VERB)," "to muster the courage to (VERB)." 社交する, an unusual "noun + する" combination, is perhaps a coinage by Yoshimoto.

彼女は「じゃあ誰か呼んで来るわね!」と言って わね is a sentence-final

美しさ

particle used almost exclusively by women. It sounds kind of old-ladyish these days.

「この人が先ですよ」と私を優先し   Think of と as an abbreviation of と言って.

「よかったわね、呼んで来てみて」   よかった ("It was a good thing") is often used in conversation when something fortunate has happened. Usually it follows rather than precedes a verb in the -**te** form, but it is the nature of colloquial speech that people often reverse the order.

とにっこり笑った   笑う can be used for smiling as well as laughing.

6   お金持ちには二種類いると思う   Literally, "When it comes to rich people, I think there are two types." The absence of が after 二種類 makes this sentence sound more colloquial, as the omission of particles is one characteristic of spoken Japanese.

お金があることで余裕ができて本来の人格をいいほうに発揮している人と   お金があること ("the fact of having money") is the cause for not only 余裕ができる but also 本来の人格をいいほうに発揮している. 余裕 ("elbow room," "leeway") is broadly used for having the space emotionally or in terms of time and money to do something; often 余裕がある/ない. できる after it is used in the sense of "have [a quality]."

今でもその蘭の鉢を見るたびに   "Dictionary form of a verb + たび (に)" is used for "each/every time (SUBJECT) (VERB)." The tense of the verb that follows it (in this case, 思い出す ["to recall"] in the next line) is always non-past.

いい思い出として思い出すのだった   This is unusual. Because of 今でも ("even now") in the previous clause, we would normally expect to see 思い出すのだ (non-past form) instead of 思い出すのだった (past form). But perhaps Yoshimoto chose this wording because she wanted to make the sentence sound retrospective.

1 **昔から、文は人なり** 文は人なり ("The style is the man himself") is a saying imported from the West. It is a famous quote from the French naturalist George-Louis Leclerc de Buffon (1707–88).

なんてなことが言ってあるが なんてな can be thought of as a truncated なんていうような, where なんて itself is mildly disparaging (see also paragraph 3 of「真っ白な嘘」).

 The pattern "**-te** form of a verb + ある" is used to indicate that the results of some action (represented by the verb) remain in effect: "People have long said 文は人なり and this saying remains in our collective consciousness" is the idea. The が at the end is not really contrastive and doesn't mean "but"; rather, it is closer to "and."

考えてみればその通りで その通り is a fixed expression meaning "it's true," "that's right," "it is exactly as you/they say."

文章にはそれを書いた人の人間性が如実に現れる それ, of course, refers to 文章.

2 **奥ゆかしい人の書いた文章には細やかな気づかいのなかにどこか凛とした気品が漂うし** 気づかい is a noun deriving from the verb 気づかう (気遣う) and means "care." 奥ゆかしい人 are people who are not only "modest" or "refined," but tactful and skilled in using language appropriate to the situation. The idea seems to be something like "In a refined person's writing, a dignified elegance seems to waft from the elaborate attention the writer has given to detail (as exemplified by his tactful, well-crafted sentences)."

匂いたつような色気が感ぜられ 感ぜられる is the spontaneous form of 感ずる. The spontaneous form looks just like the passive but expresses spontaneity.

なんともいえぬ飄逸、諧謔 なんともいえぬ is a more literary form of なんともいえない (何とも言えない). It gives the sentence an air of sophistication, and also works better with the already stiff-sounding 飄逸 and 諧謔. The comma (called *ten* in Japanese) between 飄逸 and 諧謔 can be thought of as や. It makes the sentence less wordy.

3 **一方** 一方 can also be used in the pattern 一方では...他方では... ("On the one hand...and on the other..."). Often, though, 一方 appears by

itself, without では and without the "other hand." Here I've translated it as "on the other hand" because that's what seems to work best given the flow of this essay.

さもしい人の書いた文章には　の is replacing が here, probably for variety: the sentence has four がs already.

もの欲しげな表現が　欲しげな is a **-na** adjective derived from 欲しい ("wanted"). げ can be added to certain words for the meaning "give the impression of being": 悲しげ "sad-looking," 満足げ "satisfied-looking," etc. Note also 可愛げ in paragraph 18.

さほどに文章というものは難しいものであり　The pattern "noun Aというものは noun Bである" is the same "AはBです" pattern that you've seen since day one of your studies, but is effectively used to put forward a comment on the universal nature of noun A. である, as you know by now, is a formal, written form of the copula.

まずその人間性から直していかなければならない　その might be thought of as meaning 自分の ("one's"), and その人間性 "that personality of yours." The pattern "negative stem of a verb or adjective + なければならない/なければいけない" corresponds to "must," "should," etc. Note, however, that the verb in question is 直していく rather than just 直す. The auxiliary いく in this case expresses progression into the future. Literally, one must "go and fix their personality first."

4 **わが国には**　わが (我が) is a formal form used in speeches or in writing for "my" or "our." Here it is used for humorous effect.

むかしから人間性を直す方法がいくつか伝わっている　The **-te iru** form here does not indicate ongoing action but a state in effect as a result of an action, i.e., the state of being available as a result of the action of handing down.

大方の社会人は　社会人 is a common term for full-fledged adults who have left school and are out in society.

そんな面倒なことはやっていられない　The assumption is that to do things like practice Zen meditation, one needs to go to a temple. Likewise with standing under a waterfall: the most practical option would be to make a reservation for a guided outing with a temple. That's why these activities are "troublesome" (面倒な) for busy people.

On a grammatical level, the いられない is the negative potential form

どう書いても嫌な奴は嫌な奴

of いる, as in やっている ("doing"). It might help to think of "**-te** form + いられない" as a pattern meaning "can't tolerate" doing whatever action it is that the verb expresses.

米国から自己啓発セミナーなんてなのも入りごんでいる　Again, なんてな is a bold shortening of なんていうような (see also paragraph 1).

入りごんでいる is a verb of Machida's own invention, in the -**te iru** form. The standard form is 入り込む (こ, not ご), and that's what you'll find in the dictionary at the back of this book.

それもそう効果を期待できない　Machida is saying that the imported self-improvement seminars are ineffective, but not that they are ineffective *like* Zen meditation or the act of standing in a waterfall. The Zen practices may be effective for all we know, but because the average member of society cannot easily take advantage of them—at least consistently, over a long period—the result is the same: little or no self-improvement. That the result is the same seems to be the sense in which それも is used.

5　**だから仕方ない**　仕方(が)ない ("It cannot be helped," "There is nothing for it") is a very common expression in spoken Japanese. しようがない is another way of saying the same thing.

腐った人間性のままで　まま is used to mean "as is." 腐った人間性のままで means, literally, "in the unchanged state of [having] a rotten human nature." Other examples: 黙ったままで "keeping silent," 自然のままで, "in its/one's natural state."

腐った奴と思われよう　思われよう is the volitional form of the passive verb 思われる. The idea is "Let's be thought of as rotten blokes."

そう思って諦めている人がいま全国に約二千万人程度いる（らしい）　This is a joke. There is no apparent reason for the figure 20 million (a little more than a sixth of Japan's population). The らしい makes the statement sound more convincing, like the author really heard this as a fact even though it is obviously baloney.

6　**そんな人間性の腐ったあなたでも**　そんな modifies あなた, not 人間性. 人間性の腐った is a fixed adjectival phrase meaning, roughly, "whose nature has gone rotten."

読者をして、なんとなくよい人だ、と思わしむる方法　読者をして...と思わしむ＝読者に...と思わせる. しむ is a remnant of classical Japanese, equivalent to the causative せる/させる; it is in its noun-modifying form, しむる, because it modifies 方法. The をして is also classical, and is equivalent to に or を. なんとなく ("somehow") modifies よい人だ, not 思わしむる. This is made clear by the use of commas.

やり方は超簡単　超 is a prefix used by young people to intensify the meaning of the adjective, e.g., 超面白い "super interesting." It is used here in humorous contrast with the surrounding formal language.

勿体ぶってずらずらずらずらいろんなことを言って　ぶる is a suffix that attaches to nouns and the stems of adjectives, turning them into verbs meaning "to behave (in the manner suggested by the noun or adjective)": 天才ぶる "to act like one is a genius," えらぶる "to behave arrogantly" (from the adjective えらい "great").

9　**一般にこれをどのように使い分けているかというと**　かというと is used here to bring up a question—"How are these two styles used, generally speaking?"—in order to address it. The explanation that follows is for written Japanese and is somewhat oversimplified; the use of verb endings in both spoken and written Japanese is complicated.

えらそうに傲然と言いたいときは　えらそうに and 傲然と are both adverbs that modify 言う.

という風に使い分けている　風 ("manner," "style") is synonymous with よう.

これはあくまで方法論に過ぎない　あくまで is an adverb that, when followed by an assertion, expresses the speaker's/writer's strong belief. The pattern "noun + に過ぎない" corresponds to "be nothing more than (NOUN)" and, like its English translation suggests, downplays the importance of whatever it follows. Here に過ぎない is used after a noun, but it can also be used after an adjective or a verb in one of its plain forms.

10　**方法に過ぎない使い分けが逆転**　逆転 is short for 逆転して and signals a reversal whereby "what is no more than a mere means at the writer's disposal ends up determining his entire personality in the minds of his readers."

文章上の傲然とした態度　The suffix 上 is often hard to translate. Here 文章上 could be rendered as "throughout his writing," "upon the page," "in his sentences," and so on.

肉付き面のように 肉付き面 (or 肉付きの面) comes from a folktale in which an old woman puts on a demon mask in order to frighten her daughter-in-law, and it becomes attached to her face and cannot be removed. The idea of 肉付き面のように is that the writer's personality as judged from his writing becomes permanently fixed to him.

その文章の内容、書き手の実際の性格の如何にかかわらず 如何にかかわらず is a combination of the noun 如何 ("the how"), the particle に, and かかわらず, a verb in the classical negative, meaning "regardless/irrespective of." かかわらず itself is often used in the pattern "noun + にも + かかわらず" for the same meaning.

へりくだったよい人 This is two adjectives, へりくだった ("humble") and よい ("good"), modifying 人.

と思い込んでしまう傾向にあるのである 思い込む often means "to believe mistakenly," and that seems to be the meaning here. Machida could have ended with 傾向があるのである ("there is a tendency for"), but he uses に instead. This gives us the feeling that readers are "oriented," as it were, "toward the tendency" of mistakenly believing that those who write with the **da/de aru** style are overbearing and arrogant, and those who write with the **desu/-masu** style are humble and decent.

11 **お分かりであろう** "お + -**masu** stem + でしょう/であろう" is a polite pattern.

12 **以下、その方法を実地に試してみよう** 以下 is a word for "below" used when referring to the position of information in a text. –てみよう is the volitional form of –てみる.

13 **いまだにその最右翼である** いまだに is a mostly written expression equivalent to まだ ("still").

   最右翼 means "the best or leading person" and derives from the custom of seating students in the classroom in order of grades, with the top student in the front right-hand seat (最 "most," 右 "right," 翼 "wing").

   あらゆる価値を破壊・転倒せよ せよ is one of two blunt imperative forms of する. The other is しろ, seen in paragraph 2 of「美しさ」.

14 **けっこうよい人に見える** 見える can mean "to seem" as well as "to be able to see," "to be visible," and so on.

15 **僕は反キリスト主義者なのです** The original lyric is "I am an antichrist." "Antichrist" in Japanese, by the way, would be 反キリスト教者.

僕はいろんなものすべてを壊してしまいたいのです　ものすべて is two words: もの ("things") + すべて ("everything"). Machida could have also written ものをすべて. The ending しまいたい is the -**tai** form of しまう.

なぜなら僕はアナーキーでありたいからです　でありたい is the -**tai** form of である and means what it looks like it should mean: "to want to be."

16　みたいなニュアンスが漂って　みたい is an auxiliary -**na** adjective meaning "like" in reference to what comes before it. Here it could be interchanged with というような.

それはそれで仕方ないかなあ、という気がしてくる　かなあ, as you'll recall from paragraph 3 of「美しさ」, is an emotive particle. くる in 気がしてくる expresses the onset of the feeling: one would *begin to* feel that events couldn't be otherwise.

18　可愛げというものがまるでない　もの in this case can be thought of as "aspect" or "element." まるで is an intensive adverb.

おまえにも少しくらい反省するところがあるだろう　おまえ is a rough, masculine way of saying あなた. ところ does not mean "place" but something more like "room," i.e., "room for self-reflection/soul-searching."

と言いたくなる　Literally, "one begins to want to say."

19　通常の随筆の場合もそうで　そう seems to refer to the phenomenon by which we feel differently about a writer, regardless of the content of the piece we are reading, depending on whether he uses **desu**/-**masu** or **da**/**de aru**.

20　ゴミ集積所　In Tokyo there are set places on the street to put out the trash on certain days of the week (burnable trash two days a week, nonburnable trash once a week, etc.—the rules vary from place to place).

21　ゴミに弱い僕　に弱い can be used for things one has a weakness for in a positive sense, such as a fondness for sweets (あまいものに弱い), as well as in a negative sense, such as being weak in math (数字に弱い) or a poor drinker (酒に弱い).

ゴミから受ける精神的ダメージの度合いが違うからです　Technically, words ending with the suffix 的 are -**na** adjectives, but sometimes you can omit the な, as Machida has done here.

2 **これは、拙著『博士の愛した数式』の帯の文句であり** 拙著 is a humble word for referring to one's own book.

In the Japanese publishing industry, an 帯 is a strip of paper fitted over the bottom third of a book cover. It contains blurbs, quotes from reviewers and the like, and is used as a sales tool to catch the attention of customers in bookstores. It also helps bookstore employees understand a book's content at a glance.

つまりは つまり is used to state a conclusion: "that is to say . . ."; the は adds a certain degree of emphasis.

作者である私自身 である could be replaced by の in this case. Remember, である is just a written form of です, but unlike です it can modify other words, as it does here.

自身 is a noun that attaches directly to other nouns for emphasis. The meaning is "myself," "herself," "itself," depending on the context.

ずっと変わらず 変わらず is a negative form of 変わる that in this case is equivalent to 変わらなく. It modifies the verb at the end of the sentence, 出会い続けている.

3 **読んでいるうち** うち has at least two meanings, depending on whether what comes before it is affirmative or negative. Here the meaning is "while": "while reading whatever mathematics-related books I could find as reference material."

イメージが微妙に変わってゆく ゆく is another word for いく, and is used as an auxiliary verb to indicate motion moving away; くる is used for motion moving closer, as in 浮かび上がってくる in paragraph 14.

私にとって天才とはつまり は marks the topic. と makes it clear that the topic is *the meaning of* 天才, not 天才 by itself. But it is sometimes more helpful to remember とは as a particle combination used in stating definitions and equivalent to というものは.

4 **1から100まで足し算しなさい** なさい is the polite imperative form—the form teachers use when telling their students to do something.

という問題を出したところ The pattern of "-**ta** form of a verb + ところ" indicates that when A happened, B was the result.

6 　基本中の基本　This "noun + （の）中の + noun" pattern is used to express the quintessence of something: 男の中の男 "a man's man."

この発想があまりにも鮮やかすぎて　あまりにも (usually followed by an adjective, but sometimes by a verb) is a set phrase used for emphasis. It can mean "too ..." (あまりにも暑い "too hot") or just "extremely" (あまりにも有名な話 "a very famous story"). It is often used in the pattern "あまりにも + adjective stem + すぎる," where すぎる—itself an auxiliary verb meaning "too"—gives added emphasis.

めまいを起こしそうになる　The pattern "-**masu** stem + そうになる" expresses the idea of the subject's being in danger of something happening to him/her/it. Here, of course, Ogawa is saying that the concept is so dazzling as to make one faint.

7 　ただ単に難しい問題を解くのが天才ではない　ただ and 単に both have the meaning of "only," "merely"; their use together is particularly emphatic.

その結果として問題が解けるだけなのだ、と　This と refers all the way back to the first sentence of the paragraph: そこで私は感づいた "That's when I realized it." It marks the content of what Ogawa realized, which is to say everything after the first sentence.

8 　傷だらけになりながら　だらけ is a suffix used to indicate that the noun to which it attaches is full of or covered in negative things: 間違いだらけ "full of mistakes," 傷だらけ "covered in scratches."

凡人が自分の足元にばかり囚われている間に　ばかり is a particle that is similar in meaning to, and often interchangeable with, だけ. It follows a noun or a noun and another particle for the meaning "only" or "and nothing else." Here Ogawa seems to be saying that while the ordinary person's full powers of concentration are focused on his or her footing (*and nothing else*), the genius is elsewhere, seeing the big picture.

思わず、「ずるいじゃないか」と口走りそうになる　Since this is what one thinks or mutters to oneself, it is in the plain spoken style rather than the **desu**/-**masu** style.

本当にずるいほどお見事なのだ　The polite prefixes お or ご can be added to certain adjectives when used to praise others: お見事! "Splendid!" おえらい! "Well done!" ご立派! "Magnificent!" Here Ogawa seems to be using お見事 somewhat playfully.

9 たちまち世界を美しく統制する<u>だけ</u>の力を備えている In this case, だけ expresses extent, i.e., "to have a power *to the extent* sufficient to control…"

まだ<u>見ぬ</u>ものへの憧れ The ぬ of 見ぬ is a classical negative verb ending.

10 当然私に予感や憧れが沸いてくる<u>はずもなく</u> はずもない/はずはない indicates the impossibility of something being so. なく is the continuative form of ない.

才能がないばかりか根気もない "Aばかりか Bも/まで" is a pattern (usually only written) for saying "not only A but also B." When A is a verb in the negative form, as it is here, what follows is often something undesirable—less desirable, even, than A.

先生から赤字で大きな<u>バツ</u>をもらい In Japan, an X mark (バツ) is used to indicate a wrong answer or rejected choice, and a circle (丸) to indicate a correct answer or selected choice.

12 これが凡人と天才の違い<u>であろう</u> であろう is a formal, written equivalent to the spoken でしょう.

13 数学者の藤原正彦先生と<u>お話しした</u>時も "お + -**masu** stem + する" is humble and here shows respect for the professor.

15 あのように素晴らしい公式が隠れている<u>とすれば</u> Often とすれば is used to make a hypothetical clause, i.e., "If it is true that…" Here, however, Ogawa uses とすれば to grant the existence of a situation she recognizes as real: "If there is such a wonderful formula hidden in 1 + 2 + 3 + …etc.—and there is, of course—then…"

16 <u>ひとしきり</u>感心している間に ひとしきり＝しばらく "for some time."

新星が見つかる<u>のと同じく</u>数の秘密も…隠れている のと同じく is used to connect two clauses and indicate they are similar in some way. The の nominalizes (turns into a noun) everything in the sentence up to it. 同じく is the adverbial (-**ku**) form of 同じ.

数の秘密も寄り添い合って隠れている<u>もの</u>らしい もの functions to turn the otherwise straightforward statement of hearsay 隠れているらしい into a sentence that resonates with feeling, and at the same time to make the sentence a comment on the nature of mathematical secrets: "mathematical secrets seem to hide together in clusters."

『博士の愛した数式』を巡って

17 『世にも美しい数学入門』(筑摩書房)を読んでいただきたい   Note the humble/polite language Ogawa uses when she addresses us, the readers.

ああ、神様は何と不思議な技を見せて下さる   Note the honorific pattern –てくださる. くださる by itself is an honorific verb for "to give" and shows respect toward the one who gives. In this case, it is used as an auxiliary and shows respect for God.

天を仰ぎ両手を合わせずにはいられない   ずにいる denotes being in a state of not doing the action of the verb. Here the root verb is 合わせる ("to put [one's hands] together"), and いる is in the negative potential form. The literal meaning of the phrase 両手を合わせずにはいられない is "to not be able to not put both hands together," hence my translation "cannot help but clasp one's hands together." For an introduction to ずに, see「電車の中で若者に注意」(paragraph 2).

結果が得られている   得られている is the passive form of 得る ("to obtain"). The results (結果) here are those obtained (the formulas discovered) from adding up numbers raised to the power of 2 or 3.

19 何とまあくだらない小説だ   何と is for emphasis. The colloquial まあ, used before an opinion, expresses the speaker's hesitancy: "What a, well, stupid novel."

フン   フン here is the sound of someone scoffing—kind of like *ha!* or *bah!* in English.

22 桁外れに頭のいい人々の集まりに違いない   桁外れに is a set phrase meaning "extraordinarily." 桁 is a column of numbers or a decimal place, so 桁外れ (or 桁違い) is something out of the bounds of the usual, beyond the norm.

高校時代の数学が、いつも赤点すれすれだった   すれすれ is used for physical actions that just narrowly escape something, such as a bullet almost grazing a person or a boat narrowly missing rocks, and by extension for nonphysical situations in which one narrowly escapes something (barely legal, narrowly elected, barely passing a class).

23 まるで学園祭のようでもある   School festivals open to the public are held at Japanese universities and colleges in the fall, with booths run by various clubs selling snacks or knickknacks, or hosting special concerts, contests, or other events.

24 **学会の方々が揃っておられた**　Note Ogawa's use of the polite 方々 (rather than 人々) and おられた (the honorific form of the auxiliary いる, in the -**ta** form).

かちこちに緊張しながら　Ogawa has combined かちかち and こちこち, both of which mean "stiff."

25 **あとはもう一言も言葉は浮かんでこず**　こず ＝ こなく (from the auxiliary verb くる, indicating movement toward the speaker). The form ず (or なく) in this case indicates attendant circumstances. That is, Ogawa finished her tea "without a single word springing to mind."

緊張感はどんどん高まるばかりだった　ばかり in the pattern "dictionary form of a verb ＋ ばかりだ（った）" can indicate a one-way change for the worse, in this case "does nothing but increase."

26 **視線を宙に泳がせ**　泳がせ is the -**masu** stem of 泳がせる. Though it looks like the causative form of 泳ぐ ("to swim"), the verb actually has another, more figurative meaning: "to allow to wander/move freely." The professor allows his gaze (視線) to wander freely in the air (宙), as it were. He is shifting his gaze here and there.

27 **失礼に当たるではないかと思われたが**　思われる is a special form of 思う: the spontaneous form. It looks just like the honorific or passive, but the context tells you it isn't either of these. The sense is that it "struck" Ogawa that to say such a thing in front of a mathematician might be insulting.

黙っているよりは多少ましな気がした　ましな (a -**na** adjective) is used for the better of two bad alternatives.

28 **小説の中に書いておきながら**　ながら after the stem of an adjective or verb means "while" or "although." Here it attaches to the -**masu** stem of the auxiliary おく, which indicates that the effect of the action of the root verb (書く) is ongoing. 書いておく means, in other words, "to write so as to be written," and 書いておきながら "although I have written (so as to remain in print, so that people can read)..."

いまだによく分からないんです　We first saw いまだに in paragraph 13 of 「どう書いても嫌な奴は嫌な奴」. There it was followed by an affirmative expression; here it is followed by a negative one. In either pattern, いまだに translates as "still." However, when used with a negative, it

『博士の愛した数式』を巡って

expresses the writer's sense of surprise or frustration more strongly than a plain old まだ would.

33 **にもかかわらず**　にもかかわらず is a set phrase meaning "nevertheless," or "despite" whatever comes before it. Usually it is used after some other word or clause, but this sentence-initial position is also possible and perfectly understandable.

理屈ではeの仕組みが理解できたつもりでいても　Note that つもり is used not only in the sense of "to plan to" or "to intend to," but also for supposition (sometimes mistaken supposition). A very literal rendering of this clause would be something like: "Even though I am of the thinking that, on a theoretical level, I understand the working of *e*...," with the implication being, "I don't really understand it." If Ogawa really understood *e*, and had not just convinced herself that she had, she would understand why it is referred to as "natural" (自然). She doesn't, though, as we learn in the next clause.

35 **ゼロを起点とする真っすぐな線グラフである**　とする in this context means "to set it at": to put the starting point of the line on the graph at zero. It is interchangeable with にする, as in "Aにする" ("to make something A").

37 **縦軸、横軸の単位が何であったかは**　何であった is 何である in the -**ta** form, followed by the interrogative particle か and, finally, the topic-maker は.

そのグラフは...変わらないあるがままの姿で　あるがまま is a set phrase meaning "as it is." 変わらない ("unchanged") and あるがままの both modify 姿. This kind of redundancy is okay in Japanese.

38 **こうしてグラフという、目に見える図で表わすと**　という modifies 図; 目に見える further modifies it.

42 **無知にも程があるこの私に**　にも程がある is a set expression used for emphasis. Ogawa is saying that she is ignorant to the extreme when it comes to math—"the limit of ignorance," as I put it in the translation. The expression can also be used to warn someone not to do something excessively: お冗談にも程がある "You joke too much."

44 **そろそろ桜が散りはじめようか、という季節**　散りはじめよう is the volitional form of 散りはじめる (散り始める) ("to begin to scatter"). ようか

can be thought of as an abbreviation of ようとするではないか. The pattern "volitional form + とする" (first seen in paragraph 3 of「料理」) can also mean "to be about to do/happen," and that's what it means here: "the season when the cherry blossoms were about to start falling."

電車の中は部活動帰りらしい高校生 部活動 are extracurricular activities. 帰り (note the reading) can function as a suffix meaning "returning from," as it does here.

47 **訪ねたことの<u>ある場所</u>** が can also be used.

久しぶりに戻ってきた<u>かのような</u>気持になった "Dictionary/-**ta** form of a verb + かのよう" is used, like "as if I were/had" in English, to liken a feeling or situation to one that doesn't in fact exist. The idea here is "I felt as if I had returned, after a long time away…"

何もかもすべて 何もかも and すべて both mean "everything," or "all." The use of both is for added emphasis.

それが不思議<u>でならなかった</u> One uses "-**te** form of a verb/adjective + ならない" to indicate that a naturally occurring, often uncontrollable feeling or sensation (expressed by the verb/adjective) is strong and cannot be easily quelled. "I could not help feeling it was eerie" might be another decent translation of this sentence.

48 **博士の書棚に置かれた本<u>たち</u>は** たち is a suffix added to nouns (usually ones that refer to human beings) to make the noun plural and, sometimes, to show reverence for it as well. Ogawa uses it here to indicate her affection and respect for the books.

広大な数の世界を<u>前にした</u>時の人間のささやかさ …を前にする literally means "to put…in front of one"; by extension, "to face" "to confront."

49 **正面から寺尾聰さんが<u>歩いてこられた</u>** こられる is the honorific form of the auxiliary verb 来る, indicating movement toward the speaker/writer.

50 **子供と<u>阪神タイガース</u>を愛した博士** The Hanshin Tigers are a professional baseball team in Japan.

無常ということ

1　**少し前のことになるが**　This sort of sentence, with こと, is often used to introduce an episode, as was also seen in「電車の中で若者に注意」(paragraph 1).

私は或る評論家が　In contemporary usage, 或る and other adverbial expressions are usually written in hiragana. Hirano deliberately uses kanji for many such words throughout this essay, giving the piece a very formal texture.

八坂神社の前にコンヴィニエンス・ストアが出来たことは　The Yasaka (Shinto) Shrine is a major tourist attraction in Kyoto. Sometimes it is also called by its former name, the Gion Shrine.

コンヴィニエンス・ストア is usually abbreviated to コンビニ, but this sounds too informal for a serious essay of this sort.

怪しからんと憤慨しながら　怪しからん is a contraction of 怪しからぬ and is used to express anger at some impertinence or shameful behavior: まったく怪しからん "How disgraceful!" "What impertinence!" It is somewhat old-fashioned.

書いているのを読んで　の is acting as a nominalizer here. See「真っ白な嘘」(paragraph 1) for more on the nominalizing の.

乱暴な口調の割には　As my translation suggests, の割りに has the meaning "considering...," "for all..."

何事に於いても　に於いて (usually において) is a literary expression. Here it basically means the same as について but is more formal. も is used for emphasis.

それならば　それならば, or それなら, is a set phrase meaning "If that is so...," "In that case..."

そもそも祇園の交差点...どうなるのだろう?　そもそも is often used rhetorically, as it is here, for emphasis: "what on earth," "whatever," etc.

In Japan, intersections are often named and used as points of reference. どうなるのだろう? asks "what about...?" (どうだろう?, どうなの?) in a somewhat exasperated tone.

あれほどの量の自動車　あれほど is a set phrase meaning "to that extent," "that much." Literally, then, this would be "automobiles of that much volume."

高級車<u>も</u>走っていれば、市バス<u>も</u>轟音を鳴り響かせている　The pattern "noun + も + conditional (-**ba**) form + noun + も" is used for an emphatic listing of examples.

目が<u>ゆかず</u>　ゆく is a variant of いく; ゆかず is equivalent to いかないで.

殊更にコンヴィニエンス・ストアなどに着目して<u>みせる</u>ところが　みせる is an auxiliary verb that adds a nuance of "to make a show of (VERBing)." The ところ here can be thought of as "the place where"—"the place (part) where he focuses his attention"—although a more natural English translation would be "his focusing loudly on…" or, as I translated it, "the way he focused loudly on…"

私には<u>何とも</u>安易な語り口のように<u>思われた</u>のである　何とも is an intensive adverb meaning "quite," "really." 思われる is the same spontaneous form of 思う that we encountered in paragraph 27 of「『博士の愛した数式』を巡って」.

2　昔からよく京都を訪ね、この町に特別の思いがある<u>という</u>人の間では　昔から does not mean "from centuries ago," which it could mean in another context; here it just means "for a long time."

　　という has a somewhat indirect and softening effect that Hirano seems to favor, and which he makes frequent use of throughout the essay (二条城などというもの in this paragraph, for instance, and 京都という町 in the next one).

ちょっとした流行な<u>の</u>かもしれない　The use of の makes the statement softer and expresses more certainty than the sentence would without it.

これはしかし　This is a rhetorical phrase equivalent to しかしこれは in meaning but somewhat more emphatic.

<u>今に始まったことではないであろう</u>　This is a set phrase meaning "there is nothing new about it."

<u>流石は</u>田舎侍の御大将　The は makes 流石 more emphatic. Kyotoites referred to samurai from other regions with the derogatory term *inaka* samurai. The "chief of the *inaka* samurai" who built Nijō Castle in 1603 was Tokugawa Ieyasu, founder of the Tokugawa Shogunate and one of the most influential warlords in Japanese history.

<u>とんでもないものを造ってくれたわい</u>　とんでもない is a set phrase meaning "outlandish," "outrageous," "terrible," "unbelievable," or "ridiculous"

when it modifies another word. When it is used alone, in response to a proposition, it means "No way!" "Are you kidding?" and so on.

わい is an exclamatory sentence-final particle now used mainly by older men. The –てくれた is used sarcastically.

人達も多かったのではあるまいか？ まい is from classical Japanese and means, in this case, ということではないだろう. But it's easier to think of ではあるまいか as a fixed expression equivalent to ではないだろうか. These are all very formal, very "written" turns of phrase.

3 **どうも昨今のその手の議論に胡散らしさを感じて仕方がない** When used with a negative expression, どうも tends to mean "no matter what I do," "whatever one may do." In this sense, it is similar to どうしても.

胡散らしさ is unusual. Usually one says 胡散臭さ (from 胡散臭い) if the noun form is needed.

"**-Te** form of a verb/adjective + 仕方がない" means "can't help feeling…" and is similar to, and often interchangeable with, "**-te** form + ならない" from paragraph 47 of 「『博士の愛した数式』を巡って」.

何でも好き放題にぶち壊して 放題 is added for the meaning of "as much as one wants," or "left to its own devices" as in 荒れ放題 in paragraph 5.

高層ビルだろうとパチンコ店だろうと だろうと…だろうと is a set pattern having the meaning "be it…or be it…" and the implication "it does not matter which," "regardless." Usually だろうが …だろうが.

幾らでも建てれば良いなどと乱暴なことは言わない The pattern "**-ba** form + いい/よい" is used to recommend doing such and such. Here, of course, Hirano is not recommending that people build as many tall buildings and pachinko parlors as they like; he is saying that he is not going so far to say that to do so would be okay.

どういう京都を残したいと思っているのかと問えば かと問えば (using 問う "to ask") is a more formal equivalent of かと聞けば.

先の評論家ではないが It may look like Hirano is saying that 「あの日、あの時見た京都」 does not apply to the above-mentioned critic, but in fact he is saying, indirectly, that it does. ではないが is used in this way to indirectly cite someone. Here you can think of it as being a less-direct が いうように.

ということでしかないのではあるまいか "Noun + でしかない" is equivalent to にすぎない ("to be nothing more than…").

無常ということ

それは**いかにも**恣意的である　いかにも is an intensifier meaning "indeed," "absolutely," "certainly."

京都という町の長い歴史に**比して**　に比して (from 比する) is a more formal equivalent of に比べて ("compared with").

何とちっぽけなもの**であろう**　何と…だろう is a mostly written pattern used for emphasis: 何と難しい本だろう "What a difficult book it is!" 何と … ものであろう is a variation on this pattern. In spoken Japanese, people tend to say なんて…んだろう.

4　同じことは京都の**町屋**を巡る議論についても**言える**　町屋 are townhouses built by well-to-do merchants in the Edo period (1603–1867) with a slatted wooden façade and overhanging tiled eaves.

そこで保存すべきと主張されている風景**にしても**　にしても is used to cite an example with the implication of negation: "even when it comes to…," "no matter if it is…," etc.

一向に議論に**ならない**　Usually 議論されない; 議論にならない means "not rise to the level of a (valid) argument."

5　では何故**そう**なのであろうか　i.e., why such a counterargument is persuasive.

この問題は　i.e., the problem of preservation versus change.

『伊勢物語』の…ではないが　The *Tales of Ise* (mid-tenth century) is a collection of poems with short prose passages. In this particular poem, Narihira revisits the pavilion where he used to meet his former lover. The translation is by F. Vos in *Anthology of Japanese Literature*, ed. Donald Keene (N.Y.: Grove Press, 1955).

　　　The ではないが is the same one you saw in paragraph 3, only here you might think of it as meaning のように.

昔の愛人、知人を訪ねて　The use of (、) in this case is similar to omitting the "and" or the "or" in English.

風景**もまた**絶え間なく変化する　また風景も is also possible. もまた is one word, though it may help to think of it in terms of its constituent parts, も and また.

そうした**存在**の絶望的な不安を慰める**為にこそ**　存在 here refers to existence, to beingness or *esse*. こそ is an intensifier: "indeed," "the very…"

かくも膨大な数 かくも is a literary phrase meaning こんなに.

膨大な数築かれねばならなかった 築かれねば = 築かれなければ. 築く ("to build") is in the negative passive form but with ぬ instead of ない. ぬ's **-ba** form is ねば.

いわば凄みなのではあるまいか? いわば means "as it were," "so to speak." み in 凄み is a suffix that can attach to a limited number of nouns and adjectives to mean, as its kanji indicates, "a taste of…," "a touch of…," "-ishness."

6 **八坂神社の前が今のような景色になったのは** 今のような景色 is the scene in front of Yasaka Shrine "as it is now."

高々この数十年ほどのことであろう この数十年 is, as my translation suggests, "these past few decades." (数 functions much like a prefix meaning "several.") And ほど means "about," "approximately" when used with a figure.

千二百年間の長きに亘って絶えざる変遷を繰り返してきた の長きに亘って ("extending for the period of…") is a formal set phrase used in writing. 長き is a classical form that is equivalent to modern 長さ. 絶えざる, another classical form, means the same as 絶えない ("unceasing," "incessant," "constant"). Don't confuse it with 絶えず, an adverbial form that means "unceasingly," "incessantly," "constantly."

たまたま千百何十年目かに出現した一つの風景に決定し たまたま ("by chance") modifies 出現した ("appeared").

目 in 何十年目 is a suffix used to express an ordinal number (二年目 "the second year"). The use of か makes the exact year sound indefinite, and に marks that indefinite year as a point in time.

それを永遠に保存するなどということこそ Note that など, in addition to meaning "and so forth," can be used to single things out in a slightly derogatory or emphatic way.

ということ nominalizes what comes before it, and こそ adds emphasis. "That very thought of preserving such a landscape for eternity" is one way to translate this phrase.

最も甚だしき誤解 甚だしき ("terrible," "gross") is another throwback to classical Japanese, a more literary equivalent of 甚だしい.

それは京都が… それ refers to the "act of barbarity" of arbitrarily picking, and trying to preserve in amber, one moment in time in Kyoto.

生成と 消滅とを繰り返し続けている　As in the previous paragraph, the second と can be omitted.

一体人は…考えるであろうか？　一体 is an intensifier meaning "why on earth," "who in the world." 人 here refers to people in general, not any one individual.

子供の頃の美しい母親の姿を愛しているからといって　からといって is a set phrase meaning "just because."

現実の生きた京都ではない　Here, and in 死んだ町 three sentences later, Hirano could have used either the **-ta** or the **-te iru** form of the verb: 生きた/死んだ or 生きている/死んでいる are both possible as modifiers. The difference, if there is any at all, is perhaps that 生きている/死んでいる is more emphatic. Hirano probably chose the **-ta** form simply because there is no reason to stress "alive"/"dead" in this context.

京都そのものの破壊　そのもの is a set phrase meaning "itself": "the destruction of Kyoto itself."

変化することがなくなった時　Because the tense before it is past, 時 refers to the point at which the process of "ceasing to change" has been completed. If the clause were 変化することがなくなる時, change would still be going on, though diminishing. This is an important distinction only because it helps us understand 最早 in the next clause.

最早博物館のガラス・ケースの中に収められたミイラと同じ、死んだ町となる　最早 ("already" or, followed by a negative, "no longer") is often used to introduce a bad result. Here it modifies なる for the meaning "by that time, Kyoto will *already be* a dead city."

以前の内装と殆ど同じだったという　In this case, という is used for indirect quotation: "they say that it is almost the same."

それとてどれほどのことであろうか？　それとて is a formal phrase meaning "even so," and is similar in meaning to そうであっても, そうだとしても.

百年、二百年経ってみれば　Note that "**-te** form of a verb + みれば/みると" can be used not only for doing something and thereby discovering something through intentional action (読んでみると面白かった "When I read it, I found it was interesting"), but also for non-intentional action (その時になってみれば分かる "You'll understand then").

一瞬現れては消えた幻のようなもの　"Verb A ては verb B" is a pattern,

無常ということ

here meaning "no sooner does the action of verb A take place than the action of verb B takes place." 消える instead of 消えた would perhaps have been a better word choice.

そうした幻_{まぼろし}がどれほどあったことであろう　A sentence like this one with an interrogative pronoun and こと (and often a か at the end) acts as an intensifier: "how many there must have been!"

今眼前に眺めている光景ですら一つの幻であることを疑わせる　すら is a more literary equivalent of さえ ("even"). The use of 疑わせる in 幻であることを疑わせる ("cause one to suspect that [the very scene in front of one's eyes] is a phantasm") is hard to make sense of if one thinks of 疑う as always equivalent to the English "doubt." Although 幻ではないかと疑う would be more usual, 幻であると疑う can be used for the same meaning. Here it is better to think of 疑う as meaning "suspect" or "wonder if." (In English as well "wonder if it might be" and "wonder if it might not be" have roughly the same sense.)

一度として何かであったことがない　一度 is "once," として is "as," 何か is "something," である is the copula, and ことがない is "there are no times/cases of…" So a literal translation would be: "There are no cases of something existing for one time." Hirano is saying that everything is ever-present and ever-changing.

京都であるとしか言いようのない　としか言いようの[が/も]ない is a set phrase meaning "can only be described as…"; 言いよう is "way of saying."

7　パリやローマといったヨーロッパの古い都市　といった is a set phrase meaning "such as," "like": "ancient European cities such as Paris or Rome." It was also seen in paragraph 3 of「真っ白な嘘」.

その町並の保存状態の良さを強調する人は多い　Hirano uses は to take up "people who stress…" as the topic in order to make a comment about them. The comment he makes is a long one of almost three and a half lines. The idea is: "There are many who stress how well preserved the houses are in European cities are, but the comparison between Kyoto and Paris and Rome is an unreasonable one to make."

誰が住もうと　The pattern "volitional form + と" is a more formal, written-style equivalent of the "even if" sense of "-**te** form of a verb + も."

木造の故に　の故に is a formal phrase meaning "because of," "on account of." In this case, it is equivalent to のために.

そもそも同一に並べて議論すること自体が<u>無理な話</u>である　無理な話 is a set phrase used to describe an unreasonable case or argument.

8　<u>所詮は余所者である</u>　所詮 is a more literary equivalent of 結局 ("ultimately," "in the end"). The は is for emphasis.

<u>それこそ生粋の京都人という人達からしてみれば</u>　こそ is, as we have seen, an intensifier, but それこそ is a word in its own right that means 本当に, まちがいなく, etc. からしてみれば, meanwhile, is a set phrase meaning "from the standpoint of." Here again we see Hirano's favored use of the という pattern (first seen in paragraph 2).

9　<u>文句一つ言わずに好きなことをさせてくれた</u>　ずに was seen also in paragraph 21 of「電車の中で若者に注意」. This is the same usage: "without a single complaint."

させてくれる is the causative form of する in the -**te** form, followed by くれる. The meaning is "to let one do as one pleases."

<u>それらの別々の顔とのつきあいが一通り終えたあとになって</u>　一通り is a more formal equivalent of 大体 ("in a general way," "by and large"), and 終える is equivalent to 終わる, although 終わる is intransitive and 終える transitive. To be strictly grammatical, the structure should be either つきあい<u>を</u>一通り<u>終えた</u> or つきあい<u>が</u>一通り<u>終わった</u>, but as it is, the sentence is not likely to bother ordinary Japanese readers.

<u>私は初めてその奥に秘せられた本当の顔本当の顔とも言うべきもの</u>　秘せられた is the causative-passive form of 秘する, a literary word meaning "to conceal," "to hide." とも言うべき can be thought of as とも言える.

無常ということ

バカヤロー、お前なんか、文学者じゃない　バカヤロー is a very strong insult in Japanese. お前 is, as we saw in「どう書いても嫌な奴は嫌な奴」 (paragraph 18), a rough, masculine form of "you." Here it sounds particularly insulting because it is used together with なんか ("the likes of"). じゃない, too, is quite forceful.

座談会　Transcripts of conversations of several people (座談会), or of two people (対談), are a staple of Japanese magazines and newspapers.

1　**日本とアメリカの間を行ったり来たりして**　One of the uses of を is to indicate the "space" in which an action takes place. In this example, 間 refers to the space between Japan and America *through* or *across* which Levy traveled back and forth.

日本で耳に入ったことば　耳に入る is a set phrase meaning "to hear something"; also 耳にする (paragraph 10).

特に文学に関する、…発想や表現　Note how the comma after 特に文学に関する helps signal that the phrase does not modify the very next noun, アメリカ, but the noun group at the end of the アメリカ clause, 発想や表現. Such a piling up of modifying clauses before a noun is very common in written Japanese.

一種のよろこび　The primary meaning of 一種 is "a kind," "a sort," as in a particular sort of wine or variety of grape, but it can also be used adjectivally (with the addition of の) as here to indicate a degree of qualification: "something like joy," "something of a genius."

2　**よろこびに近い満足感**　This is a common phrasing also seen in the title of the best-selling novel by Murakami Ryu,『限りなく透明に近いブルー』(*Almost Transparent Blue*).

何となく通用している概念　何となく means "more or less," "somehow or other"; it is used a lot in Japanese as a softener. Also used in a similar fashion is 一応.

当然問われるとはかぎらない概念を問うてみる　とはかぎらない is a set phrase meaning "not at all," "not always": どのアメリカ人もコーヒーが好きだとはかぎらない "Not all Americans like coffee." See also「文学者」だとはかぎらない in paragraph 7.

問うて is the -**te** form of 問う ("to question," "to inquire into"), so the meaning is "to attempt (undertake) an inquiry into…"

3　日本であれだけこだわっている文学者という言葉　あれだけ (or あれほど, あんなに) means "to that extent," "that much." こだわる means "to be very particular" about something, often with the nuance of being too particular or obsessive (about one's dress, about crossing every t and dotting every i, about winning, etc.).

一体どうやって英語に翻訳できるか　一体 adds emphasis to どうやって ("how"): "How *on earth* can one translate…into English?"

「あの人は文学者である」というより…と否定された方が　The pattern "AというよりB" is used to say that B is more adequate in some respect than A.

というものが浮び上ってくる　くる is used since the image *comes* to mind in an action that moves *toward* one.

6　文学の単なる学者　単なる is used for emphasis: "just a scholar." See also 単なる「作家」in paragraph 12.

生物学者のように　*Furigana* (or *rubi*) are used here to give an alternate pronunciation with the same meaning. This method is used to amplify the meaning or, in the case of Chinese or Korean names written in kanji, to give the original pronunciation.

文学の学者の中には「文学者」もたまにはいるが　Don't get tripped up by the hiragana here: it is the particle も + たまに ("occasionally") + は (for emphasis/contrast) + be-verb いる + が ("although"). Writers sometimes use が at the end of a sentence to comment on the previous sentence.

7　「あいつはもの書きではない」　もの書き is generally used for professional writers for hire, but authors sometimes use it when humbly referring to themselves.

8　何となく文学を「道」とする　道 is used here in the abstract sense of a vocation or calling, a way of life; the same kanji is used in 茶道 ("the way of tea"), 武士道 ("the way of the warrior"), and 剣道 ("the way of the sword"). The particle と is usually used in this pattern of "AをBとする" ("deciding on A as B").

9　実際には…事実だ　実際に means "in fact," and 事実だ "it is a fact." This repetition of similar words or ideas would be regarded as redundancy or poor style in English, but in Japanese it is perfectly acceptable. Good redundancy was also seen in 「『博士の愛した数式』を巡って」 (paragraph 37).

「文人」という日本語 文人 is a somewhat old-fashioned term for a "man of letters," a "literatus."

「文学者」が持っているまじめさ まじめさ is a noun formed by dropping な and adding the suffix さ. We saw another example of this in 「料理」. There the root adjective was an -**i** adjective: おいしさ (paragraph 6). See also あいまいさ in paragraph 10 and 単純さ and もろさ in paragraph 24 of this essay.

he's no literatusとは誰も言わないし は is used for emphasis.

かりに言ったとしても The pattern "かりに + -**ta** form of a verb + としても" is used for the meaning "even if someone did something," "even if something were to happen."

10 **どうも存在しない** どうも used with a negative serves as an intensifier.

「書く人」という意味で 書く人 is not a normal usage in Japanese.

あの「読む人、書く人、もしくは読んだり書いたりすることによって生きる人」 The quotation marks are used here to set off the rough definition of a 文学者 from the rest of the sentence. もしくは is a formal "or."

という不思議なあいまいさ 不思議な can be used for things that are strange or unusual in a good way, a weird way, or a mysterious way: 不思議な人 "an amazing/strange/mysterious person."

écrivainはむしろ「作家」である 作家 is a neutral term equivalent to "writer" in English.

それは…ちょっと違うのではないだろうか のではないだろうか ("Isn't it that …?") is a common form for a rhetorical question in written Japanese.

「あいつは本を何冊書いても何も分っていない」 何も分っていない is a colloquial phrase expressing exasperation at someone's lack of understanding or lack of common sense. Often the いない is contracted to ない, just as it was in 調べてない in paragraph 6 of 「真っ白な嘘」.

…というニュアンスもありうるとすれば ありうる means "to be possible," "can be"; it is derived from ある plus うる, an auxiliary verb that expresses possibility. とすれば in this case means "assuming that…" or "accepting that…" and signals that the writer is about to give an assessment based on what comes before とすれば.

「文学者」たりうるかどうかという判断の中には　たりうる breaks down as たり (a classical copula indicating qualification), followed by the verb うる (indicating possibility). See also 「文学者」になりうる in the next paragraph.

11 「日本文学研究家」　The marks attached to 研究家 indicate emphasis, like italics or underlining in English.

日本文学の内部において「文学者」になりうるとは誰も考えもしなかった
において is a formal expression that in this case means "in," indicating a place in which an action occurs. The pattern "-**masu** stem + も + しない" is emphatic: 驚きもしない "to show no signs at all of surprise," 聞きもしない "to not even [have the courtesy to] ask."

13 アメリカの作家が他の作家を徹底的にけなしたときの米語　The marks above 作家 show that the subject is American 作家, not American 文学者. 米語 is English used in America (米国).

14 面白いことに　The pattern of "adjective or verb in the -**ta** form + ことに" is used in the written language to express a certain emotion about what follows: 残念なことに "regrettably," 困ったことに "in an awkward development," 驚いたことに "surprisingly."

それらの、ほとんどが書くという行為自体をめぐる侮蔑から成り立っている
それら (the insults) goes together with ほとんど: "almost all of them."

あの人の書くものはすべてうそだ、コンマやピリオドまでもうそだ　Levy may be referring here to a famous incident in 1979 in which Mary McCarthy said on a TV talk show that every word Lillian Hellman wrote was a lie, including "and" and "the."

といったことばを放つように　ように is used to give an example, by way of illustration, of how "almost all of them are made up of insults concerning the *act* of writing itself."

てにをは　This word is used to refer to being able to use "て," "に," "を," "は," and other particles correctly, i.e., to write or speak correct Japanese. In this case, は is pronounced *ha* rather than *wa*.

15 他の作家を片づける最も有名な例は　The primary meaning of 片づけ

「文学者」の国に、ぼくがいる

98 • Notes to pp. 116–20

る is "to tidy" a room or desk, for example, but it is also used more broadly for settling a debt or claim and colloquially for getting rid of or killing someone. Here, of course, Levy uses it to mean "to destroy" someone.

おそらく<u>そのままでは</u>　そのまま is a set phrase meaning "as is."

<u>ちょうど</u>…一九五〇年代に　ちょうど is used to mean "exactly" with periods of time as well as amounts. 一九五〇年代 is often abbreviated to 五〇年代.

（世界ではじめてだったのだろうか）　This phrase in parentheses connects with what follows it and not with what precedes it.

17　**アメリカ文学史を少し<u>かじった</u>ことがある人なら**　The primary meaning of かじる is "to bite into" or "to nibble at" some food, and the extended meaning is "to dip into" or "to dabble at" some subject.

<u>誰でも知っている</u>、あまりにも有名な「暴言」なのだが　Here we have another example of a comma signaling that the phrase that comes immediately before it (誰でも知っている) modifies a noun later on in the sentence (「暴言」), not the words that come immediately after it (あまりにも有名な). See paragraph 1 for the first such instance.

<u>どうして</u>日本語に訳せるか　Here どうして means "how" rather than "why."

ぼくは<u>日米</u>の間を行ったり来たりしている間に　日米 is a contraction of 日本 ("Japan") and 米国 ("America").

18　**あれはライティングじゃない。単なるタイピングにしかすぎない**　This is Levy's attempt at a translation of Capote's insult.

19　**とカタカナで<u>ごまかせば</u>**　The primary meaning of ごまかす is "to deceive," "to trick," "to cheat," but it can also be used to mean "to dodge" or "to gloss over" some issue.

そう<u>ごまかしたところで</u>　The pattern "-**ta** form of a verb + ところで" can mean "despite," "even though," and in this sense it is equivalent to ても, as in そうごまかしても. The idea here is, despite our efforts at translating Capote's insult into Japanese by using katakana loan words, and thereby making it somehow understandable, it still won't be clear to the average Japanese why, owing to the remark, Kerouac was in an instant refused admittance to the pantheon of American literature.

「文学者」の国に、ぼくがいる

ピンと来ない　ピンと来ない is an idiom meaning "to not ring a bell"; ピンと来る means "to realize," "to understand instinctively (a work of art)."

22　**問題は**　Usually a sentence beginning with 問題は will end with という ことだ/ということである, but here that ending is omitted. The というこ とにもなる at the end instead refers to the connotations of the English word "writing" and the difficulty of translating it into Japanese.

　しかし、もっと正確に訳せば…　This long sentence can be parsed into the first and last elements, しかし、もっと正確に訳せば and というニュ アンスがふくまれている, with everything in between being a descrip- tion of that ニュアンス.

　動名詞であって　The であって in this case indicates a reason for what follows. To paraphrase this segment of the sentence: It is because of the nature of the word "writing"—it being a gerund—that…

　書いているという行為でもあれば…ということにもなる　The でもあれば may be confusing at first, until you realize that it functions to set 行為 up as something to be negated. That is, 行為 is negated by にはなって いない just as テキスト is.

　「テキスト」にはなっていない　i.e., "text" as used in deconstructionist lit- erary theory. The は is used for emphasis.

　文章にはなっていない、とか、文体がない、という以前に「あれは文では ない」　文章 is a collection of sentences, or a piece of writing, and 文体 is the style of one's writing. 文, meanwhile, can have various meanings according to context: sentence, style, text, writing, literature. In this case, it probably means "sentences" in the most basic sense of gram- matically arranged words that mean something.

　　という以前に in this case means "on a more fundamental level" than what came before it in the sentence.

　強いていえば　This is a set phrase meaning "if forced to say." If forced to translate Capote's insult one way or the other, Levy would say…

23　**それだけ苦々しいもの**　それだけ is a set phrase meaning "to that extent," "to that degree."

24　**ケルアックの全面否定がなされ**　Literally, "Kerouac's total dismissal was brought about." なされ is the passive form of なす ("to create," "to make").

「文学者」の国に、 ぼくがいる

おまけに　おまけに is used to mean "on top of that," "to boot" for both positive and negative things. It comes from the word おまけ, a price reduction or an extra something thrown in at a shop (also called サービス).

というこちらの全面否定と違って　こちら refers to "this side," in other words, to Japan's literary insult.

ないしは　A formal "or," "or else." ないし is usually used between words, while ないしは is used between clauses.

ひたすら指摘している　ひたすら means to do something "single-mindedly" or "devotedly," to throw oneself into something.

最も痛切な否定としてはいささか狭いというきらいもある　きらいもある is a set phrase referring to there being an undesirable trait in a person or an undesirable aspect of some action or policy. It is used mostly in writing.

という英訳不可能なニュアンスに相当する響きがまったくない　まったく ("completely," "absolutely") is an intensifier. When used with a negative, the meaning is "not at all."

右の名言について日本語で考えれば考えるほど　右の is used instead of "the above-mentioned" since Japanese is written from right to left.

「作家」の最高峰に置かれるカポーティ　置かれる is the passive form of 置く ("to place").

もしかすると「文学者ではなかった」かも知れない　もしかすると is a formal set phrase used together with an expression of conjecture (in this case, かも知れない) for the meaning "Perhaps," "It might be that…," etc.; also もしかしたら, もしかして.

産業国アメリカの絶頂期における生産の結果として　における is a formal, written phrase meaning "in."

単純さ、もろさがあったことは　The primary meaning of もろい is "fragile" or "brittle," as of physical objects, but the word can also mean "emotionally fragile" or "vulnerable." 単純さ is probably used here with a slightly negative nuance, implying a lack of complexity or sophistication.

今となって見えるのである　The set phrase 今となって (also 今になって) is used to express something now having become clear with the benefit of hindsight, new information, etc.

「文学者」の国に、ぼくがいる

25 それが「書くこと」の必然的な崩壊であるかのように The pattern "verb + plus かのように" means "as if it were…"

カポーティのキャリアが…崩壊したのと…重なるようにも見える In other words, AがBと重なる "A concurs/overlaps with B."

27 もし「文学者」が現代語として使えるとすれば とすれば was also seen in paragraph 10. Here it forms a pattern with もし ("if"): もし + verb + とすれば "If it is to be the case that…"

一度純化される必要があるかも知れない Here 一度 is used adverbially for emphasis. It does not have the literal meaning of "one time."

28 日本語の表現の必然的な方向づけは…西洋語のそれとも中国語や韓国語のそれとも違う In other words, the orientation of A is different from both the orientation of B and the orientation of C and D.

が、「文学者」がいるということが が is sometimes used this way, at the beginning of a sentence, to mean "but" with somewhat more force than the usual しかし.

日本の特性であることに変わりはないだろう "Noun + に変わりはない" is a pattern meaning "there is no change in (NOUN)," "is the same (NOUN)" (no matter where, etc.).

29 「文学者である」こととと The clause from 「文学者である」 up to はっきりとした modifies 定義.

よりはっきりとした、そしてより本物の定義 When より is used before an adjective or adverb, it forms the comparative of that adjective or adverb: よりはっきりとした ("clearer"), より本物の ("more genuine"), より効果的 ("more effective").

30 一度は「近代語化」を経過してしまったコトバで表現をするのだから Levy is probably referring to the language reforms of the Meiji period (1868–1912) when a national language emerged. The written language gradually moved away from classical forms based on Chinese, and much new vocabulary was created by coining new words and borrowing from Western languages.

コトバ is in katakana to distinguish it as being used in the sense of "language" rather than "words."

それは当たり前なこと それ refers to the fact that, for 日本語の表現者,

there is always a part of their work that can be translated into a foreign tongue and a part that cannot be.

かならずしも自覚されているとはいえない　かならずしも is a written expression that is always used with a negative to mean "not always," "not necessarily." とはいえない ("It cannot be said that…") is a common sentence ending in written Japanese.

31 **外のまぶしい光にさらしたとき、はじめて自覚できる**　The pattern "-**ta** form of a verb + とき（は）はじめて" is used to express the idea that one first notices or learns something as a result of some action (the action expressed by the verb in the -**ta** form).

というか、はじめて自覚を強いられるのではないだろうか　This is the same というか that we saw in「真っ白な嘘」(paragraph 3). The meaning is: "We could say A (はじめて自覚できる), but perhaps it would be better to say B (はじめて自覚を強いられる)."

34 **アメリカの常識に合わせすぎていたのかもしれないと反省をしている**　反省 is self-reflection in the sense of soul-searching, of reconsidering the wisdom of a past action.

35 **もっと素直に答えればよかった**　The word 素直 is perhaps even more difficult to translate into English than 文学者, also due to cultural differences. It is very positive in its connotations, reflecting the value placed on sincerity in Japanese culture. It seems close in meaning to the British expression "to have no side": to be open, straightforward; to be cheerful and not have a "difficult" personality; to be meek, sincere. Here Levy seems to mean to not be overly self-conscious about how his answer would sound to an American—to answer more openheartedly.

"-**Ba** form + よかった" means "It would have been better had I done such and such." Don't confuse it with "-**te** form + よかった," which means almost the opposite: "I'm glad I did such and such."

Read Real Japanese

Essays

Read Real Japanese

Contemporary Writings by Popular Authors

EDITED BY Janet Ashby

NARRATED BY Reiko Matsunaga

KODANSHA INTERNATIONAL
Tokyo · New York · London

Note from the publisher

All Japanese names are given in the Japanese order, sur-
name first (except on the jacket, title page, copyright page,
and CD).

Photo Credits: Copyright © Roland Kelts, p. 11. Copyright © Shōichi
Nakamura, p. 19. Copyright © The Asahi Shimbun Company, p. 109.
Photo on p. 33 courtesy of Mitsuyo Kakuta. Photo on p. 45 courtesy
of Banana Yoshimoto.

CD narration by arrangement of PSC Produce & Management. Re-
cording and editing by The English Language Education Council Inc.

Dictionary, pp. 3–47 (starting from the back of the book), compiled
by Nihon IR Inc. Copyright © 2008 Kodansha International Ltd.

Distributed in the United States by Kodansha America LLC, and in the
United Kingdom and continental Europe by Kodansha Europe Ltd.

Published by Kodansha International Ltd., 17–14 Otowa 1-chome,
Bunkyo-ku, Tokyo 112–8652.

English text copyright © 2008 by Janet Ashby

First edition, 2008
18 17 16 15 14 13 12 11 10 09   12 11 10 9 8 7 6 5 4 3

Library of Congress Cataloging-in-Publication Data

Read real Japanese essays : contemporary writings by popular
authors / edited by Janet Ashby ; narrated by Reiko Matsunaga.
    p. cm.
  ISBN 978-4-7700-3057-3
  1. Japanese essays—20th century. 2. Japanese essays—21st
century. I. Ashby, Janet. II. Matsunaga, Reiko.
  PL772.65.R43 2008
  895.6'4508—dc22
                          2007052675

www.kodansha-intl.com

Starting from the back of the book and
running in the opposite direction . . .

PREFACE

Fifteen years have now passed since I published *Read Real Japanese* and many, many more since I first started studying Japanese. Much has changed during that period. The advent of the DVD and the Internet have made it possible for those living outside Japan to have much more exposure to spoken Japanese. And who, in the days of Japan, Inc. and its accompanying vision of robotic businessmen toiling around the clock for the economic takeover of the West, could have imagined the spread of Japanese anime and manga throughout the world and the touting of "cool Japan"?

Yet Japanese remains a deeply frustrating language to study. So much so that I remember finding it positively *encouraging* when my Japanese professor remarked one day that it took seven years to learn the language—I had despaired of ever being able to pick up a Japanese magazine or newspaper and read it more or less easily.

The problem is not only the kanji barrier, high though that can be for Western learners of Japanese, but also the differences in the spoken and written language and the unfamiliar vocabulary, set expressions, sentence patterns, and even the way of thinking. And despite all the changes in the learning environment over the years, there still aren't many intermediate reading materials available, especially ones that can be used for independent study.

It is my hope that this collection of eight essays by some of Japan's best writers will provide a relatively painless experience in reading real Japanese. I believe that I have succeeded in finding lively, well-crafted essays covering a range of topics and styles, for students of all interests and backgrounds.

ON USING THIS BOOK

There are three parts to this book: the Japanese essays and translations, the notes and dictionary at the back, and the CD. The essays are arranged roughly in order of ascending difficulty and printed in Japanese style—that is, from right to left. They are exactly as originally published with the exception of the addition of *furigana* and paragraph numbers at the top of the page.

The paragraph numbers tell you where on the facing page to look for the translations. The translations—done by phrase or sentence rather than word-for-word or as a complete text—are meant to be as natural as possible without being so idiomatic as to cause confusion.

The notes, located toward the back of the book, use the same paragraph numbers, but the text runs in the opposite direction—from left to right, the English way—for ease of reading. They provide additional information to help you understand the essays. Besides giving background cultural information, they explain idiomatic usages, unfamiliar or tricky sentence patterns, words that get "lost" in translation, nuances in usage, and so on.

The dictionary starting at the very back of the book, and also running from left to right, contains entries for nearly all of the words used in the essays. It is there for you to use as you wish. Note, however, that it provides only the sense or senses of the words as they are used in the essay(s). This means that you don't have to wade through long, complicated lists of equivalents to find the one you're looking for. Verbs there are entered under the dictionary form.

The CD contains all the essays in the book, read aloud by a professional actress at natural speed. Repeated listenings will help you acquire a sense of the sounds and rhythms of Japanese. When using the CD for self-directed study, you should (1) listen to the track once before reading the essay, to get a feel for the vocabulary and content, (2) read along silently with the narrator after fully understanding the essay, and, as a further challenge, (3) try "shadowing" the narrator, repeating aloud after her like a simultaneous interpreter. Don't be discouraged if you don't understand much of the content at first listening, or if you can't read as fast as she can. Understanding Japanese spoken at natural speed, and especially speaking it yourself at such speed, is another challenge altogether, and one that comes with time (usually time spent in Japan). It will be enough if you can absorb her intonation and enunciation of the expressions you find interesting.

SOURCES

In compiling the translations and notes, I consulted numerous reference works. Particularly to be recommended is *Nihongo bunkei jiten* (Kurosio Publishers, 1998). Also helpful were the dictionaries *Daijirin* (2nd Edition; Sanseidō, 1995), *Kōjien* (5th Edition; Iwanami Shoten, 1998), and *Kenkyusha's New Japanese-English Dictionary* (5th Edition; Kenkyūsha, 2003), as well as *A Dictionary of Basic Japanese Grammar* and *A Dictionary of Intermediate Japanese Grammar* by Seiichi Makino and Michio Tsutsui (Japan Times, 1989 and 1995).

ACKNOWLEDGMENTS

I would like to acknowledge here the unflagging efforts of my editor Michael Staley in all aspects of the production of this book, particularly in the preparation of the notes, and for the help of Kobayashi Chieko in answering questions and of Suzuki Shigeyoshi in checking the notes.

村上春樹

Murakami Haruki

Murakami Haruki is one contemporary Japanese author who needs no introduction. Born in Kyoto in 1949 and a graduate of Waseda University, he has won popularity worldwide with his postmodern existentialist stance and idiosyncratic humor in such works as *A Wild Sheep Chase*, *Norwegian Wood*, *The Wind-Up Bird Chronicle*, and *Kafka on the Shore*. His fiction has been translated into more than forty languages, but Murakami has also published numerous nonfiction works, only one of which, *Underground: The Tokyo Gas Attack and the Japanese Psyche*, is available in English. If you'd like to read more of Murakami's nonfiction, several volumes of short essays with charming illustrations by Anzai Mizumaru are available in paperback (*bunko-bon*) from Shinchōsha. Murakami's *Wakai dokusha no tame no tampen shōsetsu annai* (*Guide to Short Stories, for Young Readers*) is a selection of and introduction to six stories by Japanese authors for, as the title indicates, younger Japanese readers.

The essays in *Murakami Radio* (published in hardcover by Magazine House in 2001, and in *bunko* paperback by Shinchōsha in 2003), from which the light-hearted essay here on lying was taken, were originally written for *AnAn*, a fashion magazine popular with female readers in their twenties. My personal recommendation for further reading, though, are the several volumes of Murakami's postings on a Web site occasionally opened for questions from readers, and published by Asahi Shimbun Co. The questions range from "What's your favorite color?" to Dear Abby letters to literary discussions; Murakami's answers are cool but never cynical.

真っ白な嘘

村上春樹

僕は嘘をつくのは得意ではない。でも嘘をつくこと自体はそれほど嫌いではない。変な言い方だけど、つまり「深刻な嘘をつくのは苦手だけど、害のない出鱈目を言うのはけっこう好きだ」ということです。

昔、ある月刊誌で書評を頼まれたことがある。僕は本を書く人間で、批評する人間じゃないから、書評ってできればやりたくないんだけど、そのときは事情があって、「まあいいや、やりましょう」と引き受けた。でも普通どおりにやっても面白くないから、架空の本をでっちあげて、それを詳しく評論することにした。実在しない人の伝記の書評とかね。これはやってみると、なかなか愉快でした。でっちあげをするぶん頭は使うけれど、本を読む時間は節約できる。それに取り上げた本の著者に「あの野郎、ろくでもないことを書きやがって」と個人的に恨まれたりすることもないですしね。

真っ白な嘘 Little White Lies

1 僕は I ▪ 嘘をつくのは telling a lie ▪ 得意ではない is not something I'm good at ▪ でも嘘をつくこと自体は but telling a lie in itself ▪ それほど嫌いではない is not something I particularly abhor ▪ 変な言い方だけど it may sound odd, but ▪ つまり...ということです in a word... ▪「深刻な嘘をつくのは苦手だけど I'm bad at big lies, but ▪ 害のない出鱈目を言うのはけっこう好きだ」I'm quite fond of telling harmless and absurd lies

2 昔 in the past ▪ ある月刊誌で書評を頼まれたことがある I was asked by a certain monthly magazine to do book reviews ▪ 僕は本を書く人間で I'm someone (lit., "a person") who writes books and ▪ 批評する人間じゃない not someone who writes reviews ▪ から because ▪ 書評ってできればやりたくないんだけど if possible, I would rather not do reviews, but... ▪ そのときは事情があって because of circumstances at the time ▪「まあいいや、やりましょう」と引き受けた I accepted, saying, "Oh, okay, I'll do it" ▪ でも普通どおりにやっても but if you do it the usual way ▪ 面白くない it's no fun ▪ 架空の本をでっちあげて make up an imaginary book and ▪ それを詳しく評論する comment upon it in depth ▪ ...ことにした I decided to... ▪ 実在しない人の伝記の書評とかね like a review of a biography about a person who doesn't exist ▪ これはやってみると when I ventured to do this ▪ なかなか愉快でした it was quite amusing ▪ でっちあげをするぶん insofar as thinking it (i.e., an imaginary book) up went ▪ 頭は使うけれど it required brainwork, but ▪ 本を読む時間は節約できる I didn't have to read a book (lit., "I could save the time required to read a book") ▪ それに in addition ▪ 取り上げた本の著者に by the author of a book I chose to review ▪「あの野郎、ろくでもないことを書きやがって」 "that rat, writing such trash about my book!" ▪ ...と個人的に恨まれたりすることもないですしね there wouldn't be any holding it personally against me, saying...

この偽書評を書いたときには、あとで誰かから「ろくでもない嘘をつくな」という苦情の手紙とか、「どこに行けばこの本が手にはいるのか」といった問い合わせが来るんじゃないかと覚悟していたんだけど、一通も来なくて気が抜けたというか、まあそれはそれでほっとした。結局のところ、月刊誌の書評なんて誰も真剣に読んでないんだろうという気もしなくはないんだけれど、どうなんだろうね。

それから、今はわりにまじめに答えているけど、生意気盛りの若い頃は、インタビューでもしばしばいい加減なことを言っていた。どんな本を読んでいるかときかれて、「そうですねえ、最近は明治時代の小説をよく読んでいます。初期言文一致運動に関わったマイナーな作家が好きで、具体的に言うと、牟田口正午とか、大坂五兵なんかの作品は、今読んでも刺激的だと思いますよ」とか答えたりしてね。

もちろんどっちの作家も実在しない。完全なでっちあげである。でもそんなこと誰にもわからない。僕はそういう口からでまかせのことをすらすらと並べ立てるのがわりに得意です。得意というか、苦労がないというか。

3 | この偽書評を書いたときには when I wrote such fake reviews ▪ あとで誰かから…来るんじゃないかと覚悟していたんだけど I was prepared for…to come afterward from someone or other, but ▪ 「ろくでもない嘘をつくな」 "don't tell such stupid lies!" ▪ という苦情の手紙とか such letters of complaint as ▪ 「どこに行けばこの本が手にはいるのか」といった問い合わせ [or] inquiries like "where do I go to get hold of this book?" ▪ 一通も来なくて not a single such letter came, so ▪ 気が抜けたというか it was something of a letdown ▪ まあそれはそれでほっとした but, well, it was also a relief ▪ 結局のところ in the end ▪ 月刊誌の書評なんて誰も真剣に読んでないんだろう no one really reads the book reviews in monthly magazines ▪ …という気もしなくはないんだけれど I couldn't avoid the feeling that…but ▪ どうなんだろうね it's hard to know for sure

4 | それから and also ▪ 今はわりにまじめに答えているけど though I now answer relatively straightforwardly [in interviews] ▪ 生意気盛りの若い頃は in my young days when I was a smart aleck ▪ インタビューでもしばしばいい加減なことを言っていた I would often fool around (lit., "say larky things") even in interviews ▪ どんな本を読んでいるかときかれて when I was asked what sort of books I was reading ▪ 「そうですねえ "well… ▪ 最近は明治時代の小説をよく読んでいます recently I've been reading a lot of Meiji-period [1868–1912] novels ▪ 初期言文一致運動に関わったマイナーな作家が好きで I like minor authors involved in the early movement to write in the vernacular ▪ 具体的に言うと to be more specific ▪ 牟田口正午とか大坂五兵なんかの作品は、今読んでも刺激的だと思いますよ」 I find the works of Mudaguchi Shōgo or Ōsaka Gohei exciting to read even today" ▪ …とか答えたりしてね I'd say things like…

5 | もちろんどっちの作家も実在しない of course, neither of those authors actually exist ▪ 完全なででっちあげである they are complete fabrications ▪ でもそんなこと誰にもわからない but no one noticed that ▪ そういう口からでまかせのことをすらすらと並べ立てるの smoothly tossing off such casual remarks ▪ わりに得意です is something I'm quite good at ▪ 得意というか、苦労がないというか well, good at, or at least I have no trouble with it

日本語では「真っ赤な嘘」っていうけど、どうして嘘は赤いのか知ってますか？　奈良時代の日本では、悪質な嘘をついて世間を惑わせた人には、赤い大福餅を12個口に詰め込んで窒息死させるという酷い刑罰があったからです——というのは例によって嘘だ。どうして嘘が赤いのか、昔から気になっていて、いつか調べようと思っていたんだけど、この数十年ずっと忙しくて手がはなせなくて（嘘つけ）まだ調べてない。

英語には white lie という言葉がある。これは「罪のない（方便の、儀礼的な）嘘」のことです（これはほんと）。文字どおり「真っ白な嘘」。僕の嘘はどっちかというとこっちに近い。害はない、と思う。だって赤い大福餅を12個無理に食べさせられたりしちゃ、たまらないものね。

6 | 日本語では in Japanese ▪ 「真っ赤な嘘」っていうけど we say *"makka na uso"* (lit., "red lie"), but ▪ どうして嘘は赤いのか知ってますか？ do you know why a lie is red? ▪ 奈良時代の日本では in Japan, in the Nara period [710–784] ▪ 悪質な嘘をついて世間を惑わせた人には… という酷い刑罰があったからです it's because people who told malicious lies and disturbed the public order received the cruel punishment of… ▪ 赤い大福餅を12個口に詰め込んで窒息死させる being choked to death by having twelve red [actually pink] *daifuku* [a traditional Japanese sweet of *mochi* stuffed with bean paste] stuffed into their mouth ▪ というのは例によって嘘だ which is of course a lie too ▪ どうして嘘が赤いのか、昔から気になっていて I've wondered for a long time why lies are red and ▪ いつか調べようと思っていたんだけど I've thought I would investigate it someday, but ▪ この数十年ずっと忙しくて手がはなせなくて I've been busy without a break for the past few decades and haven't had a hand free [to do it] ▪ （嘘つけ）(liar!) ▪ まだ調べてない I still haven't investigated it yet

7 | 英語にはwhite lieという言葉がある in English there's the expression "white lie" ▪ これは「罪のない（方便の、儀礼的な）嘘」のことです this is a harmless (expedient, courteous) lie ▪ （これはほんと）(this is the truth) (i.e., I'm not lying this time) ▪ 文字どおり「真っ白な嘘」literally this is a *"masshiro na uso"* ▪ 僕の嘘はどっちかというとこっちに近い my lies are, if anything, close to this ▪ 害はない、と思う I believe they are harmless ▪ だって after all ▪ 赤い大福餅を12個無理に食べさせられたりしちゃ if I were forced to do something like eating twelve *daifuku* ▪ たまらないものね I really couldn't stand it

酒井 順子

Sakai Junko

The acerbic essayist Sakai Junko started publishing while still in high school, but it was the controversy over her 2003 book *Makeinu no tôboe* (*The Howl of the Loser Dogs*) that made her a household name in Japan. In this best-selling work she called on *makeinu*—unmarried and childless professional women over the age of thirty, like herself—to embrace their "loser" status in Japanese society and make the best of life in this new demographic category. The book touched a nerve in a society already concerned over so-called "parasite singles" (young, unmarried adults living with their parents) and the falling birth rate, and much of the subtlety of Sakai's position was lost in the ensuing rush to divide women into unmarried *makeinu* and married *kachiinu*.

Born in Tokyo in 1966 and a graduate of Rikkyō University's College of Sociology, Sakai worked at a large advertising agency, Hakuhōdō, for three years. Her socially observant eye and dry wit are evident in the essay reprinted here on changing public manners on the train, the means by which most students and workers commute to school or work in Japanese cities. It is one of the essays Sakai wrote for *Shûkan Gendai*, a weekly magazine read mainly by men. In 2001 it was published in the collection *Kakekomi sêfu?* (*Safe Inside the Train before the Door Closes?*), issued by Kodansha. For a similarly smart take on Japanese society, readers might try Sakai's *Makeinu no tôboe* or any of her other works.

電車の中で若者に注意

酒井順子

1　先日、新幹線に乗っていた時のこと。私の前の席に、若い男性二人連れが座っていたのでした。

2　彼等は二人で、携帯テレビのようなものを、ずーっと観ていました。それも、イヤホンを使用せずに、音は出しっぱなし。新幹線の中のことですから電波は悪く、「ガーッ、シャーッ」という雑音も混じって、とてもうるさいのです。

3　私は、車掌さんが彼等に注意をしてくれるのを待ちました。が、なかなか車掌さんは通りかからない。通路を挟んだ反対側の席には、中年のサラリーマンが座っていたので、彼が注意してくれないだろうかと期待し、「お願いだから、こいつらにひとこと注意してくれーっ」と念を送ってみたものの、彼は週刊誌をずっと読んでいるのみ。

4　静寂を好む私は、「では私が注意するしかないのであろうか?」と、悩んだのでした。

電車の中で若者に注意 Admonishing Young People on the Train

1 先日 the other day ▪ 新幹線に乗っていた時のこと it happened when I was on the bullet train ▪ 私の前の席に in the seats ahead of me ▪ 若い男性二人連れが座っていたのでした two young men were sitting

2 彼等は二人で…ずーっと観ていました they were watching…together for the longest time ▪ 携帯テレビのようなもの some sort of portable TV ▪ それも and that [was] ▪ イヤホンを使用せずに without using head-phones ▪ 音は出しっぱなし everyone could hear (lit., "the sound was streaming out") ▪ 新幹線の中のことですから since it was inside the bullet train ▪ 電波は悪く the reception was poor ▪「ガーッ、シャーッ」という雑音も混じって there was a lot of static, and ▪ とてもうるさいのです it was very annoying

3 私は、車掌さんが彼等に注意をしてくれるのを待ちました I waited for the conductor to admonish them ▪ が、なかなか車掌さんは通りかからない but the conductor just didn't come by ▪ 通路を挟んだ反対側の席には in the seat across the aisle from them ▪ 中年のサラリーマンが座っていたので was sitting a middle-aged businessman, and therefore ▪ 彼が注意してくれないだろうかと期待し I kind of hoped he would say something to them and ▪「お願いだから、こいつらにひとこと注意してくれーっ」と念を送ってみたものの though I tried to send him the thought to please, please, say something to them ▪ 彼は週刊誌をずっと読んでいるのみ he just continued to read his (weekly) magazine

4 静寂を好む like peace and quiet ▪「では私が注意するしかないのであろうか？」well, is there nothing for it but for *me* to admonish them? ▪ と悩んだのでした I fretted, thinking…

が、最近は若者に注意した大人が、逆ギレされてひどい目に遭うという事件が多発しています。そういえば先日も、駅のホームにおいて、化粧をしている若い女性に注意した年配の女性が、反対につきとばされて電車に接触し、大怪我をする事件がありましたっけ。

若い女性の側は、

「化粧用スポンジで汗をぬぐっていただけ。化粧をしていたわけではない」

とコメントをしていたわけですが。

ホームで化粧というのは、女大学的女子のたしなみと照らし合わせてみれば、あってはならぬ行為でしょう。が、電車内化粧が当たり前となってきた今では、

「みっともないからやめろ」

と大人が言ったとしても、

「私は別に平気だし―」

ということで話は終ってしまう。携帯電話における電磁波とか、携帯ステレオのシャカシャカ音とか、わかりやすい実害が無い限りは、「みっともない」とか「恥ずかしい」だ

- が、最近は however, recently ■ 若者に注意した大人 adults who have admonished young people ■ 逆ギレされてひどい目に遭う have on the contrary met the (unfortunate) fate of [the youths] blowing up at them in anger ■ …という事件が多発しています there have been a lot of cases of… ■ そういえば come to think of it ■ 先日も just the other day ■ 駅のホームにおいて on the station platform ■ 化粧をしている若い女性に注意した年配の女性が an elderly woman who had scolded a young woman putting on makeup ■ 反対につきとばされて電車に接触し was shoved (by the young woman) and was brushed by a train and ■ 大怪我をする be gravely injured ■ 事件がありましたっけ I seem to remember an incident in which ■ 若い女性の側は as for that young woman

5 化粧用スポンジで汗をぬぐっていただけ I was only wiping off sweat with a cosmetic sponge ■ 化粧をしていたわけではない I wasn't putting on makeup

6 とコメントをしていたわけですが she commented that…

7 ホームで化粧というのは (putting on) makeup on a train platform ■ 女大学的女子のたしなみと照らし合わせてみれば if judged by (lit., "compared with") eighteenth-century standards of comportment ■ あってはならぬ行為でしょう is no doubt unacceptable behavior ■ 電車内化粧が当たり前となってきた今では in the present day, when putting on makeup in the train has become commonplace

8 みっともないからやめろ stop such disgraceful behavior!

9 と大人が言ったとしても even if an adult should say to her

10 私は別に平気だし— well, I don't see anything wrong with it!

11 ということで話は終ってしまう she will [just say]…and that will be the end of it ■ 携帯電話における電磁波とか electromagnetic waves from a cell phone or ■ 携帯ステレオのシャカシャカ音 the irritating sound [of music] leaking from someone's headphones ■ わかりやすい実害が無い限りは as long as there's no obvious disturbance ■ 「みっともない」とか「恥ずかしい」だけでは just for being "unseemly" or "shameful"

けでは、注意もできないのです。

とはいえ携帯テレビの音っていうのは十分に実害に値するだろう、と私は思いました。たとえ逆ギレして殴りかかってきたとしても、相手はアンガールズっぽい若者だからさほど痛くはないはず。いやでも、その手の若者の方が刃物とか持っていたりして、キレると手をつけられなくなるかも……。

思いは千々に乱れましたが、あまりの騒音に耐えきれなくなって、私はついに立ち上がったのです。そして相手が怒り出さないように満面の笑みを湛えつつ、

「すみません。あのう、ちょーっと音を小さくしていただけますかぁ?」

と、ソフトに語りかけた。
突然、座席の背後から注意されて彼等はビクッとしたらしく、

「あ、すすすいません」

とか言って、ボリュームを下げたのでした。

私は、一応の結果には満足したものの、『ちょーっと音を小さくしていただけます

■ 注意もできないのです one can no longer admonish another

12 とはいえ but still… ■ 携帯テレビの音っていうのは the audio of a portable TV ■ 十分に実害に値するだろう amply qualifies as a disturbance ■ と私は思いました I thought ■ たとえ逆ギレして殴りかかってきたとしても even had they flown into an uncalled-for rage and come over to sock me ■ 相手はアンガールズっぽい若者だから these opponents of mine were hardly tough he-men, so ■ さほど痛くはないはず it surely wouldn't have hurt so much ■ いやでも but then again ■ その手の若者の方が just such a type of youth ■ 刃物とか持っていたりして might carry some sort of knife, and ■ キレると if they were to get angry ■ 手をつけられなくなるかも…… things could get out of hand…

13 思いは千々に乱れましたが I fretted over this and that, but ■ あまりの騒音に耐えきれなくなって no longer able to endure the racket ■ 私はついに立ち上がったのです I finally took action ■ 相手が怒り出さないように so they wouldn't blow up ■ 満面の笑みを湛えつつ while smiling broadly

14 あのう uh… ■ ちょーっと音を小さくしていただけますかぁ? could you please turn down the volume a teensy bit?

15 と、ソフトに語りかけた I asked non-threateningly

16 突然 suddenly ■ 座席の背後から from behind (lit., "from behind their seats") ■ 注意されて having been admonished ■ 彼等はビクッとしたらしく seeming startled, they…

17 あ、すすすいません oh, s-s-sorry

18 とか言って said something like… and ■ ボリュームを下げたのでした they turned down the volume

19 私は、一応の結果には満足したものの although I was satisfied with such fair to middling results ■『ちょーっと音を小さくしていただけますかぁ?』っていうのは saying, "Could you please turn down the volume a teensy bit?"

かぁ?』っていうのは、本当に音を小さくしろってことじゃなくて、その携帯テレビの電源を切れってことなんだよッ」とまだ思っていましたし、通路の向こうのサラリーマンに対しても、「自分だってうるさいって思っていたクセに注意もしないでホッとしたような表情だけしているとは小さい奴だなぁ!」とも思っていた。

もっと前だったら、たとえ同じ状況でも、私は注意などできなかったことでしょう。

と言うより、うんと若い頃は公共の場において、注意される側だったはずです。

たとえば高校時代、学校帰りに電車の中で友人同士でおしゃべりをしていたら、おじさんが何も言わずに「SHUT UP」と書いてある紙を差し出して去っていったので、

「シャットアップって何?」

「……あっ、シャラップってこと?」

「シャラップだってさ、変なおじさん! アハハハハ!」

と全く懲りずに大笑いしたり。

また大学時代にハワイに行った帰りは、楽しかった旅の興奮さめやらず、飛行機の中で

■ 本当に actually ■ 音を小さくしろってことじゃなくて does not mean "Turn down the sound" ■ その携帯テレビの電源を切れってことなんだよッ it means "Turn that portable TV off!" ■ …とまだ思っていましたし I was still thinking…and moreover ■ 通路の向こうのサラリーマンに対しても even with regard to the businessman sitting across the aisle ■ 「自分だってうるさいって思っていたクセに in spite of finding it noisy yourself ■ 注意もしないで you say not a word to them, but ■ ホッとしたような表情だけしているとは just sit there, looking relieved ■ 小さい奴だなぁ！」what a poor excuse for a man! ■ とも思っていた I was thinking…

20 もっと前だったら at an earlier time (lit., "had it been earlier") ■ たとえ同じ状況でも even in the same situation ■ 私は注意などできなかったことでしょう I probably wouldn't have been able to admonish anyone ■ と言うより or rather ■ うんと若い頃は when I was much younger ■ 公共の場において in public places ■ 注意される側だったはずです no doubt I would have been on the receiving end of an admonishment

21 たとえば for example ■ 高校時代 in my high school days ■ 学校帰りに電車の中で in the train on the way home from school ■ 友人同士でおしゃべりをしていたら when I was chattering away with my friends ■ おじさんが何も言わずに without saying anything, an older man ■ 「ＳＨＵＴ　ＵＰ」と書いてある紙を差し出して去っていった handed us a piece of paper on which he had written "Shut up" and walked away ■ ので because…

22 シャットアップって何？ what does "Shut up" mean?

23 ……あっ、シャラップってこと？ maybe it's "Shaddup"?

24 シャラップだってさ Shaddup!? ■ 変なおじさん！ what a weirdo! ■ アハハハハ！ ha-ha-ha!

25 と全く懲りずに大笑いしたり and we had a big laugh without learning any lesson from it at all

26 大学時代に in my college days ■ ハワイに行った帰りは on our way back from a trip to Hawaii ■ 楽しかった旅の興奮さめやらず still excited by our fun vacation ■ 飛行機の中で in the airplane

友達とずーっとしゃべったり歌を歌ったりし続けた結果、イケメンのスチュワードさんに、

「シーッ！」

と咎められて、恥ずかしい思いをしたりもしましたっけか。

そんな時代のことを思い出してみると、若い時代というのは周囲のことが全く見えていなかったのだなあ、ということがよくわかるのでした。電車の中で円陣を組んでおしゃべりしている女子高生にとっては、周囲の乗客なんていないも同然。今、自分達がおしゃべりをしている話題こそが世の中において最も大切なことであり、自分達こそが世界の中心、くらいに思っている。

今、電車の中で化粧をする女性のメンタリティーも、同じようなものなのでしょう。自分以外の乗客はいないも同然だから、アイラインをひく時の顔を見られても、何ら恥ずかしくない。同じように、自分達が今興味を持っていることが世の中において最も大切なことだから、新幹線の中でも観たい番組があれば携帯テレビを観る。

- 友達とずーっとしゃべったり chatting the whole time with my friends
- 歌を歌ったり singing songs ▪ …し続けた結果 as a result of continuously doing things like… ▪ イケメンのスチュワードさんに by the handsome steward

27 シーッ！ Shhh!

28 と答められて we were rebuked and ▪ 恥ずかしい思いをしたりもしましたっけか if memory serves me, I even had an embarrassing experience [of being on the receiving end of a rebuke] (lit., "didn't I even have an embarrassing experience?")

29 そんな時代のことを思い出してみると thinking back on those days ▪ 若い時代というのは when one is young ▪ 周囲のことが全く見えていなかったのだなぁ one doesn't see those around one at all ▪ …ということがよくわかるのでした I fully realize that… ▪ 円陣を組んでおしゃべりしている女子高生にとっては for high-school girls who are standing in a circle and chattering away ▪ 周囲の乗客なんていないも同然 it is as if the other passengers don't even exist ▪ 今、自分達がおしゃべりをしている話題こそが what they are talking about right then ▪ 世の中において最も大切なことであり is the most important thing in the universe, and ▪ 自分達こそが世界の中心、くらいに思っている they think they themselves are the center of the world

30 今 at present ▪ 電車の中で化粧をする女性のメンタリティーも the mentality of women who apply makeup in the train ▪ 同じようなものなのでしょう is probably something similar ▪ 自分以外の乗客はいないも同然だから since other passengers are as good as nonexistent ▪ アイラインをひく時の顔を見られても even if they are seen applying eyeliner ▪ 何ら恥ずかしくない [such women] feel not the slightest bit embarrassed ▪ 同じように by the same token ▪ 自分達が今興味を持っていることが…だから because what a couple of young men are most interested in at the moment is… ▪ 世の中において最も大切なこと the most important thing in the world (to them) ▪ 新幹線の中でも even if they are in the bullet train ▪ 観たい番組があれば if there is a program they want to watch ▪ 携帯テレビを観る they will watch it on a portable TV

しかし人は大人になるにつれ、次第に自分達が世界の中心ではないことに気付いてきます。結果、「人前ですべきでないこと」が見えてきて、公序良俗を守るようになってくる。その手の人はおそらく、「あ、今は電車の中で化粧をしてもいい時代なんだ」と思うのですが、それは大きな勘違い。電車内化粧というのは、まだ周囲が見えていない若者にのみ許されているのであって、同じことを大人がやってしまうと、たいへん痛々しいものなのです。

東京でもこの度、女性専用車両が各社で導入されました。関西で女性専用車両に乗ると、そこは誰の視線も気にせず化粧する女性で溢れているのですが、おそらく東京でも、同じ光景がくりひろげられているにちがいない。

「堂々と化粧ができる車両」の登場によって、電車内の道徳感は微妙に変化することでしょう。子供の頃から女性専用車両にしか乗らなかった女性がどのような大人になるのか、恐いような興味深いような気分がいたします。

31 しかし however ▪ 人は大人になるにつれ as people reach adulthood ▪ 次第に little by little ▪ 自分達が世界の中心ではないこと that they are not at the center of the world ▪ …に気付いてきます they come to realize… ▪ 結果 as a result ▪ 「人前ですべきでないこと」that which should not be done in front of others ▪ 見えてきて becomes clear to them (lit., "comes to be seen") and ▪ 公序良俗を守るようになってくる they come to observe "public order and standards of decency"

32 たまに occasionally ▪ いい大人なのに even though she is fully an adult ▪ 電車の中で化粧をする人を見るものです you see someone putting on makeup in the train ▪ その手の人はおそらく…と思っているのだと思うのですが I think that such women probably think…but ▪ 「あ、今は電車の中で化粧をしてもいい時代なんだ」ah, these days it's all right to put on makeup in the train ▪ それは大きな勘違い that is a major misconception ▪ 電車内化粧というのは putting on makeup in the train ▪ まだ周囲が見えていない若者にのみ許されているのであって is only forgiven for young people who are not yet fully aware of their surroundings, and ▪ 同じことを大人がやってしまうと when an adult does the same thing ▪ たいへん痛々しいものなのです it is a very painful sight to see

33 東京でも in Tokyo too ▪ この度 recently ▪ 女性専用車両が各社で導入されました the "women-only" car has been adopted by all the railway companies ▪ 関西で in the Kansai area ▪ 女性専用車両に乗ると when you ride in the women's car ▪ そこは there [in that car] ▪ 誰の視線も気にせず化粧する女性で溢れているのですが it is overflowing with women putting on makeup who are utterly unconcerned with the eyes of others, and ▪ おそらく…にちがいない probably ▪ 東京でも in Tokyo also ▪ 同じ光景がくりひろげられている the same scene is unfolding

34 「堂々と化粧ができる車両」の登場によって with the rise of cars in which one can unapologetically put on makeup ▪ 電車内の道徳感は微妙に変化することでしょう train ethics will no doubt be subtly changing ▪ 子供の頃から from childhood ▪ …にしか乗らなかった女性がどのような大人になるのか what sorts of adults will women who have only ever ridden in…become? ▪ 恐いような興味深いような気分がいたします [the thought] both frightens and intrigues me

角田光代

Kakuta Mitsuyo

Why is Kakuta Mitsuyo such a prolific writer, having produced over forty works of fiction and essays since she won the Kaien Literary Prize for New Writers in 1990? One might attribute it to the particular nature of the publishing scene in Japan, in which—like in the age of Dickens or Conan Doyle—short stories, novellas, and serializations are published in numerous weekly and monthly magazines, making it possible for writers to produce in large volume. But the truth is, Kakuta Mitsuyo is so prolific simply because she is so hardworking. In one interview she revealed that she had twenty-eight deadlines a month for separate columns and serials; reportedly she goes to her office and writes from 7:30 am to 5 pm, Monday through Friday.

Born in Yokohama in 1967 and a graduate of Waseda University, Kakuta got her start writing Cobalt Novels, or romantic fiction for high school girls. Her popular short stories and novels reflect the lifestyles and problems of women in their twenties and thirties. At the time of writing, she had won eight literary awards, including the Naoki Prize—Japan's most prestigious for popular fiction—for *Taigan no kanojo* (published in English as *Woman on the Other Shore*). Most recently she won the Chūōkōron-Shinsha Literary Prize for her suspense novel *Yōkame no semi* (*Eighth Day of the Cicada*) in 2007.

Kakuta's light essay here, a listing of her complaints about the male philosophy of cooking, shows well her wit and polished writing style. It comes from her essay collection *Ima, nani shiteru?* (*What're You Doing Now?*), published in 2003 by Asahi Shimbun Co.

料理

角田光代

1

男の手料理というやつが私はだいきらいである。

2

もちろん、この広い世界のどこかには、私が好きになれる男の手料理というものも存在するにちがいない。だからただしくは、今まで喰らってきた男の料理を私は好きにはなれなかった、と言うべきなんだろう。

3

まず、男の手料理にはやたらコストがかかる。男はいい素材を買おうとする。しかしいい素材を見わけられないから単純に値段の高いものを買う。もしこれがその男の日常ならば結構な話である。ビバ！ エンゲル係数。ところがほとんどの男は違う。奮発して、高い食材を買う。

4

この買いものにつきあっている時点で、私はもう、少々頭にきはじめている。高いパスタ、高いチーズ、高い魚、高い野菜、高いオイル。日々私が買おうか、いや無駄だ、で

料理 On Cooking

1　男の手料理というやつが that thing which is men's home cooking ▪ 私はだいきらいである I really despise it

2　もちろん of course ▪ この広い世界のどこかには somewhere in this broad world ▪ 私が好きになれる男の手料理 men's home cooking that I could like ▪ というものも such a thing as ▪ 存在するにちがいない no doubt exists ▪ だから therefore ▪ ただしくは…と言うべきなんだろう more correctly I should say… ▪ 今まで喰らってきた男の料理を of the men's cooking I have eaten up to now ▪ 私は好きにはなれなかった I wasn't able to like it

3　まず first of all ▪ …にはやたらコストがかかる the costs involved in… run ridiculously high ▪ 男はいい素材を買おうとする men go out of their way to buy [particularly] good ingredients ▪ しかし however ▪ いい素材を見わけられないから because they cannot tell which ones are good (lit., "because they cannot tell good ingredients [from bad ones]") ▪ 単純に値段の高いものを買う they simply buy expensive ones ▪ もしこれがその男の日常ならば if this were the guy's everyday routine ▪ 結構な話である that would really be something (lit., "would be fine") ▪ ビバ! エンゲル係数 long live Engel's coefficient! ▪ ところが however ▪ ほとんどの男は違う most men are not like that ▪ 奮発して they splurge and ▪ 高い食材を買う buy expensive ingredients

4　この買いものにつきあっている時点で when I am along [with my man-friend] on this kind of shopping excursion [and see his wild spending] ▪ 私はもう、少々頭にきはじめている I start to feel annoyed ▪ 高いパスタ expensive pasta ▪ 高いチーズ expensive cheese ▪ 高い魚 expensive fish ▪ 高い野菜 expensive vegetables ▪ 高いオイル expensive [salad/olive/sesame] oil ▪ 日々私が…などといじいじしているものを things that I vacillate about [buying] on a daily basis, thinking… ▪ 買おうか、いや無駄だ shall I buy it? No, it's a waste [of money]

も買ってみたい、じゃあ来客のあるときに買おう、などといじいじしているものをパン！と買うその横柄な態度。

しかも、素材がよくないと料理はどうたらという蘊蓄つき。これがただの蘊蓄でないところが始末に悪い。高いものイコールいい素材、いい素材イコールおいしい食事と、彼らはピューリタンのごとく純粋に信じているのである。

それから調理にやたら時間がかかる。食事に求められるものは多々あるが——栄養バランスだの、しあわせ感だの、心の交流だの——しかしそのなかでもっとも求められているものは、空腹を満たす、一刻もはやく満たす、ということのはずだが、男はこの一点を忘れがちである。

七時にきちんと夕飯になるのなら、料理にどんなに時間をかけてくれてもかまわない。しかし、五時に作り出して、八時になろうとしているのにまだ作業中、ではこまるのだ。

どんな肉体的欠陥か知らないが、私は極度に腹が減ると、血の気がさがり、脂汗がにじんできて、手がふるえ、それでもほうっておくとめまいを起こして倒れる。冗談ではない。脂汗の時点で、いそいで食事をとる、もしくはチョコレートを食べる、というのが

■ でも買ってみたい but I'd like to buy it ■ じゃあ来客のあるときに買おう well then, I'll buy it when I'm having a guest over ■ パン！と買う he just buys it with a snap of his fingers その横柄な態度 that high-handed attitude ■ しかも moreover ■ 素材がよくないと料理はどうたら about what will happen to the food if the ingredients aren't good ■ という蘊蓄つき that pontificating ■ これがただの蘊蓄でないところが that this is not harmless pontificating ■ 始末に悪い is what's hard to take ■ 高いものイコールいい素材 that expensive ingredients equal good ingredients ■ いい素材イコールおいしい食事 that good ingredients equal a good-tasting meal ■ と、彼らはピューリタンのごとく純粋に信じているのである they genuinely believe, as unequivocally as a puritan, that…

5　それから and also ■ 調理にやたら時間がかかる their cooking takes an excessive amount of time [to do] ■ 食事に求められるものは多々あるが many things are asked of meals, but ■ 栄養バランスだの for example nutritional balance ■ しあわせ感だの a feeling of happiness ■ 心の交流だの a heart-to-heart exchange ■ しかしそのなかで however, of these (i.e., what can be asked of a meal) ■ もっとも求められているものは…ということのはずだが what is most sought after is surely…but ■ 空腹を満たす to satisfy one's hunger ■ 一刻もはやく満たす to satisfy it without delay ■ 男はこの一点を忘れがちである men are apt to forget this one thing ■ 七時にきちんと夕飯になるのなら if dinner were ready by seven sharp ■ 料理にどんなに時間をかけてくれても no matter how much time the guy spent on cooking it ■ かまわない I wouldn't care ■ 五時に作り出して starts fixing it at five and ■ 八時になろうとしているのに even though it is nearing eight ■ まだ作業中 he is still in the midst of fixing it ■ では in that case ■ こまるのだ that won't do

6　どんな肉体的欠陥か知らないが I don't know what physical defect [is to blame for it], but ■ 私は極度に腹が減ると when I get extremely hungry ■ 血の気がさがり my blood drains away ■ 脂汗がにじんできて I break out in a sweat ■ 手がふるえ my hands shake, and ■ それでもほうっておくと if I am nevertheless left in that condition ■ めまいを起こして倒れる I get dizzy and keel over ■ 冗談ではない I'm not joking ■ 脂汗の時点で at the point of starting to sweat ■ いそいで食事をとる hurriedly eating a meal ■ もしくは or else ■ チョコレートを食べる eating some chocolate ■ …というの such things as…

解決策なのであるが、もちろん、料理中の男に、このような特殊な事情はまったく無関係、かたわらで私が青白い顔をしていようが、脂汗をだらだら流していようが、とにかく、時間をかけて納得のいくものをつくろうとする。そう、彼らは信じている。高いものイコールいい素材、と同じように、調理時間と食事のおいしさが比例すると。

気に入らない点はまだまだある。彼らは料理をつくるというその一点にのみ集中しているわけで、その集中力といったら無心な子供のようにすさまじく、結果鍋は焦がす、台所は必要以上によごす、何枚も皿をつかう、声をあらげる、舌うちをする、空腹で脂汗を流す女を無意識にこきつかう。

しかも、彼らに組み合わせの妙、という発想はなく、これだけ騒いで、たとえばその日の夕食は、カレーだったらカレー一品だったりする。もしくはパスタ一品。肉料理一品。魚一品。夕食としてテーブルにのるのが一品であることの、むなしさ、さびしさ、貧乏くささ、間のもたなさは、彼らには通用しない。なぜならその一品は、素材を選び抜いて、奮発して、時間をかけて、腕によりをかけて、凝りに凝って出された逸品なのだから。

解決策なのであるが are cures for that, but ■ 料理中の男に for a man in the midst of cooking ■ このような特殊な事情は these sorts of special circumstances ■ まったく無関係 are completely irrelevant ■ かたわらで [standing] beside him ■ 私が青白い顔をしていようが even if I'm pale and sickly looking ■ 脂汗をだらだら流していようが even if I'm pouring with sweat ■ とにかく no matter what the case ■ 時間をかけて he takes his time and ■ 納得のいくもの something fully satisfactory ■ …をつくろうとする he is determined to make… ■ そう yes, that's right ■ 彼らは信じている men [really] believe it ■ 高いものイコールいい素材、と同じように in the same way [that they believe that] expensive ingredients equal good ingredients ■ 調理時間と食事のおいしさが比例すると [they believe that] how good a meal tastes is directly proportional to how long it takes to fix it

7 | 気に入らない点はまだまだある there are many more points that annoy me ■ 彼らは料理をつくるというその一点にのみ集中しているわけで needless to say, they are focused [entirely] on that one thing, cooking, and ■ その集中力といったら as for their concentration ■ 無心な子供のようにすさまじく it is as fierce as the single-mindedness of a child ■ 結果 as a result ■ 鍋は焦がす they scorch pots ■ 台所は必要以上によごす they dirty the kitchen more than is necessary ■ 何枚も皿をつかう they use lots and lots of dishes ■ 声をあらげる they raise their voice ■ 舌うちをする in irritation they make disgusted sounds (lit., "they click their tongues") ■ 空腹で脂汗を流す女を無意識にこきつかう they obliviously boss around a woman who is sweating from hunger

8 | しかも moreover ■ 彼らに組み合わせの妙、という発想はなく they have no sense of the art of combining dishes ■ これだけ騒いで even though they have made such a big production [of fixing dinner] ■ その日の夕食は、カレーだったら if that day's dinner is curry ■ カレー一品だったりする they just make the one dish of curry alone ■ もしくはパスタ一品 or only pasta ■ 肉料理一品 one meat dish ■ 魚一品 one fish dish ■ 夕食として as a dinner ■ テーブルにのるのが一品であることの of there being a single dish of food on the table ■ むなしさ the desolation ■ さびしさ the loneliness ■ 貧乏くささ the beggarliness ■ 間のもたなさは the awkwardness ■ 彼らには通用しない doesn't get through to them at all ■ なぜならその一品は…逸品なのだから that is because that single dish is a masterpiece ■ 素材を選び抜いて [for which] he has carefully selected the ingredients

そして最終的に私が気にくわないのは、彼らに、料理にたいする長期的な向上心が

ないことである。その証拠に、彼らはとんでもなく傷つきやすい。少し塩味が濃いだの、

全体的に味が薄いだの、粉っぽいだのと、その逸品についてマイナス要素の目立つ意見を

口にすると、信じられないほど男は落ちこむ。じゃあ次回はこうしようという、ほがらか

な屈託のない心意気が欠けているのである。そこで、料理ごときで他人を傷つけたくない

私は連発することになる。おいしい。おいしい。おいしいよ！ とっても！

男が料理をせんとするとき、食欲よりもグルメ欲よりも、イベント性よりデート性よ

り、とにかくまず美学が優先されるらしい。ロマンと美学。なぜか男のそれは、仕事でも

人間関係でも日常生活でもなく、料理というどうでもいい場において遺憾なく発揮され

ている、と私は思う。

それでも私は、好きな男が料理をつくると宣言するとき、心のどこかでうんざりしなが

ら、けっしてやめさせることはしない。

ロマンと美学。男のそれは、滑稽で、どこかせつなくて、いつだってもろくて、さびし

■ 腕によりをかけて put to work all his cooking skills ■ 凝りに凝って taken pains upon pains

9 そして and ■ 最終的に finally ■ 私が気にくわないのは…ことである what I don't like is the fact that... ■ 彼らに、料理にたいする長期的な向上心がない they don't have any interest in improving their cooking skills over time ■ その証拠に attesting to that ■ 彼らはとんでもなく傷つきやすい their feelings are hurt ridiculously easily ■ 少し塩味が濃いだの for example, it's a little too salty ■ 全体的に味が薄いだの or overall the flavoring is on the weak side ■ 粉っぽいだの or it's a little lumpy ■ その逸品について about his masterpiece ■ マイナス要素の目立つ意見を口にすると if you give voice to a negative opinion ■ 信じられないほど男は落ちこむ a man becomes unbelievably crestfallen ■ じゃあ次回はこうしよう okay, next time I'll try this instead ■ という、ほがらかな屈託のない心意気 such a cheerful and resilient spirit ■ 欠けているのである is lacking [in men] ■ そこで so ■ 料理ごときで他人を傷つけたくない私は not wanting to hurt anyone's feelings just over something [relatively unimportant] like cooking, I... ■ 連発することになる end up saying over and over ■ おいしい it's delicious

10 男が料理をせんとするとき when a man sets his mind on cooking ■ 食欲よりも even more than the appetite [of the person eating his food] ■ グルメ欲よりも even more than [the other party's] desire to eat gourmet food ■ イベント性より more than [the concern of] making the meal a special occasion ■ デート性より more than creating the atmosphere of a date ■ とにかく above all else ■ まず美学が優先されるらしい it seems that aesthetics are given precedence ■ ロマンと美学 romanticism and aesthetics ■ なぜか for whatever reason ■ 男のそれは…遺憾なく発揮されている that side of men is amply exhibited ■ 仕事でも人間関係でも日常生活でもなく not in work nor in interpersonal relations nor in daily life but ■ 料理というどうでもいい場において in the [relatively] inconsequential area of cooking ■ と私は思う that's what I think

11 それでも nevertheless ■ 私は…けっしてやめさせることはしない I by no means stop him ■ 好きな男が料理をつくると宣言するとき when a man I like proclaims that he is going to cook ■ 心のどこかでうんざりしながら even while my stomach sinks (lit., "even while I feel fed up somewhere in my heart")

12 男のそれは that side of a man ■ 滑稽で is absurd ■ どこかせつなくて is somehow poignant

げである。 男の子なんだから、 などとおそらく言われ続けてきたであろう彼らの、 そのば
かばかしくも孤高の精神を、 やはりどうしたって私はきらいにはなれないのである。

▪ いつだってもろくて is always fragile ▪ さびしげである is lonely (lit., "is with a trace of loneliness") ▪ 男の子なんだから、などとおそらく言われ続けてきたであろう彼ら they, who have no doubt been told over and over to be a man and the like (lit., "they who have no doubt been told, 'Because you're a man [you should be such and such]'") ▪ そのばかばかしくも孤高の精神を that ridiculous, proudly independent spirit ▪ やはりどうしたって for the life of me ▪ 私はきらいにはなれないのである I cannot bring myself to hate

よしもとばなな*

Yoshimoto Banana

* She changed her name from 吉本ばなな to よしもとばなな in August 2002.

With six of her books available in English, you probably already know who Yoshimoto Banana is. More than twenty years have now passed since she debuted with her phenomenally successful novella *Kitchen* in 1987, soon after she graduated from Nihon University. Born in Tokyo into a literary family in 1964 (her father, Yoshimoto Takaaki, is a well-known poet and literary critic, her mother a haiku poet, and her sister, Haruno Yoiko, a cartoonist), she is one of only a few Japanese writers whose works have become inter-

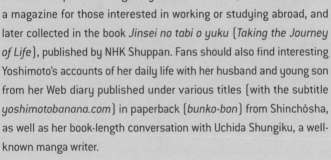

national bestsellers. Her themes of spirituality, the search for selfhood, and the fleetingness of life continue to strike a chord with younger readers both in Japan and abroad. Recently she has herself chosen the pieces for a four-volume anthology of her works, *Yoshimoto Banana senshū* (*Collected Works of Yoshimoto Banana: An Author's Selection*), organized by theme: (1) Occult, (2) Love, (3) Death, and (4) Life.

Yoshimoto's rather intuitive style can be seen in the short essay here, on a chance meeting in a flower shop. It was originally written for *Wish*, a magazine for those interested in working or studying abroad, and later collected in the book *Jinsei no tabi o yuku* (*Taking the Journey of Life*), published by NHK Shuppan. Fans should also find interesting Yoshimoto's accounts of her daily life with her husband and young son from her Web diary published under various titles (with the subtitle *yoshimotobanana.com*) in paperback (*bunko-bon*) from Shinchōsha, as well as her book-length conversation with Uchida Shungiku, a well-known manga writer.

美しさ

よしもとばなな

1

ある夜、用があって高級スーパーに行った。品揃えの多さについつい買いこんでしまい、大荷物を抱えて併設の花屋に行った。

店員さんはひとりしかいなくて、前の中年女性はものすごく複雑なことを頼んでいた。

いちばん高い胡蝶蘭をプレゼント用に包装し、かつ高級仏花を別のところに、しかるべき包装をして配達してほしい、という感じのこと。全身から金持ち光線と金持ちを優先しろ光線をびんびん出していた。

2

私は「たったこれだけです！」というのをアピールするために、チューリップ十本二千円というのをすでに手に持ち、風呂場に置く予定の蘭の小さな鉢も抱え、先にやってくれないかな－、というムードを出して待ってみたが、私の前の人が私と同じ作戦で優先されてしまい、店員さんはこれ以上はもうだめ、胡蝶蘭を包むことに専念します、という

3

美しさ On Beauty

1 ある夜 one evening ▪ 用があって I had an errand [to run] and ▪ 高級スーパーに行った I went to an upscale supermarket ▪ 品揃えの多さについつい買いこんでしまい because of the large selection of goods, I ended up buying a lot, and ▪ 大荷物を抱えて loaded with bags ▪ 併設の花屋に行った I went to the attached flower shop

2 店員さんはひとりしかいなくて there was only one clerk [there] and ▪ 前の中年女性はものすごく複雑なことを頼んでいた the middle-aged lady before me [in line for the register] had an extremely complicated order ▪ いちばん高い胡蝶蘭をプレゼント用に包装し [she wanted] the most expensive phalaenopsis orchids wrapped as a present ▪ かつ and also ▪ 高級仏花を別のところに、しかるべき包装をして配達してほしい she wanted premium shrine flowers suitably packaged and delivered to a different place ▪ という感じのこと it was that sort of order ▪ 全身から...をびんびん出していた from every pore of her body came bursting forth... ▪ 金持ち光線と金持ちを優先しろ光線 a ray saying "I am a rich person" and a ray saying "Rich people deserve preferential treatment"

3 私は「たったこれだけです！」というのをアピールするために in order to make the point "This is all I have!" ▪ チューリップ十本二千円というのをすでに手に持ち I already had in hand [a bunch of] the ten-for-¥2000 tulips, and ▪ 風呂場に置く予定の蘭の小さな鉢も抱え I also was carrying a small potted orchid plant that I planned to put next to the bath ▪ 先にやってくれないかなー、というムードを出して待ってみたが I tried to stand and wait, giving off the feeling "Couldn't you let me go first?" but ▪ 私の前の人が私と同じ作戦で優先されてしまい the customer ahead of me had already used the same strategy and was taken first ▪ これ以上はもうだめ "this is all I can handle" (lit., "I can't take more than this") ▪ 胡蝶蘭を包むことに専念します "I am going to concentrate on wrapping the orchids"

体勢に入ってしまった。

やむなく二十分くらい私は待った。すると後ろからどんどん人が来ては、あら、時間が

かかりそうね、という感じで去って行くのが感じられた。順番を保つために私はその持

ち場を離れにくくなり、他の店員さんを呼んで来て何とかしてもらうということもできな

かった。待つのは全然苦手じゃないけど、店の中に漂う「できればあきらめて出直してほ

しい」感じが気持ちをうさませた。その複雑なことを頼んでいた人がひとことでも「時間

がかかってごめんなさい」とか何とか言ってくれれば、それで気は軽くなったのだが、そ

の人は私と肩が触れるような距離にいるのに私を絶対に見ないのだった。下町育ちの私に

とっては異様な感じのする雰囲気だった。

そこにものすごく美しい人……強いて似ているタイプをあげれば篠ひろ子のような感じ

の身なりのいい中年女性が、風のようにやってきてチューリップ十本二千円を取り「先

にやってくれないかなー」という感じで店内の様子を見はじめた。私はまずい！ と思

い、「実はさっきからずっと待っているのですが、終わりそうもないのですー」と言って

- という体勢に入ってしまった had adopted a [defensive] position that…

4 やむなく二十分くらい私は待った I had no choice but to wait for around twenty minutes ▪ すると while doing so ▪ 後ろからどんどん人が来ては people kept lining up behind me and then ▪ あら、時間がかかりそうね my, it looks like it will take a long time ▪ という感じで去って行くのが感じられた I could sense them leaving as if thinking… ▪ 順番を保つために in order to keep my place in line ▪ 私はその持ち場を離れにくくなり it became harder for me to leave my post and ▪ 他の店員さんを呼んで来て何とかしてもらうということもできなかった I couldn't even go fetch another employee to help out ▪ 待つのは全然苦手じゃないけど [as a general rule] I don't mind waiting (lit., "I'm not at all bad at waiting"), but ▪ 店の中に漂う「できればあきらめて出直してほしい」感じが the feeling hanging in the air in the shop of that clerk wanting us to give up and come again another time ▪ 気持ちをすさませた put me in a disagreeable mood ▪ その複雑なことを頼んでいた人が that woman making such a complicated order ▪ ひとことでも「時間がかかってごめんなさい」とか何とか言ってくれれば if she had said just one word such as "Sorry to take so much time" or the like ▪ それで気は軽くなったのだが that would have lightened my mood, but ▪ その人は私と肩が触れるような距離にいるのに although we were close enough to touch shoulders ▪ 私を絶対に見ないのだった she refused to meet my eye (lit., "she absolutely would not look at me") ▪ 下町育ちの私にとっては for me, having been raised in the *shitamachi* ▪ 異様な感じのする雰囲気だった it was a bizarre atmosphere

5 そこに thereupon ▪ ものすごく美しい人 an extremely beautiful woman ▪ 強いて似ているタイプをあげれば if I were forced to say whom she resembled ▪ 篠ひろ子のような感じの身なりのいい中年女性 a well-dressed middle-aged woman with the aura of Shino Hiroko ▪ 風のようにやってきて blew in (like the wind) and ▪ チューリップ十本二千円を取り gathered up [a bunch] of the ten-for-¥2000 tulips and ▪ 「先にやってくれないかなー」という感じで with the feeling of "Couldn't you let me go first?" ▪ 店内の様子を見はじめた she started to take in the situation inside the shop ▪ 私はまずい！と思い fearing the worst (lit., "thinking Uh-oh!") ▪ 「実はさっきからずっと待っているのですが "Actually, I've been waiting quite a while, but ▪ 終わりそうもないのですー」 it doesn't look like she'll be done anytime soon…" ▪ と言ってみた I ventured to say

みた。黙って順番を主張することもできたのだが、それではこのぎすぎすしたムードに

飲まれてしまうという気がして、思い切って社交してみたのです。彼女は「じゃあ誰か呼

んで来るわね！」と言って去って行き、他の店員さんを呼んで来て、「この人が先ですよ」

と私を優先し、「よかったわね、呼んで来てみて」とにっこり笑った。

お金持ちには二種類いると思う。お金があることで余裕ができて本来の人格をいいほう

に発揮している人と、その逆になっている人と。私はそのとき、まだ若い世代としてその

両方にはさまれていた。その人の笑顔はほんとうに美しく、その美しさこそを求めてみ

んな自分に投資したりいいところに嫁に行ったりしているのだが、最終的にはお金じゃ

なくて、その人の持っている本質がこういうところで出て、人生の質を変えてしまうんだ

なぁ……！　金持ちでも美しくもない私はしみじみ考え、今でもその蘭の鉢を見るたび

に、あの柔らかい笑顔をいい思い出として思い出すのだった。

■ 黙って順番を主張することもできたのだが I could well have silently asserted my being first, but ■ それではこのぎすぎすしたムードに飲まれてしまうという気がして I felt [that if I remained silent] I would be done in by this cold, prickly mood [in the shop] and so ■ 思い切って社交してみたのです I bravely mustered my social graces ■ 彼女は「じゃあ誰か呼んで来るわね！」と言って saying, "Well, I'll just go and fetch someone!" ■ 去って行き、他の店員さんを呼んで来て she went off and came back with another clerk and (lit., "she went off and called for another clerk and came back, and then") ■「この人が先ですよ」と私を優先し said, "This person was ahead of me" and let me go first, and then ■「よかったわね、呼んで来てみて」とにっこり笑った she smilingly said, "Good thing I went and got someone"

6 お金持ちには二種類いると思う I believe there are two types of rich people ■ お金があることで余裕ができて [those for whom] money allows them breathing space and ■ 本来の人格をいいほうに発揮している人と brings out their true character in a good way, and ■ その逆になっている人と [secondly] those for whom money does the opposite ■ 私はそのとき at that time I ■ まだ若い世代として as one of the younger generation ■ その両方にはさまれていた stood between (lit., "was sandwiched between") those two [types] ■ その人の笑顔はほんとうに美しく the smiling face of that woman was truly beautiful, and ■ その美しさこそを求めて it is for just such beauty ■ みんな自分に投資したり that everyone works on enriching themselves (i.e., in ways that cost money) or ■ いいところに嫁に行ったりしているのだが does things like marry into a good (i.e., rich) family, but ■ 最終的には ultimately ■ お金じゃなくて it is not money but ■ その人の持っている本質がこういうところで出て a person's true nature that comes out in this sort of situation and ■ 人生の質を変えてしまうんだなぁ……！ [that nature] changes the quality of their life ■ 金持ちでも美しくもない私は I who am neither rich nor beautiful ■ しみじみ考え reflect deeply and ■ 今でも even now ■ その蘭の鉢を見るたびに every time I look at that orchid [next to the bath] ■ あの柔らかい笑顔をいい思い出として思い出すのだった I would fondly recall that softly smiling face

町 田 康

Machida Kou

Machida Kou—musician, actor, poet, novelist—is a difficult figure for an outsider to fully grasp. Born in Sakai, to the south of Osaka, in 1962, and the only non-college graduate among the authors featured in this book, he formed a punk-rock band while still in high school and forged a career as a musician and actor in TV dramas, movies, and TV commercials, until gradually concentrating on writing. He has won various literary prizes for his powerful use of language in works written in a variety of styles but often containing a mix of nonsense and pastiche, as in references to Natsume Sōseki or Jimmy Cliff in a historical novel set in the Edo period, to entertain and jolt the reader.

Machida made his literary debut first as a poet, then as a novelist. *Kussun daikoku* (*Weeping Daikoku*), his first piece of fiction, is a marvelously plotless work that won him both the Noma Award for New Writers and the Bunkamura Deux Magots Literary Prize. In 2000 he won the Akutagawa Prize for *Kiregire* (*Shreds*). Machida has written much nonfiction as well: *Ejiki*, his second work, is part essay, part diary, and *Herahera botchan* is a mind-bending collection of essays on random topics.

The piece you are about to read, on the ramifications of the level of diction in one's writing style, is written in a deadpan manner. Machida treats the topic with an exaggerated seriousness. You'll find that it becomes funnier and funnier on repeat readings. The essay is from *Tēsuto obu nigamushi 4* (*Taste of a Scowl 4*), the fourth volume of collected columns from Machida's long-running series in the *Yomiuri Weekly*. It was published by Chūōkōron-Shinsha in 2007.

どう書いても嫌な奴は嫌な奴

町田　康

1　昔から、文は人なり、なんてなことが言ってあるが考えてみればその通りで、文章にはそれを書いた人の人間性が如実に現れる。

2　奥ゆかしい人の書いた文章には細やかな気づかいのなかにどこか凜とした気品が漂うし、セクシーな人の書いた文章には匂いたつような色気が感ぜられ、愉快な人の書いた文章にはなんともいえぬ飄逸、諧謔の気配がたちこめる。

3　一方、自己主張の激しい人が書いた文章には、私が、僕が、という主語が頻出するし、さもしい人の書いた文章にはどことなくもの欲しげな表現があちこちに目立つ。さほどに文章というものは難しいものであり、よい文章を書こうと思ったらまずその人間性から直していかなければならない。

4　わが国にはむかしから人間性を直す方法がいくつか伝わっているが代表的なのは滝に

どう書いても嫌な奴は嫌な奴 No Matter How He Writes, a Creep Is Still a Creep

1 昔から from olden times ▪ 文は人なり the style is the man himself ▪ なんてなことが言ってあるが it has been said that…and ▪ 考えてみればその通りで if you think about it, it's true ▪ 文章にはそれを書いた人の人間性が如実に現れる the personality of a writer is clearly evident in a sentence he or she has written

2 奥ゆかしい人の書いた文章には in a modest person's writing ▪ 細やかな気づかいのなかにどこか凛とした気品が漂うし a dignified elegance seems to waft from his or her well-considered sentences, and ▪ セクシーな人の書いた文章には in a sexy person's writing ▪ 匂いたつような色気が感ぜられ one can feel an alluring sexiness, and ▪ 愉快な人の書いた文章には in a cheery person's writing ▪ なんともいえぬ飄逸、諧謔の気配がたちこめる there is an indefinable hint of easygoingness and good humor

3 一方 on the other hand ▪ 自己主張の激しい人が書いた文章には in the writing of someone who is very self-assertive ▪ 私が、僕が、という主語が頻出するし there are many [sentences] containing "I" (lit., "'I' is frequently the subject of the sentence"), and ▪ さもしい人の書いた文章には in a mean-spirited person's writing ▪ どことなくもの欲しげな表現があちこちに目立つ expressions stand out here and there which are somehow selfish and grasping ▪ さほどに文章というものは難しいものであり thus, writing is a complicated thing, and ▪ よい文章を書こうと思ったら if you want to write well ▪ まずその人間性から直していかなければならない you must start by reforming your personality

4 わが国には in our country ▪ むかしから人間性を直す方法がいくつか伝わっているが there are several traditional methods of self-improvement (lit., "several methods for correcting our nature have been handed down over the ages"), and ▪ 代表的なのは as for the [most] representative ones ▪ 滝にうたれる standing in a waterfall

うたれる、或いは座禅を組む、このふたつである。しかし大方の社会人は忙しいからそん

な面倒なことはやっていられない。最近では米国から自己啓発セミナーなんてなのも入り

ごんでいるが、それもそう効果を期待できない。

だから仕方ない。腐った人間性のままで腐った文章を書いて腐った奴と思われよう。そ

う思って諦めている人がいま全国に約二千万人程度いる（らしい）。

しかし諦めるのはまだ早い。そんな人間性の腐ったあなたでも、読者をして、なんとな

くよい人だ、と思わしむる方法がある。しかもやり方は超簡単、ちょっとしたコツを覚

えれば、すぐにできてその瞬間から効果が現れるという画期的な方法である。これが嘘

や詐欺なら勿体ぶってずらずらずらいろんなことを言ってなかなか本題に入らないの

だけれども嘘や詐欺ではないのですぐ言う。

それは文末の方法である。

御案内の通り、文末には、だ・である調、と、です・ます調がある。

一般にこれをどのように使い分けているかというと、えらそうに傲然と言いたいとき

■ 或いは or ■ 座禅を組む practicing Zen meditation ■ このふたつである there are these two ■ しかし however ■ 大方の社会人は忙しいから since most working people are busy ■ そんな面倒なことはやっていられない they can't go to the trouble to do such things ■ 最近では recently ■ 米国から自己啓発セミナーなんてなのも入りごんでいるが so-called self-improvement seminars have entered Japan from America, but ■ それもそう効果を期待できない one can't expect all that much from them

5 | だから仕方ない therefore, there's no help for it ■ 腐った人間性のままで rotten human beings that we are ■ 腐った文章を書いて write rotten sentences and ■ 腐った奴と思われよう let's accept being thought of as rotten guys ■ そう思って諦めている人が those who have resigned themselves to this fate ■ いま全国に約二千万人程度いる（らしい）now number as many as 20 million nationwide (apparently)

6 | しかし諦めるのはまだ早い but wait! It's too soon to be resigned ■ そんな人間性の腐ったあなたでも even for you who are rotten to the core ■ 読者をして、なんとなくよい人だ、と思わしむる方法がある there is a way to make your readers think of you as, somehow, a good guy ■ しかも moreover ■ やり方は超簡単 it's ultra-simple ■ ちょっとしたコツを覚えれば if you master a simple technique ■ すぐにできて you can soon do it and ■ その瞬間から効果が現れる you will be able to see the results from that very moment ■ という画期的な方法である it is that sort of revolutionary method ■ これが嘘や詐欺なら if this were a lie or a scam ■ 勿体ぶってずらずらずらずらいろんなことを言って I would grandly go on and on with various claims and ■ なかなか本題に入らないのだけれども not soon get to the point, but ■ 嘘や詐欺ではないのですぐ言う this is not a lie or a scam, so I'll just come right out and say it

7 | それは文末の方法である it is the sentence-ending method

8 | 御案内の通り as you already know ■ 文末には、だ・である調、と、です・ます調がある sentences can end in the **da/de aru** or **desu/-masu** style

9 | 一般にこれをどのように使い分けているかというと as to how these are used, we can in general say that… ■ えらそうに傲然と言いたいときは when one wants to speak arrogantly, with an air of superiority

は、だ・である調、へりくだって丁寧に言いたいときは、です・ます調という風に使い分

けている。これはあくまで方法論に過ぎない。

ところが一般に人々は、文は人なり、と信じているから、方法に過ぎない使い分けが逆

転、文章上の傲然とした態度、へりくだった態度が肉付き面のようにその書き手の性格と

なってしまうのである。つまり、その文章の内容、書き手の実際の性格の如何にかかわら

ず、読み手は、だ・である調で書く人は傲岸不遜な人、です・ます調で書く人はへりく

だったよい人と思い込んでしまう傾向にあるのである。

というと、もはやお分かりであろう。文末をです・ます調に変えるだけであなたは、文

は人なり、の原則に則って周囲の人によい人だ、と思われるのである。

以下、その方法を実地に試してみよう。

パンクロックの歌詞にはラディカルなものが多いが一九七六年に英国でデビューした

セックス・ピストルズはいまだにその最右翼である。既成の秩序を罵倒・冷笑し、あら

ゆる価値を破壊・転倒せよ、と呼び掛けた。

■ へりくだって丁寧に言いたいときは when one wants to be modest and polite ■ という風に使い分けている that is how they are differentiated ■ これはあくまで方法論に過ぎない the question of which style to use is no more than a simple question of means

10　ところが however ■ 一般に人々は、文は人なり、と信じているから because people generally believe that the style is the man ■ 方法に過ぎない使い分けが逆転 what is nothing more than a mere means [at the writer's disposal] backfires, so that ■ 文章上の傲然とした態度、へりくだった態度が the haughty attitude, or the humble attitude, that comes across in the writing ■ 肉付き面のように like a veritable *nikuzuki-men* ■ その書き手の性格となってしまうのである becomes that writer's personality ■ つまり in other words ■ その文章の内容、書き手の実際の性格の如何にかかわらず no matter what the content of the writing, and no matter what the actual personality of the writer might be ■ 読み手は…と思い込んでしまう傾向にあるのである readers tend to imagine that… ■ 傲岸不遜な人 an overbearing and arrogant person ■ へりくだったよい人 a humble and nice person

11　もはやお分かりであろう you must be able to guess where this is going ■ 文末をです・ます調に変えるだけで by simply switching your sentence endings to the **desu**/-**masu** style ■ 文は人なり、の原則に則って in line with the principle that the sentence is the man ■ 周囲の人に by those around you ■ と思われるのである you will be thought of as

12　以下、その方法を実地に試してみよう below, let's try putting this method into practice

13　パンクロックの歌詞には among punk rock lyrics ■ ラディカルなものが多いが there are many that are radical, but ■ 一九七六年に英国でデビューしたセックス・ピストルズは the Sex Pistols, who made their debut in England in 1976 ■ いまだにその最右翼である still take the prize [for radical lyrics] ■ 既成の秩序を罵倒・冷笑し they hurled abuse and sneered at the established order and ■ あらゆる価値を破壊・転倒せよ、と呼び掛けた they called for the destruction and overturning of all values

そんなパンクロックの歌詞もです・ます調にすればけっこうよい人に見える。

僕はアナーキストです。僕は反キリスト主義者なのです。僕は破壊をしたいのです。僕はいろんなものすべてを壊してしまいたいのです。なぜなら僕はアナーキーでありたいからです。僕はアナーキーでありたいのです。僕は僕に残された最上の方法を採ります。

それは僕がアナーキーであることです。

なにか深い事情があってアナーキストになった。けれどもそれを聞くのは気の毒だ、みたいなニュアンスが漂って、この人が駅を爆破したり、通信を混乱させたりしてもそれはそれで仕方ないかなあ、という気がしてくる。これが、です・ます調の魔力である。これを通常の、だ・である調でやると、

私はアナーキストだ。反キリスト主義者でもある。私はありとあらゆるものを破壊した

14 | けっこうよい人に見える seem like quite a decent fellow

15 | 僕はアナーキストです I am an anarchist ■ 僕は反キリスト主義者なのです and I am anti-Christian, you see ■ 僕は破壊をしたいのです I would like to destroy ■ 僕はいろんなものすべてを壊してしまいたいのです I'd like to totally demolish lots of things ■ なぜなら僕はアナーキーでありたいからです that's because I want to be anarchy ■ 僕は僕に残された最上の方法を採ります I will adopt the best means left to me ■ それは僕がアナーキーであることです and that is for me to be anarchy

16 | なにか深い事情があってアナーキストになった there must surely be some profound circumstances behind his becoming an anarchist ■ けれどもそれを聞くのは気の毒だ but it would be intrusive to ask him about it ■ みたいなニュアンスが漂って there is such a nuance here, and ■ この人が駅を爆破したり通信を混乱させたりしても even if this person were to blow up a train station or disrupt communications ■ それはそれで仕方ないかなあ、という気がしてくる somehow one would feel that events could not have been otherwise (i.e., that the man had no choice but to do it) ■ これが…の魔力である this is the magic of… ■ これを通常の…でやると to put this in the usual…

17 | 私はアナーキストだ I am an anarchist ■ 反キリスト主義者でもある I am also an anti-Christian ■ 私はありとあらゆるものを破壊したいのだ it is my desire to destroy everything conceivable

いのだ。なぜなら私は常にアナーキーでありたいと念願しているからである。　私に残された唯一最上の道はアナーキーであることのみなのである。

或いは歌詞だけではなく通常の随筆の場合もそうでけっこうエゴイスティックで我が儘な随筆を書いても、です・ます調でやるといい人みたいに思える。

可愛げというものがまるでない。アナーキストになる前におまえにも少しくらい反省するところがあるだろうと言いたくなる。

その日、僕は朝から嫌な気分でした。なぜならその日はゴミ収集の日だったからです。　僕はゴミ収集の日はいつも憂鬱な気分になります。　僕の家の前がゴミ集積所になっているからです。　僕はゴミが嫌いです。　僕はゴミやヘドロよりも花や音楽が好きな人間なのです。　ところが僕の家の前がゴミ集積所になってしまったのです。　なぜこんなことになったかというと、ゴミ集積所が回り持ちだからです。　去年までは左隣の青沼さんのと

■ なぜなら私は常にアナーキーでありたいと念願しているからである for it is my long-held ambition to be in a perpetual state of anarchy ■ 私に残された唯一最上の道はアナーキーであることのみなのである the sole path left to me is anarchy

18 | 可愛げというものがまるでない there is nothing charming or likeable here ■ アナーキストになる前に before becoming an anarchist ■ おまえにも少しくらい反省するところがあるだろう you ought to search your conscience a little; you, too, must have faults to correct (lit., "in you, too, there must be a little room for self-reflection [on past conduct]") ■ と言いたくなる one wants to say…

19 | 或いは or ■ 通常の随筆の場合もそうで also in the case of typical personal essays ■ けっこうエゴイスティックで我が儘な随筆 a fairly egotistical and self-indulgent essay ■ いい人みたいに思える people will be able to think you seem like a decent fellow

20 | その日 that day ■ 僕は朝から嫌な気分でした I was in a bad mood from the morning ■ なぜならその日はゴミ収集の日だったからです that was because that day was a garbage day ■ 僕はゴミ収集の日はいつも憂鬱な気分になります on garbage days I always get depressed ■ 僕の家の前がゴミ集積所になっているからです because the front of my house has become a trash-collection area ■ 僕はゴミが嫌いです I hate garbage ■ 僕はゴミやヘドロよりも花や音楽が好きな人間なのです I am a person who loves flowers and music rather than garbage and slime ■ ところが however ■ なぜこんなことになったかというと the reason things have come to such a pass ■ ゴミ集積所が回り持ちだからです is because the trash-collection area rotates ■ 去年までは until last year ■ 左隣の青沼さんのところでした it was in front of the house of my left-hand neighbor, Aonuma-san

ろでした。今年は僕のところで、来年から右隣の江部さんのところに移動します。

でも僕は我慢できません。僕は僕のところを飛ばして今年から江部さんのところにして欲しかったのです。なぜなら回り持ちというのは一見公平に見えて公平でないからです。なぜなら花や音楽が好きでゴミに弱い僕と、もともとヘドロみたいな人間性の江部さんとではゴミから受ける精神的ダメージの度合いが違うからです。公平というならそこまで考慮して欲しいと僕は思います。

僕は家の前のゴミを江部さんのところに移動しました。

さすがにこんな人は文末の小細工では救えない。

■ 今年は僕のところで this year it's at my place, and ■ 来年から右隣の江部さんのところに移動します from next year it will move to the front of Ebe-san's house, to the right of me

21 でも僕は我慢できません but I just can't take it anymore ■ 僕は僕のところを飛ばして今年から江部さんのところにして欲しかったのです I wanted them to skip me and make it Ebe-san this year ■ 回り持ちというのは一見公平に見えて rotating looks fair at first glance, but ■ 公平でない it's not fair [at all] ■ 花や音楽が好きでゴミに弱い僕と … とでは between me, who loves flowers and music and has trouble with garbage, and ■ もともとヘドロみたいな人間性の江部さん Ebe-san, who is fundamentally slimy by nature ■ ゴミから受ける精神的ダメージの度合いが違うからです the degree of psychological damage from trash is [completely] different ■ 公平というなら if you think it is fair ■ そこまで考慮して欲しいと僕は思います I would like you to take that into account too

22 僕は家の前のゴミを江部さんのところに移動しました I moved the garbage from in front of my house over to Ebe-san's place

23 さすがにこんな人は文末の小細工では救えない there's no two ways about it—this sort of fellow cannot be saved merely by tinkering with sentence endings

小川 洋子

Ogawa Yōko

Ogawa Yōko is in the enviable position of being a serious writer who has won a popular fan base. Winner of the Akutagawa Prize in 1991 (and recently serving as a judge for it), she became a million-selling author with *Hakase no aishita sūshiki* (published in English as *The Housekeeper and the Professor*), which in 2004 received the Yomiuri Literary Prize and the first annual Japanese Booksellers' Prize. This novel, soon made into a film, details the growing relationship among an aging professor of mathematics with a memory problem (he can only remember things for eighty minutes), his housekeeper, and her ten-year-old son.

Ogawa was born in 1962 in Okayama Prefecture and graduated from Waseda University. She lives in Ashiya, in Hyogo Prefecture, with her salaryman husband and son. Her account here of four experiences she had in relation to *Hakase no aishita sūshiki* was written for a collection of essays, *Inu no shippu o nadenagara* (*While Petting a Dog's Tail*, published by Shūeisha in 2006), which also contains pieces on the impact Anne Frank had on her life.

Although her works have been widely translated in Europe and are especially popular in France, Ogawa is only starting to be published in English. *The Diving Pool: Three Novellas* includes "Pregnancy Diary" (winner of the Akutagawa Prize), which was published in the *New Yorker* in 2005. And *The Housekeeper and the Professor* was released in 2009 by Picador (in the U.S.) and Harvill Secker (in the U.K.).

『博士の愛した数式』を巡って

小川洋子

「世界は驚きと歓びに満ちている……」

これは、拙著『博士の愛した数式』の帯の文句であり、つまりは読者の方々に向けたメッセージなのだが、作者である私自身が、最も強くこの言葉を嚙み締めている。小説を書くための下調べをしている間も、執筆の最中も、そして本が出版された今になってもずっと変わらず私は、世界に隠された驚きと歓びに出会い続けている。

資料として数学に関わりのある本を手当たり次第に読んでいるうち、それまで抱いていた天才数学者のイメージが微妙に変わってゆくのを感じた。私にとって天才とはつまり、どんな難しい問題でも解いてしまう人、であった。混沌としてややこしく、底知れない暗闇に包まれた難問の森に果敢に分け入り、複雑な解決への道を探し出す人、なのだった。

『博士の愛した数式』を巡って Concerning *The Housekeeper and the Professor*

1 | 「世界は驚きと歓びに満ちている……」 "The world is full of surprise and joy"

2 | これは、拙著『博士の愛した数式』の帯の文句であり these words are from the *obi* of my book *The Housekeeper and the Professor* ▪ つまりは that is to say ▪ 読者の方々に向けたメッセージなのだが it is a message directed at readers, and yet ▪ 作者である私自身 I myself, the author ▪ 最も強くこの言葉を噛み締めている relish these words more than anyone ▪ 小説を書くための下調べをしている間も while doing research for the novel (lit., "in order to write the novel") ▪ 執筆の最中も and in the midst of writing it ▪ そして本が出版された今になっても and also now that the book has been published ▪ ずっと変わらず the whole time, unfailingly ▪ 世界に隠された驚きと歓びに出会い続けている I have continued to encounter the world's hidden surprises and joys

3 | 資料として数学に関わりのある本を手当たり次第に読んでいるうち while reading whatever mathematics-related books I could find as reference material ▪ それまで抱いていた天才数学者のイメージが微妙に変わってゆくのを感じた I felt my previously held image of math geniuses subtly changing ▪ 私にとって天才とはつまり…であった to my mind a genius was, in short ▪ どんな難しい問題でも解いてしまう人 a person who could solve even the most difficult of problems ▪ 混沌としてややこしく、底知れない暗闇に包まれた難問の森に果敢に分け入り would boldly make his way into a chaotic, confounding forest of hard problems—a forest enveloped in infinite darkness—and ▪ 複雑な解決への道を探し出す find a path to a complex solution

歴史上最高の数学者の一人、と言われるガウス（一七七七～一八五五）には、ある有名なエピソードがある。自習をさせるために先生が「1から100まで足し算しなさい」という問題を出したところ、ガウス少年はあっという間に答えを出してしまった。1から100まで順に大きくなる計算式と、100から1まで順に小さくなる計算式を二つ並べる、三角数の考え方を用いたのだ。

1+　2+　3+　4+・・・・・・・・・+　98+　99+100

100+ 99+ 98+ 97+・・・・・・・・・+　3+　2+　1

101+101+101+101+・・・・・・・・・+ 101+101+101 ＝ 101×100

つまり1から100までの数の和は、

101×100÷2＝5050

となる。

数学の出来る人にとっては基本中の基本、常識の問題だろうが、私のような人間に

4 | 歴史上最高の数学者の一人、と言われるガウス（一七七七〜一八五五）には concerning [Karl Friedrich] Gauss (1777–1855), who is said to be one of the greatest mathematicians of all time ■ ある有名なエピソードがある there is a famous episode ■ 自習をさせるために先生が「1から100まで足し算しなさい」という問題を出したところ when his teacher gave the class, for practice, the problem of adding up all the numbers from 1 to 100 ■ ガウス少年はあっという間に答えを出してしまった the young Gauss produced the answer in no time at all ■ 1から100まで順に大きくなる計算式と the formula for adding from 1 to 100 in ascending order and ■ 100から1まで順に小さくなる計算式を the formula for adding from 100 to 1 in descending order ■ 二つ並べる、三角数の考え方を用いたのだ he used a triangular-number approach, lining up and comparing… ■ つまり1から100までの数の和は、101×100÷2＝5050となる in other words, the sum of the numbers 1 to 100 is equal to 101 times 100 divided by 2

6 | 数学の出来る人にとっては for someone who is good at math ■ 基本中の基本、常識の問題だろうが this is probably a matter of common sense, the most basic of basics, but ■ 私のような人間にとっては for someone like me

とっては、順に大きくなる式と小さくなる式を上下に並べ、101を全部で100個作る、というこの発想があまりにも鮮やかすぎて、めまいを起こしそうになる。どこをどう叩いたらそんなことを思いつくのか、見当もつかない。計算式の問題が、ある時点から不意に図形化し、しかもそこに予想外の規則的な繰り返しが表われ出てくる……。考えれば考えるほど神秘的である。

そこで私は感づいた。ただ単に難しい問題を解くのが天才ではない。複雑な問題を単純化してしまうのが天才だ。その結果として難しい問題が解けるだけなのだ、と。

地図にある通りの道を選んだら、崖もある、沼地もある、狼もいる。凡人はそれでも、傷だらけになりながら一歩一歩進んでゆくだろう。ところが天才は、凡人が自分の足元に囚われている間に、気球を飛ばし、風に乗ってスイスイと目的の地へ到着する。天才がやってのける単純化は、本当に思わず、「ずるいじゃないか」と口走りそうになる。

言い方を変えれば、天才たちは皆、どんなに複雑に見える問題にも、裏には何かがあにずるいほどお見事なのだ。

■ 順に大きくなる式と小さくなる式を上下に並べ、101を全部で100個作る to line up, one on top of the other, one ascending and one descending formula and making 100 individual sums each equal to 101 ■ というこの発想があまりにも鮮やかすぎて、めまいを起こしそうになる such a concept is so elegant as to be dizzying ■ どこをどう叩いたら no matter how much I might rack my brains ■ そんなことを思いつくのか、見当もつかない I wouldn't have the faintest idea of how to come up with that ■ 計算式の問題が、ある時点から不意に図形化し at a certain point the problem suddenly takes a diagrammatic form and ■ しかも moreover ■ そこに予想外の規則的な繰り返しが表われ出てくる…… in it an unforeseen [pattern of] regular repetition emerges... ■ 考えれば考えるほど神秘的である the more I think about it, the more magical it seems

7 そこで私は感づいた that's when it struck me ■ ただ単に難しい問題を解くのが天才ではない merely solving difficult problems is not genius ■ 複雑な問題を単純化してしまうのが天才だ genius is making complicated problems simple ■ その結果として難しい問題が解けるだけなのだ it is just as a consequence of such simplification that difficult problems are able to be solved ■ と that is [what I realized]

8 地図にある通りの道を選んだら if one takes a mapped road ■ 崖もある there are precipices ■ 沼地もある there are bogs ■ 狼もいる there are wolves ■ 凡人はそれでも despite that, the ordinary person ■ 傷だらけになりながら becoming scratched and bruised all over in the process ■ 一歩一歩進んでゆくだろう probably plods on, step by step ■ ところが天才は the genius, on the other hand ■ 凡人が自分の足元にばかり囚われている間に in the time in which ordinary people are preoccupied with their footing ■ 気球を飛ばし flies up in a hot-air balloon and ■ 風に乗って rides the wind and ■ スイスイと目的の地へ到着する glides swiftly to his destination ■ 思わず、「ずるいじゃないか」と口走りそうになる one is tempted to blurt out, without a second thought, "That's cheating!" ■ 天才がやってのける単純化は the simplification a genius brings off ■ 本当にずるいほどお見事なのだ is so remarkable it makes one want to cry foul

9 言い方を変えれば to put it another way ■ 天才たちは皆 all geniuses ■ どんなに複雑に見える問題にも、裏には何かがある、と予感する力を備えている possess the ability to sense that that there is something [hidden] behind even the most difficult-looking problem

る、と予感する力を備えている。そしてその何かは、複雑さを一気に蹴散らし、たちまち世界を美しく統制するだけの力を備えている、と信じている。まだ見ぬものへの憧れ。これがなければ発見は生まれない。

1から100までの足し算を出題されても、当然私に予感や憧れが沸いてくるはずもなく、ぶつぶつ文句を言いながら順番に、まじめに足してゆく。才能がないばかりか根気もない私は、途中で嫌気がさし、あちこちで計算間違いを起こす。もちろん答えも間違っているわけで、先生から赤字で大きなバツをもらい、やり直しを命じられる。いつまでたっても洞窟から抜け出せない。

その隣でガウス少年は、数の世界の隠れた美しい秘密を手に入れている。洞窟に射す一本の光をつかみ取り、暗闇から抜け出し、はるか遠い地平に旅立っている。

これが凡人と天才の違いであろう。

■ そして and ■ その何かは…だけの力を備えている、と信じている they believe that that "something" has the power to… ■ 複雑さを一気に蹴散らし put to rout the complexity in one fell swoop and ■ たちまち世界を美しく統制する instantly bring the world into beautiful order ■ まだ見ぬものへの憧れ a thirst for the unseen ■ これがなければ発見は生まれない without this, discoveries would not be made

10 1から100までの足し算を出題されても if I were assigned the problem of adding up the integers from 1 to 100 ■ 当然私に予感や憧れが沸いてくるはずもなく naturally there would be no sixth sense or thirst [for the unknown] welling up in me, and ■ ぶつぶつ文句を言いながら順番に、まじめに足してゆく while grumbling, I would earnestly start adding them up, one by one ■ 才能がないばかりか根気もない not only have no (mathematical) ability, but also have no perseverance ■ 私は途中で嫌気がさし I would get fed up midway through and ■ あちこちで計算間違いを起こす make mistakes in the calculations here and there ■ もちろん答えも間違っているわけで and of course, because my answer would also be wrong ■ 先生から赤字で大きなバツをもらい I would get a big red X from my teacher and ■ やり直しを命じられる be ordered to do it over ■ いつまでたっても洞窟から抜け出せない I would be stuck forever in a dark cavern

11 その隣でガウス少年は the young Gauss sitting next to me ■ 数の世界の隠れた美しい秘密を手に入れている would have in his possession a beautiful, hidden secret of the world of numbers ■ 洞窟に射す一本の光をつかみ取り he would have seized onto the one ray of light pouring into that cavern ■ 暗闇から抜け出し made his way out of the darkness, and ■ はるか遠い地平に旅立っている be setting off for the far horizon

12 これが凡人と天才の違いであろう this is no doubt the difference between the ordinary person and a genius

以前、数学者の藤原正彦先生とお話しした時も、このガウスのエピソードで盛り上がった。しかし先生は単に盛り上がるだけではなく、

「$1^2+2^2+3^2+4^2+$……だったらどうなるか、あるいは$1^3+2^3+3^3+4^3+$……では、どうでしょう」

とおっしゃって、さらさらと計算をはじめられた。$1+2+3+$……にあのように素晴らしい公式が隠れているとすれば、2乗、3乗の足し算からは何が浮かび上がってくるか、わくわくするでしょう、小川さん。そう言って私にウインクしそうな雰囲気だった。

ここでまたしても私は驚きに打たれた。なるほど、天才は一箇所に留まっていないのだ。私がガウスの計算にひとしきり感心している間に、才能のある人はどんどん新しい方面に目を向けている。私は$1+2+3+$……の謎が解けただけで十分満足だが、決して満足しないのが天才である。一つの発見から更なる発見を生み出す。新しい恒星が発見されると、それに引っ張られるようにすぐ近くでも新星が見つかるのと同じく、数の秘密も寄り添い合って隠れているものらしい。

13 | 以前 some time ago ▪ 数学者の藤原正彦先生とお話しした時も when I was talking with the mathematician Dr. Fujiwara Masahiko ▪ このガウスのエピソードで盛り上がった we had a good talk about this episode with Gauss ▪ しかし先生は単に盛り上がるだけではなく however, the professor did not simply get excited about the topic

14 | ……だったらどうなるか how about…? ▪ あるいは…では、どうでしょう or how about…?

15 | とおっしゃって he said and ▪ さらさらと計算をはじめられた started dashing off calculations ▪ 1＋2＋3＋……にあのように素晴らしい公式が隠れているとすれば if there is such a wonderful formula hidden in 1＋2＋3＋… ▪ 2乗、3乗の足し算からは何が浮かび上がってくるか what might emerge in adding up numbers raised to the power of 2 or of 3? ▪ わくわくするでしょう、小川さん it's exciting to think about, isn't it, Ogawa-san? ▪ そう言って私にウインクしそうな雰囲気だった he said to me as if with a wink

16 | ここでまたしても私は驚きに打たれた once again, I was struck by surprise ▪ なるほど I see ▪ 天才は一箇所に留まっていないのだ geniuses do not linger in one place ▪ 私がガウスの計算にひとしきり感心している間に while I am seized with admiration for Gauss's calculations ▪ 才能のある人はどんどん新しい方面に目を向けている gifted people are quickly moving on and looking in new directions ▪ 私は…の謎が解けただけで十分満足だが I would be satisfied enough just at being able to solve the puzzle of…but ▪ 決して満足しないのが天才である never being satisfied—that is [the mark of a] genius ▪ 一つの発見から更なる発見を生み出す from one discovery they make further discoveries ▪ 新しい恒星が発見されると when a new star is discovered ▪ それに引っ張られるようにすぐ近くでも新星が見つかる as if pulled in by it, other new stars nearby are discovered ▪ …のと同じく in the same way that… ▪ 数の秘密も寄り添い合って隠れているものらしい mathematical secrets seem to hide together in clusters

2乗、3乗の和がどのような公式で表わされるかについては、藤原先生との対談集『世にも美しい数学入門』（筑摩書房）を読んでいただきたい。ああ、神様は何と不思議な技を見せて下さるのかと、天を仰ぎ両手を合わせずにはいられない結果が得られている。もちろん私はただ座っていただけで、計算して下さったのは全部、藤原先生である。

『博士の愛した数式』を発表した時、一番気がかりだったのは、数学の専門家の方々がどんなふうに読んで下さるか、ということだった。

「こんな分かりきったことを、回りくどく、大げさに書いて、何とまあくだらない小説だ。フン」

と、軽蔑されるのではないか。いや、そもそも数学の先生たちは、こんなつまらない小説は読まないであろう。などといろいろ心配をしていた。

ある日、思いも寄らない知らせが届いた。この小説が日本数学会出版賞を受賞したの

17 2乗、3乗の和がどのような公式で表わされるかについては as for how the adding up of numbers to the power of 2 or 3 is expressed in a formula ▪ 藤原先生との対談集『世にも美しい数学入門』（筑摩書房）を読んでいただきたい I refer you to (lit., "I would like you to read") the book we coauthored, *An Introduction to Extremely Beautiful Mathematics* (Chikuma Publishing Co.), in which I asked Professor Fujiwara questions ▪ ああ、神様は何と不思議な技を見せて下さるのか oh, how wondrous are the works of God! ▪ ...と、天を仰ぎ両手を合わせずにはいられない結果が得られている the results are so marvelous that you cannot help but look up to the heavens, clasp your hands together, and say... ▪ 私はただ座っていただけで I just sat there ▪ 計算して下さったのは全部、藤原先生である it was Professor Fujiwara who did all the calculations

18 『博士の愛した数式』を発表した時 when *The Housekeeper and the Professor* was published ▪ 一番気がかりだったのは the thing I was the most anxious about ▪ 数学の専門家の方々がどんなふうに読んで下さるか、ということだった was how mathematicians would read it

19 こんな分かりきったことを、回りくどく、大げさに書いて writing these sorts of obvious things in such a roundabout and overblown way ▪ 何とまあくだらない小説だ what a, well, stupid novel ▪ フン bah!

20 と、軽蔑されるのではないか wouldn't it be dismissed like that? ▪ いや but no ▪ そもそも数学の先生たちは、こんなつまらない小説は読まないであろう math professors wouldn't be reading this sort of silly novel in the first place ▪ などといろいろ心配をしていた I worried about this and that

21 ある日 one day ▪ 思いも寄らない知らせが届いた I received an undreamt-of notice ▪ この小説が日本数学会出版賞を受賞したのだ this novel had won the Mathematical Society of Japan (MSJ) Prize for Publications

だ。

私は授賞式に出席するため、日本大学理工学部駿河台校舎へ向かった。学会の会場で、講演やシンポジウムの合間に式が行われるらしい。正直、少し怖かった。文学の授賞式ならば大体どういうものか予測がつくが、何と言っても数学会だ。桁外れに頭のいい人々の集まりに違いない。ガウスや藤原先生のような人たちがうようよしているのだ。そんな恐ろしいところへ、どんな顔をして入ってゆけばよいのだろう。高校時代の数学が、いつも赤点すれすれだったこの私が。

駿河台校舎に到着すると、中は案外ざわざわした雰囲気だった。あちこちにポスターや会場の案内図が貼られ、手伝いらしい若者がうろうろしている。チェックも一切なく、出入り自由で、まるで学園祭のようでもある。

本部に案内されると、そこには他の受賞者の方々（皆さん数学の専門家ばかり）や、学会の方々が揃っておられた。私は日本数学会理事長、森田康夫先生の隣に、かちこちに緊張しながら、ぎこちなく、居心地悪く腰掛けた。

22　私は授賞式に出席するため to attend the award ceremony ■ 日本大学理工学部駿河台校舎へ向かった I set out for Nihon University, College of Science and Technology, Surugadai Campus ■ 学会の会場で at an academic conference ■ 講演やシンポジウムの合間に式が行われるらしい apparently the ceremony was to be held in between lectures and symposiums ■ 正直、少し怖かった to tell the truth, I was a little scared ■ 文学の授賞式ならば were it a literary award ceremony ■ 大体どういうものか予測がつくが I would have some idea what to expect, but ■ 何と言っても数学会だ this was a *mathematics* convention ■ 桁外れに頭のいい人々の集まりに違いない it was certain to be a gathering of phenomenally intelligent people ■ ガウスや藤原先生のような人たちがうようよしているのだ it would be swarming with people like Gauss and Professor Fujiwara ■ そんな恐ろしいところへ、どんな顔をして入ってゆけばよいのだろう how was I to act going to such an intimidating place? ■ 高校時代の数学が、いつも赤点すれすれだったこの私が I whose grades in high school math were always close to failing?

23　駿河台校舎に到着すると when I arrived at the Surugadai Campus ■ 中は案外ざわざわした雰囲気だった it was bustling inside [the convention hall], to my surprise ■ あちこちにポスターや会場の案内図が貼られ posters and directions for getting to the venue were up here and there, and ■ 手伝いらしい若者がうろうろしている young people who seemed to be assistants [for the convention] were standing about ■ チェックも一切なく there was no check-in ■ 出入り自由で people were free to come and go and ■ まるで学園祭のようでもある it felt almost like a school festival

24　本部に案内されると when I was shown into the reception area ■ そこには他の受賞者の方々（皆さん数学の専門家ばかり）や、学会の方々が揃っておられた the other prizewinners (all mathematicians) and MSJ members were assembled there ■ 私は日本数学会理事長、森田康夫先生の隣に…腰掛けた I sat down next to the MSJ Chairman, Professor Morita Yasuo ■ かちこちに緊張しながら stiff with tension ■ ぎこちなく、居心地悪く feeling awkward and ill at ease

数学会の理事長先生と自分との間に、どんな共通点があるだろう。一体何を喋ったらいいのだろう。初対面の挨拶を済ませてしまうと、あともう一言も言葉は浮かんでこず、愛想笑いを浮かべるにも限度があり、間を持たせるためのお茶はすぐに飲み干してしまった。緊張感はどんどん高まるばかりだった。

同じように森田先生も困っておられた。視線を宙に泳がせ、一生懸命、適切な話題がないかと探している気配が、こちらにも伝わってきた。しばらく二人で、もじもじとした時間を過ごした。

とうとう沈黙に耐え切れず、私は口を開いた。本当はこんなことを数学者の先生の前で口にするのは、失礼に当たるのではないかと思われたが、黙っているよりは多少ましな気がしたのだ。

「先生、小説の中に書いておきながら、私は自然対数 e が、いまだによく分からないんです」

小説の博士が愛したのは、オイラーの公式、

25 | 数学会の理事長先生と自分との間に between the MSJ Chairman and myself ▪ どんな共通点があるだろう what points in common could there possibly be? ▪ 一体何を喋ったらいいのだろう what on earth was I to say to him? ▪ 初対面の挨拶を済ませてしまうと after getting through the usual how-do-you-do's ▪ あとはもう一言も言葉は浮かんでこず not a single word sprang to mind ▪ 愛想笑いを浮かべるにも限度があり one can smile pleasantly for only so long, and ▪ 間を持たせるためのお茶はすぐに飲み干してしまった I had soon finished the tea given to me to fill the time ▪ 緊張感はどんどん高まるばかりだった my feeling of nervousness only increased

26 | 同じように森田先生も困っておられた Professor Morita was similarly at a loss ▪ 視線を宙に泳がせ as he looked around the room ▪ 一生懸命、適切な話題がないかと探している気配が、こちらにも伝わってきた I could sense him feverishly searching for an appropriate topic ▪ しばらく二人で for a while the two of us ▪ もじもじとした時間を過ごした passed the time in awkward silence

27 | とうとう沈黙に耐え切れず at last no longer able to endure the silence ▪ 私は口を開いた I opened my mouth ▪ 本当は actually ▪ こんなことを数学者の先生の前で口にするのは to say such a thing in front of a mathematician ▪ 失礼に当たるのではないかと思われたが seemed insulting, I thought, but ▪ 黙っているよりは多少ましな気がしたのだ I felt it would be somewhat better than remaining silent

28 | 小説の中に書いておきながら although I wrote about it in my novel ▪ 私は自然対数 e が、いまだによく分からないんです I still don't fully understand the Napierian logarithm e

29 | 小説の博士が愛したのはオイラーの公式 the Euler formula that the professor in my book loved

$e^{\pi i}+1=0$

ということになっている。

πは円周率、iは虚数（-1の平方根）。eはπと同じように

循環しない無理数で、

2.718281828459045……

とどこまでも続いてゆく。

これら、何の関わりもないように見えるeとπとiが結びつき、1をプラスした瞬間に0になる。オイラーが発見した公式は、永遠と無が一瞬の中で共存している、奇跡的に美しい式なのだ。

にもかかわらず頭の固い私は、理屈ではeの仕組みが理解できたつもりでいても、どうしてこの脈絡のない数字の連なりが〝自然〞と命名されているのか、分からない。感覚としてつかめない。

「ああ、それはですね……」

森田先生はすぐさま、胸ポケットから万年筆を取り出し、手近にあったパンフレットの

30 | ということになっている is expressed... ▪ π は円周率 π is pi (the circular constant) ▪ i は虚数 (-1の平方根) and i is an imaginary number (the square root of -1) ▪ e は π と同じように循環しない無理数で like π, e is a non-repeating irrational number

31 | とどこまでも続いてゆく and so on ad infinitum

32 | これら、何の関わりもないように見える e と π と i が結びつき the seemingly unrelated [elements] e and π and i are linked together and ▪ 1を プラスした瞬間に0になる the instant you add 1 [to $e^{\pi i}$], they become 0 ▪ オイラーが発見した公式は…奇跡的に美しい式なのだ this equation Euler discovered is a miraculously beautiful equation ▪ 永遠と無が 一瞬の中で共存している in which eternity and nothingness coexist in an instant

33 | にもかかわらず nevertheless ▪ 頭の固い私は for me, whose thinking is very rigid ▪ 理屈では e の仕組みが理解できたつもりでいても sure though I am that, on a theoretical level, I understand the working of e ▪ どう してこの脈絡のない数字の連なりが〝自然〟と命名されているのか、分 からない I can't understand why this series of unrelated numbers is called "natural" ▪ 感覚としてつかめない I just can't feel it intuitively

34 | ああ、それはですね…… oh, that's…

35 | 森田先生はすぐさま、胸ポケットから万年筆を取り出し [so saying] Professor Morita immediately took out a fountain pen from his chest pocket ▪ 手近にあったパンフレットの裏に on the back of the pamphlet that he had at hand

裏にさーっと座標軸を書き、一本の線を引いた。ゼロを起点とする真っ直ぐな線グラフである。

「つまり e はこのように表わされるわけなんです」

縦軸、横軸の単位が何であったかは、恥ずかしながら忘れてしまった。ただ先生の万年筆から一本の線が引かれた時、"自然"の意味が自然に身体に染み込んできたのだけはよく覚えている。そのグラフは、何の無理もなく、遥か遠い昔からずっと変わらないあるがままの姿で、どこまでも伸びていた。

「こうしてグラフという、目に見える図で表わすと、途端に霧が晴れるみたいによく分かりますね」

「ええ、そうなんですよ」

霧と一緒にさっきまでの緊張もどこかへ行ってしまい、私はうれしくなった。

森田先生もにこにこにこされていた。

日本数学会の理事長先生が、無知にも程があるこの私に、わざわざ万年筆を取り出し

『博士の愛した数式』を巡って　86

■ さーっと座標軸を書き sketched an axis ■ 一本の線を引いた drew a single line ■ ゼロを起点とする真っ直ぐな線グラフである it was a graph with a straight line running from zero

36 つまり in short ■ e はこのように表わされるわけなんです e is expressed like this

37 縦軸、横軸の単位が何であったかは what the values of the vertical and horizontal axes were ■ 恥ずかしながら忘れてしまった I am embarrassed to say, I've forgotten ■ 先生の万年筆から一本の線が引かれた時 when that one line was drawn from the professor's pen ■ 〝自然〟の意味が自然に身体に染み込んできたのだけはよく覚えている I only remember feeling the meaning of "natural" naturally permeating my body ■ そのグラフは as for the graph ■ 何の無理もなく utterly naturally ■ 遥か遠い昔からずっと変わらないあるがままの姿で in the same unchanging form from the distant past ■ どこまでも伸びていた it went on without end

38 こうしてグラフという目に見える図で表わすと when you express it in this sort of visual graphic form ■ 途端に霧が晴れるみたいによく分かりますね all of a sudden the fog lifts and you understand it clear as day, don't you?

39 霧と一緒に along with the fog ■ さっきまでの緊張もどこかへ行ってしまい the tension from a moment ago had also gone away ■ 私はうれしくなった and I became happy

40 ええ、そうなんですよ yes, you're absolutely right

41 森田先生もにこにこされていた Professor Morita was also smiling happily

42 無知にも程があるこの私に for me, the limit of ignorance ■ わざわざ万年筆を取り出して took the trouble of taking out his pen and

て、eについて教えて下さった。嫌がりもせず、軽蔑もせず、優しく教えて下さった。そのことが感動的だった。

あの瞬間、先生と私の間には、一つの数に隠された偉大な美しさを共有しているという喜びが、満ちあふれていた。

そろそろ桜が散りはじめようか、という季節、私は静岡県のローカル線に乗り、小山町へ向かっていた。土曜日の午後で、電車の中は部活動帰りらしい高校生でにぎやかだった。

商店街もバスターミナルもない小さな駅で降りると、改札口に立って手を振る、プロデューサーの荒木さんの姿が見えた。この小山町で、映画『博士の愛した数式』の撮影が行われているのだ。

細い坂道を上がってゆくと、不意に視界が開け、トラックやクレーンや大きな照明や

■ *e*について教えて下さった taught [me] about *e* ■ 嫌がりもせず un-grudgingly ■ 軽蔑もせず un-patronizingly ■ 優しく kindly ■ そのことが感動的だった that made a big impression on me

43 あの瞬間 in that moment ■ 先生と私の間には between the professor and me ■ 一つの数に隠された偉大な美しさを共有しているという喜び the joy of sharing one of the great beauties hidden in numbers ■ 満ちあふれていた brimmed

44 そろそろ桜が散りはじめようか、という季節 [it was] the season when the cherry blossoms were about to start falling ■ 私は静岡県のローカル線に乗り I had gotten on a local train in Shizuoka Prefecture and 小山町へ向かっていた was heading to Oyama-chō ■ 土曜日の午後で it was a Saturday afternoon, and ■ 電車の中は部活動帰りらしい高校生でにぎやかだった inside the train it was lively with what seemed to be lots of high school boys and girls on their way home from sports practice

45 商店街もバスターミナルもない小さな駅で降りると when I got off at a station too small for even a street of shops or a bus depot ■ 改札口に立って手を振る、プロデューサーの荒木さんの姿が見えた I saw the movie producer Mr. Araki standing at the ticket gate and waving at me ■ 映画『博士の愛した数式』の撮影が行われているのだ the shooting of the movie of *The Housekeeper and the Professor* was taking place

46 細い坂道を上がってゆくと when we had climbed up a narrow road ■ 不意に視界が開け suddenly the view opened up and ■ トラックやクレーンや大きな照明やカメラやテントが目に飛び込んできた trucks and cranes and huge lights and cameras and tents jumped into view

に、博士の住む家が建っていた。

なぜか私は、幼いころ何度も訪ねたことのあるような気持になった。壊れた呼び鈴、革の寝椅子、傷だらけの食卓、ヨーロッパ製のコーヒーカップ、手回しの鉛筆削り、擦り切れたベッドカバー……。何もかもすべてが、小説を書いている時、私の頭の中にあったのと同じ姿でそこにあったからだ。作り物のはずなのに、長い年月、博士の体温を吸い込んできた風合いが、隅々にまで行き渡っていた。一切打ち合わせなどしなかったのに、監督はどうして、私の中だけにあったイメージをこんなにも鮮やかに再現できたのか。それが不思議でならなかった。

博士の書棚に置かれた本たちは、森田先生の書斎からお借りしてきたものだった。博士の勉強机は、広大な数の世界を前にした時の人間のささやかさを象徴するように、この勉強机は、広大な数の世界を前にした時の人間のささやかさを象徴するように、こぢんまりとしたものだった。窓からは、風に散る桜の花がよく見えた。

撮影の準備が整い、正面から寺尾聰さんが歩いてこられた。

カメラやテントが目に飛び込んできた。大勢の人々が忙しく立ち働いていた。その向こう

- 大勢の人々が忙しく立ち働いていた lots of people were busy at work
- その向こうに beyond that (i.e., the scene of trucks and cranes and people working) ▪ 博士の住む家が建っていた the house where the professor lived had been built

47 | なぜか for some reason ▪ 私は、幼いころ何度も訪ねたことのある場所へ久しぶりに戻ってきたかのような気持になった I felt as if I had returned, after a long time away, to a place I had visited many times as a small child ▪ 壊れた呼び鈴 the broken doorbell ▪ 革の寝椅子 the leather couch ▪ 傷だらけの食卓 the scarred dinner table ▪ ヨーロッパ製のコーヒーカップ the coffee cups from Europe ▪ 手回しの鉛筆削り the hand-cranked pencil sharpener ▪ 擦り切れたベッドカバー…… the threadbare bedspread... ▪ 何もかもすべてが、小説を書いている時、私の頭の中にあったのと同じ姿でそこにあった absolutely everything was there exactly as it had been in my mind's eye while writing the novel ▪ からだ it was because ▪ 作り物のはずなのに even though the house was a prop ▪ 長い年月 over the long years ▪ 博士の体温を吸い込んできた風合いが a palpable atmosphere that had absorbed the professor's body heat ▪ 隅々にまで行き渡っていた had lingered in every nook and cranny ▪ 一切打ち合わせなどしなかったのに despite our never having had any discussions ▪ 監督はどうして、私の中だけにあったイメージをこんなにも鮮やかに再現できたのか how could the director have reproduced so vividly the images that were only in my head? ▪ それが不思議でならなかった it was too strange for words

48 | 博士の書棚に置かれた本たちは the books on the professor's bookshelves ▪ 森田先生の書斎からお借りしてきたものだった were ones I had borrowed from Professor Morita's study ▪ 博士の勉強机は the professor's desk ▪ 広大な数の世界を前にした時の人間のささやかさを象徴するように as if to symbolize the insignificance of humans standing before the vast world of numbers ▪ こぢんまりとしたものだった was a small one ▪ 窓からは from the window ▪ 風に散る桜の花がよく見えた I could see cherry blossoms falling in the wind

49 | 撮影の準備が整い with everything readied for filming ▪ 正面から寺尾聰さんが歩いてこられた Terao Akira came walking up to me (lit., "from the front")

博士だった。素数を愛し、オイラーの公式を愛し、子供と阪神タイガースを愛した博士

が、活字の中から、生きた人間に生まれ変わって、私の目の前に現われたのだ。

世界は驚きと歓びに満ちている。

まさに私はその言葉を、胸に深く刻みつけたのだった。

50 | 博士だった it was the professor! ▪ 素数を愛し [the professor] who loved prime numbers ▪ オイラーの公式を愛し who loved Euler's formula ▪ 子供と阪神タイガースを愛した博士が the professor who loved children and the Hanshin Tigers ▪ 活字の中から生きた人間に生まれ変わって he had stepped out of the pages of my book (lit., "he had been reborn out of the typeset letters") as a flesh-and-blood human being and ▪ 私の目の前に現われたのだ appeared in front of my eyes

51 | 世界は驚きと歓びに満ちている the world is full of surprise and joy

52 | まさに私はその言葉を、胸に深く刻みつけたのだった truly these words are now engraved in my heart

平野啓一郎

Hirano Keiichirō

A dense, kanji-packed prose style like that of Hirano Keiichirô is usually associated with older novelists, but actually he is the youngest of the writers represented in this book, having been born in 1975. Raised in Kita-Kyûshû, he was still a student at Kyoto University when he burst on the literary scene with his ambitious novella *Nisshoku* (*Eclipse*), set in Europe in the Middle Ages. *Nisshoku* won the Akutagawa Prize in 1999 and formed a loose trilogy with *Ichigetsu monogatari* (*Tale of the First Moon*), set in Meiji-era Japan, and *Sôsô* (*The Funeral*), a very long historical novel about Chopin, Delacroix, and George Sand.

Hirano spent a year in France as a cultural ambassador of Japan, but since then has been publishing works set in contemporary Japan. Concerned about a drop in the ability of many Japanese to appreciate serious literature, Hirano has also published a guide to "slow reading," *Hon no yomikata: Surô rîdingu no jissen* (*How to Read a Book: The Practice of Slow Reading*).

Hirano's meditations here on Kyoto and the nature of change were first published in the literary magazine *Shinchô*, then in the book *Urayamashii hito: '03 nenban besuto essei shû* (*Enviable People: Best Essays of 2003*), issued by Bungei Shunjû. His works have been translated into French, Korean, and Chinese, and a short story of his, "Clear Water," can be found in the second volume of the *Columbia Anthology of Modern Japanese Literature*. If you enjoy the essay here, you might consider reading Hirano's collection of writings on contemporary society, *Bunmei no yûutsu* (*The Melancholy of Civilization*), available in paperback (*bunko-bon*) from Shinchôsha.

無常ということ

平野啓一郎

少し前のことになるが、私は或る評論家がインターネットのウェブサイト上に、八坂神社の前にコンヴィニエンス・ストアが出来たことは怪しからんと憤慨しながら書いているのを読んで、乱暴な口調の割には何事に於いても紋切型の浅薄さで、一向に核心に触れないのが常のこの人らしい話だと苦笑したことがある。それならば、そもそも祇園の交差点をあれほどの量の自動車が往来していることはどうなるのだろう？　外国産の高級車も走っていれば、市バスも轟音を鳴り響かせている。そうした風景には一向に目がゆかず、殊更にコンヴィニエンス・ストアなどに着目してみせるところが、私には何とも安易な語り口のように思われたのである。

昔からよく京都を訪ね、この町に特別の思いがあるという人の間では、京都の景観破壊を嘆じてみせることはちょっとした流行なのかもしれない。これはしかし、恐らく今に

無常ということ Thoughts on Mutability

1 少し前のことになるが it was a little while ago ▪ 或る評論家がインターネットのウェブサイト上に on the Web site of a certain pundit ▪ 八坂神社の前にコンヴィニエンス・ストアが出来たことは the fact that a convenience store had been built in front of the Yasaka Shrine ▪ 怪しからんと憤慨しながら書いているのを読んで I read rantings about how improper it was ▪ 乱暴な口調の割には for all his violent tone ▪ 何事に於いても in everything he said ▪ 紋切型の浅薄さで there was a formulaic shallowness, and ▪ 一向に核心に触れないの not at all getting to the heart of the matter ▪ 常のこの人らしい話だ was typical of this person ▪ 私は…と苦笑したことがある I had the experience of smiling wryly [upon reflecting that…] ▪ それならば、そもそも祇園の交差点をあれほどの量の自動車が往来していることはどうなるのだろう? what then of such a large number of automobiles coming and going through the Gion crossing? ▪ 外国産の高級車も走っていれば on top of the foreign luxury cars running there ▪ 市バスも轟音を鳴り響かせている you have the roaring of city buses ▪ そうした風景には一向に目がゆかず without at all taking into account that sort of scene ▪ 殊更にコンヴィニエンス・ストアなどに着目してみせるところ the way he focused loudly on such things as convenience stores ▪ 私には何とも安易な語り口のように思われたのである seemed all too simpleminded

2 昔からよく京都を訪ね、この町に特別の思いがあるという人の間では among people who have long frequented Kyoto and who possess a special feeling for the city ▪ 京都の景観破壊を嘆じてみせることは loudly denouncing the destruction of the Kyoto townscape ▪ ちょっとした流行なのかもしれない might be a minor trend ▪ これはしかし、恐らく今に始まったことではないであろう it is, however, probably nothing new (lit., "not something that has just started now")

始まったことではないであろう。二条城などというものが建てられた当時も、流石は田舎侍の御大将、とんでもないものを造ってくれたわいと悲憤慷慨する人達も多かったのではあるまいか？ これは今日のビル建設などよりも、よほど深刻な決定的な「景観破壊」であった筈である。

私は、どうも昨今のその手の議論に胡散らしさを感じて仕方がない。勿論、何でも好き放題にぶち壊して、高層ビルだろうとパチンコ店だろうと幾らでも建てれば良いなどと乱暴なことは言わない。しかし、それでは一体、彼らが何時頃のどういう京都を残したいと思っているのかと問えば極めて曖昧である。先の評論家ではないが、結局は各々の記憶の中にある「あの日、あの時見た京都」ということでしかないのではあるまいか？ それはいかにも恣意的である。京都という町の長い歴史に比して、彼の個人的な愛着の歴史とは何とちっぽけなものであろう。

同じことは京都の町屋を巡る議論についても言える。こちらは実際に京都に住んでいる人達の言うことであるから議論にも迫力があるが、とはいえそこで保存すべきと主張

■ 二条城などというものが建てられた当時も even when Nijō Castle was built ■ 流石は田舎侍の御大将、とんでもないものを造ってくれたわい the head of the country bumpkin samurai has built something outlandish ■ …と悲憤慷慨する人達も多かったのではあるまいか？ were there not many people waxing indignant that…? ■ これは this [building of Nijō Castle] ■ 今日のビル建設などよりも far more, even, than the construction of buildings today ■ よほど深刻な決定的な「景観破壊」であった筈である must have been a terribly grave and decisive "destruction of scenery"

3 | 私は、どうも昨今のその手の議論に胡散らしさを感じて仕方がない somehow I cannot help feeling that there is something questionable about such arguments nowadays ■ 勿論 of course ■ 何でも好き放題にぶち壊して capriciously tear down anything and everything with abandon and ■ 高層ビルだろうとパチンコ店だろうと幾らでも建てれば build as many high-rise buildings or pachinko parlors as one likes ■ 良いなどと乱暴なことは言わない I will not say anything as reckless as it is okay to… ■ それでは一体、彼らが何時頃のどういう京都を残したいと思っているのかと問えば whenever we ask [such preservationists] exactly what period and exactly what kind of Kyoto they wish to preserve ■ 極めて曖昧である [the answer] is [inevitably] very vague ■ 先の評論家ではないが I do not mean to single out that above-mentioned pundit, but ■ 結局は ultimately ■ 各々の記憶の中にある in their individual memories ■「あの日、あの時見た京都」ということでしかないのではあるまいか？ is it not just the Kyoto seen on a particular day at a particular time? ■ それはいかにも恣意的である that is much too arbitrary ■ 京都という町の長い歴史に比して compared to the long history of the city of Kyoto ■ 彼の個人的な愛着の歴史とは the history of one's own personal feelings of affection ■ 何とちっぽけなものであろう is such a puny and insignificant thing

4 | 同じことは京都の町屋を巡る議論についても言える the same can be said of the arguments concerning [preservation of] the *machiya* of Kyoto ■ こちらは実際に京都に住んでいる人達の言うことであるから since these assertions are made by people actually living in Kyoto ■ 議論にも迫力がある the arguments have [a certain] force ■ とはいえ and yet ■ そこで保存すべきと主張されている風景にしても the townscapes that are asserted to be worth saving (lit., "that should be saved")

されている風景にしても結局は彼らが幼少時に慣れ親しんだ割と最近の町の姿である。

五百年前にその一帯がどういう風景であったのかということは一向に議論にならない。

平安時代に比べればそれらの町屋にしても十分近代建築じゃないかという反論は私は説

得力があると思う。

では何故そうなのであろうか？　私はこの問題は、京都という町の本質的な性格に

関係していると思う。京都という町は、永遠に無常をかなしみ続ける町である。『伊勢物

語』の「月やあらぬ春や昔の春ならぬわが身ひとつはもとの身にして」ではないが、昔の

愛人、知人を訪ねて荒れ放題になった家屋に愕然とするという場面は古典の中によくあ

る。人の儚さと建造物の儚さとは同じ無常の底知れぬかなしみの渦中にある。人が死ぬよ

うに、建造物も壊れる。人が移り変わるように、風景もまた絶え間なく変化する。そうし

た存在の絶望的な不安を慰める為にこそ、不変の聖所としての神社仏閣がかくも膨大な

数築かれねばならなかったのではあるまいか。永遠に変わらない場所である神社仏閣と無

常に変わりゆく江湖の人間の居住区、その残酷な対比こそが京都という町のいわば凄み

■ 結局は彼らが幼少時に慣れ親しんだ割と最近の町の姿である are in the last analysis relatively recent appearances in the city—places the preservationists became used to and fond of as children ■ 五百年前にその一帯がどういう風景であったのかということは how that district looked 500 years ago ■ 一向に議論にならない does not enter the discussion at all ■ 平安時代に比べれば compared to the Heian period [794–1185] ■ それらの町屋にしても十分近代建築じゃないか are not such structures quite modern architecture? ■ という反論は私は説得力があると思う I think such an opposing argument is persuasive

5 | では well then ■ 何故そうなのであろうか? why is that so? ■ 私はこの問題は、京都という町の本質的な性格に関係していると思う I think this matter is related to the essential nature of Kyoto ■ 京都という町は、永遠に無常をかなしみ続ける町である Kyoto is a city that is continually mourning the impermanence of worldly things ■ 『伊勢物語』の「月やあらぬ春や昔の春ならぬわが身ひとつはもとの身にして」ではないが even if we do not single out [the words of] the *Tales of Ise*: "Is not that the moon? / And is not the spring the same / Spring of the old days? / My body is the same body— / Yet everything seems different" ■ 昔の愛人、知人を訪ねて when someone goes to visit a lover or an acquaintance from the past ■ 荒れ放題になった家屋に愕然とする he is taken aback to find an abandoned house in a state of disrepair ■ という場面は古典の中によくある such a scene is often found in classical literature ■ 人の儚さと建造物の儚さとは the transience of human life and the transience of buildings [made by man] ■ 同じ無常の底知れぬかなしみの渦中にある are both caught in mutability's vortex of immeasurable sadness ■ 人が死ぬように in the same way that human beings die ■ 建造物も壊れる buildings, too, fall apart ■ 人が移り変わるように in the same way that human beings undergo change ■ 風景もまた絶え間なく変化する scenery, too, ceaselessly changes ■ そうした存在の絶望的な不安を慰める為にこそ precisely to console such existential dread (lit., "existential desperate anxiety") ■ 不変の聖所としての神社仏閣がかくも膨大な数築かれねばならなかったのではあるまいか did we not feel compelled to build shrines and temples as unchanging holy places in such huge numbers? ■ 永遠に変らない場所である神社仏閣と the eternally unchanging shrines and temples and ■ 無常に変わりゆく江湖の人間の居住区 the ever-changing dwelling places of humanity ■ その残酷な対比こそが京都という町のいわば凄み

八坂神社の前が今のような景色になったのは、高々この数十年ほどのことであろう。

私は千二百年間の長きに亘って絶えざる変遷を繰り返してきたあの場所の風景を、たまたま千百何十年目かに出現した一つの風景に決定し、それを永遠に保存するなどということこそ京都という町に対する最も甚だしき誤解に基づいた蛮行であると思う。それは京都が、今現在も生き、生成と消滅とを繰り返し続けているということを忘れた人の愚かな考えである。一体人は、子供の頃の美しい母親の姿を愛しているからといって、彼女の生の変化を認めず、殺して冷凍保存にすることなど考えるであろうか？　彼らが愛しているのは、現実の生きた京都ではない。彼らが憤っているのは、京都そのものの破壊ではない。それは単に彼らの記憶の中の京都に過ぎない。変化することがなくなった時、京都は最早博物館のガラス・ケースの中に収められたミイラと同じ、死んだ町となるであろう。それを喜ぶのは、随分と悪趣味ではあるまいか？　三条通に感じのいい――観光客の大好きな――喫茶店がある。火事になった後に、建て替わったら以前の内装と殆ど同

なのではあるまいか? isn't it precisely that cruel contrast [between the two] that could be termed the frightening but compelling power of Kyoto?

6　八坂神社の前が今のような景色になったのは、高々この数十年ほどのことであろう　it is only in the past few decades that the area in front of Yasaka Shrine took on its present appearance ▪ 千二百年間の長きに亘って絶えざる変遷を繰り返してきたあの場所の風景を、たまたま千百何十年目かに出現した一つの風景に決定し　to decide that the [proper] landscape of that location, which has been repeatedly changing without interruption over the long period of 1200 years, should be the particular one that happened to appear at a point in time after 1100 years plus several decades, and ▪ それを永遠に保存する　to preserve it forever ▪ などということこそ　such an act indeed ▪ 京都という町に対する最も甚だしき誤解に基づいた蛮行であると思う　is, I believe, an act of barbarity based on a gross misunderstanding of Kyoto ▪ それは…ということを忘れた人の愚かな考えである　it is the foolish thinking of people who have forgotten that… ▪ 京都が、今現在も生き、生成と消滅とを繰り返し続けている　Kyoto is [still] alive now and continuing to repeat [a cycle of] creation and extinction ▪ 一体人は　who on earth ▪ 子供の頃の美しい母親の姿を愛しているからといって　just because they loved the beautiful appearance of their mother when they were a child ▪ 彼女の生の変化を認めず　would refuse to accept the changes [wrought in her] by life ▪ 殺して冷凍保存にすることなど考えるであろうか?　and think of killing her and cryopreserving her? ▪ 彼らが愛しているのは、現実の生きた京都ではない　what they love is not the actual living Kyoto ▪ 彼らが憤っているのは、京都そのものの破壊ではない　the object of their indignation is not the destruction of Kyoto itself ▪ それは単に彼らの記憶の中の京都に過ぎない　it is merely the Kyoto in their memories ▪ 変化することがなくなった時　the moment she stops changing ▪ 京都は最早…死んだ町となるであろう　Kyoto will be a dead city ▪ 博物館のガラス・ケースの中に収められたミイラと同じ　like a mummy shut up in a glass case in a museum ▪ それを喜ぶのは、随分と悪趣味ではあるまいか?　isn't being pleased by that the ultimate in perversity? ▪ 三条通に　on Sanjō Avenue ▪ 感じのいい――観光客の大好きな――喫茶店がある　there's a pleasant coffee shop—a great favorite of tourists ▪ 火事になった後に、建て替わったら　when it was rebuilt after a fire ▪ 以前の内装と殆ど同じだったという　people said that

じだったという。それとてどれほどのことであろうか？

この町の長い歴史の中に一瞬現れては消えた幻のようなものではあるまいか。そうした

幻がこれまでどれほどあったことであろう。それらが無限に集積し、今眼前に眺めてい

る光景ですら一つの幻であることを疑わせる。変わり続けた結果、嘗て一度として何かで

あったことがない。しかも、その虚無の表層の目眩く衣替えの連続が、紛れもなく京

都であるとしか言いようのないような或る固有の雰囲気を醸成している。それこそが、

この町の本来の魅力なのではあるまいか？

京都の景観保護の問題を議論する際に、パリやローマといったヨーロッパの古い都市を

例に挙げて、その町並の保存状態の良さを強調する人は多い。しかし、誰が住もうと百

年、二百年という間、堅牢な石造りの建造物が変わらぬ姿のまま立ち続けているそれらの

町と、木造の故に人と家屋とがその脆さに於いて結び合い、やがては例外なく滅びること

の宿命を共有していた京都の町とでは、そもそも同一に並べて議論すること自体が無理

な話である。

the interior was almost the same as before ■ それとてどれほどのこと であろうか? even so, to what extent is that [really] so? ■ 百年、二百年 経ってみれば after a century or two have passed ■ この町の長い歴史 の中に in the long history of this city ■ 一瞬現れては消えた幻のよう なものではあるまいか won't it be like a phantasm that appeared for an instant and then disappeared? ■ そうした幻がこれまでどれほどあった ことであろう one wonders how many such phantasms there have been up to now ■ それらが無限に集積し they have accumulated ad infini- tum ■ 今眼前に眺めている光景ですら一つの幻であることを疑わせる making one suspect that even the very scene presently in front of one's eyes is a phantasm ■ 変わり続けた結果 the result of having changed continuously is that ■ 嘗て一度として何かであったことがない nothing has existed just a single time ■ しかも moreover ■ その虚無の表層 の目眩く衣替えの連続が that dizzying succession of [so to speak] sea- sonal changes of clothing at the ephemeral surface ■ 紛れもなく京都 であるとしか言いようのないような或る固有の雰囲気を醸成している has distilled a certain atmosphere that one can only describe as un- mistakably Kyoto ■ それこそが、この町の本来の魅力なのではあるまい か? and isn't it exactly that [atmosphere] which is the essential charm of this city?

7 京都の景観保護の問題を議論する際に when arguing the question of the preservation of the Kyoto townscape ■ パリやローマといったヨー ロッパの古い都市を例に挙げて、その町並の保存状態の良さを強調する 人は多い many people cite the example of European cities like Paris and Rome, and stress how well the houses there have been preserved ■ 誰が住もうと百年、二百年という間、堅牢な石造りの建造物が変わら ぬ姿のまま立ち続けているそれらの町と [to compare] such cities, whose solid stone buildings have stood unchanged for a century or two no matter who has lived in them ■ 木造の故に人と家屋とがその脆さに 於いて結び合い、やがては例外なく滅びることの宿命を共有していた京 都の町とでは with Kyoto, where on account of the wooden architec- ture people and their houses are hand in hand in their fragility and share the fate of perishing in due course without exception ■ そもそ も同一に並べて議論すること自体が無理な話である from the start, it is unreasonable to argue by placing [the two cases] on the same level

京都に住み始めて、私は今年で九年目になる。所詮は余所者である。それこそ生粋の京都人という人達からしてみれば、私がここで熱心に京都について語っていること自体が、随分と憫笑を誘う話であるのかもしれない。しかし私は、今書いたようなことに気づき始めてから、以前よりもずっとこの町のことが好きになった。

嘗て子供の頃に訪れた京都は、私を観光都市としての顔で丁寧に迎えてくれ、洗練された作り笑顔で見送ってくれた。大学時代に数年間をここで過ごすこととなった時には、学生の町としての顔で大らかに受け容れ、文句一つ言わずに好きなことをさせてくれた。

そして今、それらの別々の顔とのつきあいが一通り終えたあとになって、私は初めてその奥に秘せられた本当の顔とも言うべきものを少しずつ窺い知るようになった。それは思いの外、かなしい顔だった。なるほど、余所者に見せて良い顔ではなかった。けれども私は、それを美しいと感じた。そして、それを隠そうとすることを、やはり奥ゆかしいと思った。

8 | 京都に住み始めて、私は今年で九年目になる this year will be the ninth year since I started living in Kyoto ■ 所詮は余所者である in the final analysis, I am an outsider ■ それこそ生粋の京都人という人達からしてみれば doubtless, then, from the perspective of born-and-bred Kyotoites ■ 私がここで熱心に京都について語っていること自体 my passionately talking about Kyoto here in itself ■ 随分と憫笑を誘う話であるのかもしれない might well invite a pitying smile ■ 私は、今書いたようなことに気づき始めてから after beginning to notice what I have just written about above ■ 以前よりもずっとこの町のことが好きになった I have come to love this city even more than before

9 | 嘗て子供の頃に訪れた京都は the Kyoto I visited previously as a child ■ 私を観光都市としての顔で丁寧に迎えてくれ politely greeted me with the face of a tourist city and ■ 洗練された作り笑顔で見送ってくれ saw me off with a refined and carefully constructed smile ■ 大学時代に数年間をここで過ごすこととなった時には when I came to spend several years here in my university days ■ 学生の町としての顔で大らかに受け容れ she accepted me graciously with the face of a college town and ■ 文句一つ言わずに好きなことをさせてくれた let me act as I liked without a single word of complaint ■ そして今 and now ■ それらの別々の顔とのつきあいが一通り終えたあとになって after my relationships with those individual faces have by and large come to an end ■ 私は初めてその奥に秘せられた本当の顔とも言うべきものを少しずつ窺い知るようになった I have gradually begun to perceive, for the first time in my life, what ought be called the real face [of Kyoto] hidden behind the façade [of those other faces] ■ それは思いの外、かなしい顔だった it was an unexpectedly sad face ■ なるほど、余所者に見せて良い顔ではなかった indeed, it was not the face she should have shown to a stranger ■ 私は、それを美しいと感じた I found it beautiful ■ それを隠そうとすることを、やはり奥ゆかしいと思った I thought that her effort to hide that sad face was elegantly self-effacing

リービ英雄

Levy Hideo

「文学者」の国に、ぼくがいる Living in the Land of the *Bungakusha*

バカヤロー You idiot! ▪ お前なんか、文学者じゃない you're no *bungakusha*! ▪ （一九八〇年代の日本の文芸誌に載った有名な座談会の結末から）(from the conclusion of a famous round-table talk featured in a Japanese literary magazine in the 1980s)

1 日本とアメリカの間を行ったり来たりして生活していた時代 at a time when I was traveling back and forth between Japan and America ▪ 日本で耳に入ったことばをアメリカ人に説明することがよくあった I often had occasion to explain to Americans words that I'd heard in Japan ▪ 特に文学に関する、アメリカとは微妙に違ういろいろの発想や表現 various ideas and expressions, especially ones related to literature, which were subtly different from [those in] America ▪ アメリカの大学で at American universities ▪ 伝達することができたとき when I was able to [effectively] communicate ▪ 一種のよろこびを感じることもあった I felt a kind of joy ▪ どこまでが翻訳可能か to what extent is it possible to translate them? ▪ どこからが翻訳不可能か from what point is it impossible to translate them? ▪ 翻訳不可能なものはなぜそうなのか why are the impossible ones so impossible? ▪ たびたび考えさせられたのである I was frequently given cause to think...

2 伝達することができたとき when I [successfully] got these ideas and expressions across [to others] ▪ よろこびに近い満足感を味わった I experienced a sense of satisfaction very close to joy ▪ どうしても伝達できない、あるいはどうしても翻訳できないと分ったときにこそ it was precisely at those times when I realized I just could not convey something, or just could not translate it ▪ かえって [that] all the more ▪ 日本の中で何となく通用している概念を正確に問うことができたのである I was able to make a closer inquiry into [certain] concepts that are generally taken for granted in Japan

となく通用している概念を正確に問うことができたのである。あまりにも当然なことだが、そのプロセスの中に当然問われるとはかぎらない概念を問うてみることが、面白い。

たとえば、日本では、ある人がある人に対して、「あいつなんか文学者じゃない」と言ったコメントを、アメリカで説明しようとした時、日本であれだけこだわっている文学者という言葉を、一体どうやって英語に翻訳できるかという問題にぶつかった。しかも「あの人は文学者である」というより、「あいつは文学者じゃない」と否定された方が、逆に「文学者」というものが浮び上ってくる。

そしてその「文学者」は、実は英語では存在しないカテゴリーであることも、浮び上るのだ。

You are not a……とか、That guy's no……そのような文章を完成させる名詞が、どうしても見つからなかった。

もちろん、日本語の「文学者」は、文学の単なる学者を意味するだけではないから、──オロジストとか──シストにもならないし、ただの scholar of 生物学者のように、──オロジストとか──シストにもならないし、ただの scholar of

■ あまりにも当然なことだが needless to say ■ そのプロセスの中に in the process ■ 当然問われるとはかぎらない概念を問うてみることが、面白い it is [always] interesting to try examining concepts that do not obviously call for examination

3 | ある人がある人に対して、「あいつなんか文学者じゃない」と言ったコメント the comment made by one person about another, "He's no *bungakusha*" ■ 説明しようとした時 when I tried to explain ■ 日本であれだけこだわっている文学者という言葉 that term "*bungakusha*" that people set such store by in Japan ■ 一体どうやって英語に翻訳できるか how on earth does one translate [it] into English? ■ …という問題にぶつかった I ran into the problem of… ■ …というより than it does with… ■ 「あいつは文学者じゃない」と否定された方が、逆に「文学者」というものが浮び上ってくる the image of a "*bungakusha*" comes into sharper relief with the negative form "He's no *bungakusha*"

4 | その「文学者」は、実は英語では存在しないカテゴリーであることも the fact, too, that "*bungakusha*" is a category that does not exist in English

5 | そのような文章を完成させる名詞が、どうしても見つからなかった I just could not find the right noun to complete such sentences

6 | 日本語の「文学者」は、文学の単なる学者を意味するだけではないから because the Japanese word "*bungakusha*" does not only denote a scholar of literature ■ 生物学者のように、——オロジストとか——シストにもならないし one cannot just add "-ologist" or "-ist" as in "biologist," and ■ ただの scholar of literature ではだめだ simply [saying] "scholar of literature" will not do

literature ではだめだ。文学の学者の中には「文学者」もたまにはいるが。

特に否定形の「あいつは文学者じゃない」といったとき、「学者」とは逆に he's no writer に似た響きもあるが、そう訳してしまうと、「あいつはもの書きではない」ということになる。「文学者」はみんなもの書きである。しかし、もの書きはみんな「文学者」だとはかぎらない。

ぼくの理解でいうと、日本語の「文学者」は、文学を研究する人も、文学を批評する人も、文学を創作する人も含まれている。何となく文学を「道」とする、というニュアンスが強い。

英語には literatus ということばがある。日本文学に通じているあるアメリカ人が、日本語の「文学者」を、その literatus として翻訳したのをぼくは聞いたことがある。何となく「文学をする人」という意味にはなっているが、literatus は、文学を「道」とするよりも文学を「趣味」とする人という意味合いが強くて、実際には「文人」という日本語を英訳するのにその literatus がよく使われているのも事実だ。「文学者」が持っているまじ

■ 文学の学者の中には「文学者」もたまにはいるが although once in a while there are *bungakusha* among scholars of literature

7 | 特に否定形の「あいつは文学者じゃない」といったとき particularly when you state it in the negative form "He's no *bungakusha*" ■「学者」とは逆に…に似た響きもあるが the "*gakusha*" has, on the contrary, more of the ring of…but ■ そう訳してしまうと if one goes ahead and translates it like that ■「あいつはもの書きではない」ということになる it means "He's no *monokaki*" ■「文学者」はみんなもの書きである *bungakusha* are all *monokaki* ■ しかし、もの書きはみんな「文学者」だとはかぎらない however, not all *monokaki* are necessarily *bungakusha*

8 | ぼくの理解でいうと as I understand it ■ 文学を研究する人も people who do research in literature and ■ 文学を批評する人も people who do literary criticism and ■ 文学を創作する人も people who create literature ■ 含まれている are [all] included ■ 何となく文学を「道」とする、というニュアンスが強い ["*bungakusha*"] has the strong nuance of someone who somehow or other follows "the way" of literature

9 | 英語には…ということばがある in English there is the word… ■ 日本文学に通じているあるアメリカ人 a certain American expert on Japanese literature ■ 日本語の「文学者」を、その literatus として翻訳した had translated the Japanese "*bungakusha*" as "literatus" ■ ぼくは聞いたことがある I once heard ■ 何となく「文学をする人」という意味にはなっているが it does sort of have the meaning of "a person who does literature," but ■ …よりも more than… ■ 文学を「趣味」とする人という意味合いが強くて it has a strong sense of "a person who does literature as a hobby," and ■ 実際には「文人」という日本語を英訳するのにその literatus がよく使われているのも事実だ it is also a fact that "literatus" is often used when translating the Japanese "*bunjin*" into English ■「文学者」が持っているまじめさを欠いている [the English "literatus"] lacks the [element of] seriousness of "*bungakusha*"

めさを欠いている。he's no literatus とは誰も言わないし、かりに言ったとしても「あいつなんか文人じゃない」というコッケイな意味になってしまうのだろう。

アイデンティティーの用語としての「文学者」にあたる英語は、どうも存在しない。

écrivain というフランス語があるけれども、それは「書く人」という意味で、「文学者」がもっているあの「読む人、書く人、もしくは読んだり書いたりすることによって生きる人」という不思議なあいまいさはないようだ。écrivain はむしろ「作家」である。「あいつは作家じゃない」という日本語は耳にするが、それは「あいつは文学者じゃない」とはちょっと違うのではないだろうか。「あいつは文学者じゃない」と日本語で言ったとき、「文学者」たりうるかどうかという判断の中には、どのように書いているかだけではなく、どのように読んでいるかという資質も問われている。そして読み手の資質と書き手の資質を結びつけて、どちらの行為も超越した「何か」が問われているのではないだろうか。

■ …とは誰も言わないし no one would say [in English]…and ■ かりに言ったとしても even if someone were to say it ■「あいつなんか文人じゃない」というコッケイな意味になってしまうのだろう it would probably have the comical oddness of "He's no *bunjin*"

10 アイデンティティーの用語としての as a term of personal identity ■「文学者」にあたる英語は an English word corresponding to "*bungakusha*" ■ どうも存在しない just does not exist ■ écrivain というフランス語があるけれども there is the word *écrivain* in French, but ■ それは「書く人」という意味で that means "someone who writes" and ■「文学者」がもっている…という不思議なあいまいさはないようだ it doesn't seem to have the bizarre vagueness that "*bungakusha*" has ■ あの「読む人、書く人、もしくは読んだり書いたりすることによって生きる人」that ambiguity of "a person who reads, or a person who writes, or a person who lives by reading and/or writing" ■ écrivain はむしろ「作家」である an "*écrivain*," rather, is a "*sakka*" ■「あいつは作家じゃない」という日本語は耳にするが one sometimes hears "He's no *sakka*" in Japanese, but ■ それは…とはちょっと違うのではないだろうか isn't that somewhat different from…? ■「あいつは本を何冊書いても何も分っていない」というニュアンスもありうるとすれば if one accepts that there is the nuance "even though he's written several books, he's completely clueless [about Japanese literature]" ■「文学者」たりうるかどうかという判断の中には in judging whether he is fully a "*bungakusha*" ■ どのように書いているかだけではなく、どのように読んでいるかという資質も問われている in question are his qualifications as to not just how he writes but also how he reads ■ 読み手の資質と書き手の資質を結びつけて linking his qualifications as a reader and his qualifications as a writer and ■ どちらの行為も超越した「何か」が問われているのではないだろうか isn't there a certain "something" at issue that supersedes either of those acts?

「文学者」はいうまでもなく、近代のカテゴリーである。近代以前には「歌人」や「俳人」はいたが、「文学者」はいなかった。そして日本近代の多くのアイデンティティーのように、そこには民族や国籍の条件もついてしまった（日本文学にたずさわる外国人はよく「日本文学研究、」というラベルを張られている。近代の常識の中では、日本国籍を有しない人は日本文学の内部において「文学者」になりうるとは誰も考えもしなかったようだ）。アメリカには「作家」もいるし、「研究家」もいる。しかし、「文学者」はいない。

ぼくはある時期、単なる「作家」ではなく「文学者」になりたいと渇望した。

「お前は文学者じゃない」という日本語の侮蔑が英語ではなかなか伝わらない。逆に、アメリカの作家が他の作家を徹底的にけなしたときの米語を、どうやって和訳できるかという問題について、考えさせられたこともある。

アメリカ文学には、そのような侮蔑の「名言」はいくつかある。面白いことに、それら

11 | いうまでもなく it goes without saying ▪ 近代のカテゴリーである is a modern category ▪ 近代以前には in pre-modern times ▪「歌人」や「俳人」 "*kajin*" (tanka poets) and "*haijin*" (haiku poets) ▪ 日本近代の多くのアイデンティティーのように as is the case for much of Japanese modern identity ▪ そこには民族や国籍の条件もついてしまった conditions of ethnicity and nationality went with it ▪（日本文学にたずさわる外国人はよく「日本文学研究家」というラベルを張られている (foreigners engaged in Japanese literature are often labeled "Japanese literature *researchers*" ▪ 近代の常識の中では in the modern conventional wisdom ▪ 日本国籍を有しない人は日本文学の内部において「文学者」になりうるとは誰も考えもしなかったようだ) it appears that it never occurred to anyone that a person not holding Japanese citizenship could ever be a "*bungakusha*" and insider in Japanese literature）

12 | ある時期 during a certain period ▪ 単なる「作家」ではなく「文学者」になりたいと渇望した hungered to be not a mere "*sakka*" but a "*bungakusha*"

13 | …という日本語の侮蔑が英語ではなかなか伝わらない the contempt of…in Japanese is quite difficult to convey in English ▪ 逆に conversely ▪ アメリカの作家が他の作家を徹底的にけなしたときの米語 the English that American *sakka* use when they denigrate other writers ▪ どうやって和訳できるかという問題について about the problem of how to put into Japanese ▪ 考えさせられたこともある I have also had occasion to think about

14 | そのような侮蔑の「名言」はいくつかある there are several such "famous remarks" of the insulting type ▪ 面白いことに interestingly enough

の、ほとんどが書くという行為自体をめぐる侮蔑から成り立っているのである。アメリカ

の作家同士が衝突するときに、「あの人の書くものはすべてうそだ、コンマやピリオドま

でもうそだ」といったことばを放つように。個人的攻撃のときもかならずてにをはを取り

上げる、つまり、書く資格そのものが問われるのである。

他の作家を片づける最も有名な例は、おそらくそのままでは日本語に翻訳しにくい例で

もあるだろう。ちょうど作家がはじめてテレビに出るようになった一九五〇年代に、ノー

マン・メイラーとトルーマン・カポーティが（世界ではじめてだったのだろうか）作家の

テレビ対談をやり、その中で、ちょうどそのとき話題になっていたケルアックの『オン・

ザ・ロード』についてどう思うかという質問に対して、カポーティが即座に、

That's not writing. It is only typing.

と答えてしまった。

アメリカ文学史を少しかじったことがある人なら誰でも知っている、あまりにも有名な

「暴言」なのだが、そんな短いが究極的な「批判」を、どうして日本語に訳せるか、ぼ

■ それらの、ほとんどが書くという行為自体をめぐる侮蔑から成り立っているのである almost all of them are made up of insults concerning the *act* of writing itself ■ アメリカの作家同士が衝突するときに when American authors clash ■「あの人の書くものはすべてうそだ "everything that person writes is a lie ■ コンマやピリオドまでもうそだ」down to the very last comma and period" ■ といったことばを放つように for example, letting loose such words as… ■ 個人的攻撃のときも in personal attacks as well ■ かならずてにをはを取り上げる they unfailingly touch on the *mechanics* of writing (lit., "on the usage of particles and prepositions") ■ 書く資格そのものが問われるのである the very qualification of writing itself is questioned

15 | 他の作家を片づける最も有名な例は the most famous example of annihilating another author ■ おそらくそのままでは日本語に翻訳しにくい例でもあるだろう is probably also an example that would be hard to translate as is into Japanese ■ ちょうど作家がはじめてテレビに出るようになった一九五〇年代に in the 1950s, exactly when writers first started to appear on television ■ ノーマン・メイラーとトルーマン・カポーティ Norman Mailer and Truman Capote ■（世界ではじめてだったのだろうか）(probably for the first time in the world) ■ 作家のテレビ対談をやり took part in a TV talk show of writers ■ その中で during which ■ ちょうどそのとき話題になっていたケルアックの『オン・ザ・ロード』についてどう思うかという質問に対して in response to the question of what he thought of Kerouac's *On the Road*, which at that time was attracting much attention ■ 即座に like a shot

16 | …と答えてしまった replied…

17 | アメリカ文学史を少しかじったことがある人なら誰でも知っている、あまりにも有名な「暴言」なのだが it is a classic "low blow" familiar to anyone who knows even a smattering of the history of American literature, but ■ そんな短いが究極的な「批判」を、どうして日本語に訳せるか how that short but ultimate "criticism" could be translated into Japanese

くは日米の間を行ったり来たりしている間に、何度も思いをめぐらせたことがある。

18 あれはライティングじゃない。単なるタイピングにしかすぎない。

19 とカタカナでごまかせば、今の日本人にも何となく分かる人は少なくないだろうが、そうごまかしたところで、なぜケルアックがカポーティの毒舌によってたちまちアメリカ文学のパンテオンから門前払いになったかはピンと来ないのではないだろうか。

20 あれは書いているんじゃない。ただタイプライターを打っているだけだ。

21 と翻訳すれば、書く行為を問題にした失格宣言の内容が伝わり、「あいつは文学者じゃない」との意味合いの違いもはっきりしてくる。

22 問題は、その writing は動名詞であって、書いているという行為でもあれば書いていた

■ ぼくは日米の間を行ったり来たりしている間に while I was going back and forth between America and Japan ■ 何度も思いをめぐらせたことがある I would often turn over in my mind [the question of...]

18 あれはライティングじゃない that's not *raitingu* ■ 単なるタイピングにしかすぎない it's no more than *taipingu*

19 とカタカナでごまかせば if one thus finesses it by using loan words from English ■ 今の日本人にも何となく分かる人は少なくないだろうが not a few Japanese now would generally grasp the meaning, but ■ そうごまかしたところで despite such fancy footwork [in the interest of producing a translation] ■ なぜケルアックがカポーティの毒舌によってたちまちアメリカ文学のパンテオンから門前払いになったかは why Kerouac was in an instant refused admittance to the pantheon of American literature because of Capote's stinging remark ■ ピンと来ないのではないだろうか won't be obvious, will it?

20 あれは書いているんじゃない that's not (the act of) *writing* ■ ただタイプライターを打っているだけだ it's only striking the keys of a typewriter

21 書く行為を問題にした失格宣言の内容が伝わり the content of a declaration of disqualification making a problem of the *act* of writing will be conveyed, and ■「あいつは文学者じゃない」との意味合いの違いもはっきりしてくる the difference in meaning between this and "He's no *bungakusha*" will also become clear

22 問題は、その writing は the problem is that that word "writing" ■ 動名詞であって is a gerund, and as such ■ 書いているという行為でもあれば書いていたことの結果としての、あの時代ではまだあまり使われなかった「テキスト」にはなっていない、ということにもなる [Capote's use of it] implies that, while Kerouac's work is not only not a [proper] act of writing, it is also not even a "text"—a term not yet in wide use then—which is to say the result of the act of writing

ことの結果としての、あの時代ではまだあまり使われなかった「テキスト」にはなってい

ない、ということにもなる。しかし、もっと正確に訳せば、文章にはなっていない、と

か、文体がない、という以前に、「あれは文ではない」、強いていえば人間の行為、あるい

は人間が行為したその結果にはなっていない、猿のようにタイプライターのキーを任意に

打ちまくったたぐいのものにすぎない、というニュアンスが含まれている。

カポーティの「批判」は、それだけ苦々しいものだったし、「猿がタイプライターを百

万年打てば『ハムレット』もいつかは出てくる」という「文」の究極を暗示したもう一つ

の「名言」と妙に響き合っている。

カポーティの毒舌によってケルアックの全面否定がなされ、おまけに初期のテレビのも

つ衝撃的なインパクトによって、それもすぐ「定評」になった。しかし、日本語から逆

に考え直すと、「文学者じゃない」というこちらの全面否定と違って、アメリカでは書く

ことをめぐる生産の過程、ないしは生産の過程の結果をひたすら指摘していることが目立

ち、最も痛切な否定としてはいささか狭いというきらいもあるのではないだろうか。そう

■ もっと正確に訳せば if we were to translate it more precisely ■ 文章にはなっていない、とか、文体がない、という以前に even prior to [the problem of Kerouac's work] not being a proper piece of writing or not having any style ■ 「あれは文ではない」"it isn't even sentences" ■ 強いていえば when it comes right down to it ■ 人間の行為、あるいは人間が行為したその結果にはなっていない it's neither a human act nor the product of a human act ■ 猿のようにタイプライターのキーを任意に打ちまくったたぐいのものにすぎない it's no more than if, say, monkeys had randomly struck the keys of a typewriter ■ というニュアンスが含まれている it has such a nuance

23 カポーティの「批判」は、それだけ苦々しいものだったし Capote's "criticism" was just that harsh and ■ 「猿がタイプライターを百万年打てば『ハムレット』もいつかは出てくる」"if monkeys typed for a million years, someday they would produce *Hamlet*" ■ という「文」の究極を暗示したもう一つの「名言」と妙に響き合っている has subtle overtones of another "famous remark" suggesting the extreme of "writing," to the effect that…

24 カポーティの毒舌によって by Capote's sharp tongue ■ ケルアックの全面否定がなされ Kerouac suffered a total dismissal and ■ おまけに in addition ■ 初期のテレビのもつ衝撃的なインパクトによって because of the dramatic impact of TV in its early days ■ それもすぐ「定評」になった that [of a non-qualifying writer] soon became his established reputation ■ 日本語から逆に考え直すと if we consider [Capote's criticism] from the perspective of Japanese ■ …というこちらの全面否定と違って [we find that] it differs from the total dismissal of…and ■ アメリカでは書くことをめぐる生産の過程、ないしは生産の過程の結果をひたすら指摘していることが目立ち it is striking that the American example points exclusively to the process of production, or to the results of the process of production, and ■ 最も痛切な否定としてはいささか狭いというきらいもあるのではないだろうか as the most cutting dismissal of all, doesn't it lean toward being rather *narrow*?

25

感じるのは、「文学者じゃない」という英訳不可能なニュアンスに相当する響きがまった
くないからだろう。英語と日本語の間を行ったり来たりしすぎたから、ぼくはそんな奇
妙なことを考えだしたのか。右の名言について日本語で考えれば考えるほど「作家」の
最高峰に置かれるカポーティは、もしかすると「文学者ではなかった」かも知れない、と
疑いはじめる。そして産業国アメリカの絶頂期における生産の結果としてもっぱら強
調された writing は、「文」にも「écriture」にもない単純さ、もろさがあったことは、今

となって見えるのである。

「歌人」や「俳人」、そしてヨーロッパの前近代でそれに相当する「書く人」のカテゴ
リーを断ち切ってでき上った、アメリカ文学の純然たる「ライティング」のエネルギー
の中で、最も純然たる「ライター」であったトルーマン・カポーティの、「文学者」では
ない「作家」のキャリアを見ても、アメリカの意外なもろさがうかがえる。抒情的な中
編作家でデビューしたカポーティが、その最高の傑作として『冷血』というノンフィク
ションを上梓してから、『かなえられた祈り』という最後の失敗作で「文」の崩壊を晩年

「文学者」の国に、ぼくがいる　126

■ そう感じるのは…からだろう that one feels that way is probably because… ■ …という英訳不可能なニュアンスに相当する響きがまったくない it doesn't have any echo at all corresponding to the untranslatable (into English) nuances of… ■ 英語と日本語の間を行ったり来たりしすぎたから maybe it was because I was moving back and forth too much between [the worlds of] English and Japanese ■ ぼくはそんな奇妙なことを考えだしたのか that I began thinking about such an odd thing ■ 右の名言について日本語で考えれば考えるほど the more I think about [Capote's] famous words above in Japanese ■ 「作家」の最高峰に置かれるカポーティは、もしかすると「文学者ではなかった」かも知れない、と疑いはじめる the more I start to wonder if Capote, who stands at the pinnacle of "*sakka*," might not actually have "been no *bungakusha*" himself ■ 産業国アメリカの絶頂期における生産の結果としてもっぱら強調された writing は as for the [American] "writing," which was wholly regarded as a product in the peak period of Industrial America ■ 「文」にも「écriture」にもない単純さ、もろさがあったことは、今となって見えるのである it is now evident that it had a simplicity and fragility not present in either "*bun*" or "*écriture*"

25 「歌人」や「俳人」、そしてヨーロッパの前近代でそれに相当する「書く人」のカテゴリーを断ち切ってでき上がった、アメリカ文学の純然たる「ライティング」のエネルギーの中で amidst the energy of pure-and-simple "writing" in American literature, which developed cut off from the "*kajin*" or "*haijin*" [in Japan] or the corresponding "*kaku hito*" found in premodern Europe ■ 最も純然たる「ライター」であったトルーマン・カポーティの、「文学者」ではない「作家」のキャリアを見ても even by looking at the career of Truman Capote, a "*sakka*" and not a "*bungakusha*," who was the quintessential pure-and-simple "writer" ■ アメリカの意外なもろさがうかがえる we can glimpse the remarkable fragility of America ■ 抒情的な中編作家でデビューしたカポーティ Capote, who had made his debut as the author of lyrical novellas ■ その最高の傑作として『冷血』というノンフィクションを上梓してから after publishing his great masterpiece, the nonfiction work *In Cold Blood* ■ 『かなえられた祈り』という最後の失敗作で「文」の崩壊を晩年に体験してしまった experienced in his later years the disintegration of his "*bun*" in his last work, the failure *Answered Prayers*

に体験してしまった。しかもそれが「書くこと」の必然的な崩壊であるかのように、そんな結末を体験したのだった。しかもそれが「書くこと」の必然的な崩壊であるかのように、そんいほどのモノの生産性がたった三十年間、たったの一世代で崩壊したのと、不思議に重なるようにも見える。

「文学者」ということばはやがて日本語から消えてゆくのだろうか。経済大国日本は、経済絶頂期のアメリカと同じように「ライター」だけの国になってしまうのだろうか。それとも、近代の民族主義の文脈の中で生まれた「文学者」は、近代の後に、別の意味合いをもって生まれ変わって、生きつづけるのだろうか。

もし「文学者」が現代語として使えるとすれば、それは日本語の表現の歴史を身につけて、その中で生きる――読み手としても書き手としても――という意味として一度純化される必要があるかも知れない。

日本語の歴史、そしてその中から生まれた日本語の表現の必然的な方向づけは、いま

■ それが「書くこと」の必然的な崩壊であるかのように as if it were an inevitable breakdown of doing "writing" ■ そんな結末 that kind of end ■ まぶしいほどのモノの生産性がたった三十年間、たったの一世代で崩壊したのと with the collapse of a dazzling [degree of] productivity in only three decades, or in only one generation ■ 不思議に重なるようにも見える seems to uncannily overlap

26 「文学者」ということばはやがて日本語から消えてゆくのだろうか will the word *bungakusha* eventually disappear from Japanese? ■ 経済大国日本は Japan, the economic power ■ 経済絶頂期のアメリカと同じように just like America at its economic peak ■ 「ライター」だけの国になってしまうのだろうか become a country with only "writers"? ■ それとも or else ■ 近代の民族主義の文脈の中で生まれた「文学者」は the "*bungakusha*" born in the context of modern nationalism ■ 近代の後に in the postmodern period ■ 別の意味合いをもって生まれ変わって、生きつづける survive after being reborn with a [new and] different significance?

27 もし「文学者」が現代語として使えるとすれば if "*bungakusha*" is to be used as a contemporary word ■ それは日本語の表現の歴史を身につけて、その中で生きる——読み手としても書き手としても——という意味として defined as mastering the history of expression in the Japanese language and living within it—both as a reader and as a writer ■ 一度純化される必要があるかも知れない it may be necessary to refine it

28 日本語の歴史 the history of the Japanese language ■ そしてその中から生まれた日本語の表現の必然的な方向づけは and the inevitable orientation of Japanese expression which was born out of it ■ いうまでもなく needless to say

でもなく、西洋語のそれとも中国語や韓国語のそれとも違う。近代国家が押しつける意味づけと違って、日本の「文学者」は自分を「日本」の代表と思いこむことはできなくなるだろう。が、「文学者」がいるということが、多分、日本の特性であることに変わりはないだろう。日本がアメリカのように「作家だけ」の国になってしまう可能性が現実にはある。が、アメリカ（とか中国、とか韓国）が「文学者」の国になる可能性はゼロだろう。

「あいつは文学者じゃない」といったとき、「あいつには日本民族の感性を代表する資格はない」という意味から、「あいつには日本語の歴史も分っていないし、日本語独自の可能性も理解していない」というような意味に変われば、「文学者である」ことと「文学者ではない」という区別がむしろよりはっきりとした、そしてより本物の定義に近づくのだろう。そして日本列島の住民のわずかなマイノリティにすぎないが、「文学者」は世界との正真な関わり方、つまり一つの「アイデンティティー」として成り立ちつづけるだろう。

■ 西洋語のそれとも中国語や韓国語のそれとも違う differs from that of Western languages and also from that of languages like Chinese and Korean ■ 近代国家が押しつける意味づけと違って unlike the meaning imposed by the modern nation-state ■ 日本の「文学者」は自分を「日本」の代表と思いこむことはできなくなるだろう Japan's *bungakusha* will probably become unable to assume that they themselves represent Japan ■ が、「文学者」がいるということが but the existence of "*bungakusha*" ■ 多分、日本の特性であることに変わりはないだろう will probably not change in the respect of being a distinguishing feature of Japan ■ 日本がアメリカのように「作家だけ」の国になってしまう可能性が現実にはあるが it is true that there is a possibility for Japan to become, like America, a country with "only *sakka*," but ■ アメリカ（とか中国、とか韓国）が「文学者」の国になる可能性はゼロだろう there is zero possibility that America (or China or Korea, or any other country) will become a country of "*bungakusha*"

29 「あいつには日本民族の感性を代表する資格はない」という意味から from the meaning "He is [utterly] unqualified to represent the [unique] sensibility of the Japanese people" ■ 「あいつには日本語の歴史も分っていないし、日本語独自の可能性も理解していない」というような意味に to something along the lines of "He doesn't know the history of the Japanese language and he has no understanding of the unique possibilities of [expression in] Japanese" ■ 「文学者である」ことと「文学者ではない」という区別がむしろよりはっきりとした、そしてより本物の定義に近づくのだろう then we would be closer to a more genuine definition [of *bungakusha*] in which the distinction between "He is a *bungakusha*" and "He isn't a *bungakusha*" would be clearer ■ 日本列島の住民のわずかなマイノリティにすぎないが although being only a very small minority of the [total] residents of the Japanese Archipelago ■ 「文学者」は世界との正真な関わり方、つまり一つの「アイデンティティー」として成り立ちつづけるだろう "*bungakusha*" would continue to be an authentic way of relating to the world, that is, would constitute a particular identity

現実の生活の中で、日本語の表現者は、英訳可能な「作家」と英訳不可能な「文学者」

という二つの「アイデンティティー」の中で生きるだろう。日本語の表現者にとって、自

分の仕事には外国語で説明できる面とそうでない面が常にあるはずだ。一度は「近代語

化」を経過してしまったコトバで表現をするのだから、それは当り前なことである。し

かしそれは今の日本ではかならずしも自覚されているとはいえない。

「文学者である」とか「文学者ではない」という日本語を外へ持ち出して、外のまぶしい

光にさらしたとき、はじめて自覚できる、というか、はじめて自覚を強いられるのではな

いだろうか。

ぼく自身は、最近、アメリカの新聞記者から、「あなたのアイデンティティーはけっ

きょく何ですか」と聞かれたことがある。聞いた人はジャーナリストだから、おそらく

は、「最終的に、あなたの帰属する文化はアメリカなのか、日本なのか」という意味だっ

たのだろう。

ぼくは少し考えて、「ジャパニーズ・ライター」と答えてしまった。日本の作家、日本

30 現実の生活の中で in their actual lives ▪ 日本語の表現者は those using a Japanese form of [literary] expression ▪ 英訳可能な「作家」と英訳不可能な「文学者」という二つの「アイデンティティー」の中で生きるだろう probably live among the two identities of the translatable "*sakka*" and the untranslatable "*bungakusha*" ▪ 日本語の表現者にとって for those expressing themselves in Japanese ▪ 自分の仕事には外国語で説明できる面とそうでない面が常にあるはずだ there is, no doubt, always a part of their work that can be translated into a foreign language and a part that cannot be ▪ 一度は「近代語化」を経過してしまったコトバで表現をするのだから since they express themselves in a language that has undergone "modernization" ▪ それは当り前なことである that is only natural ▪ しかしそれは今の日本ではかならずしも自覚されているとはいえない however, it cannot be said that in present-day Japan people are necessarily aware of that

31 …という日本語を外へ持ち出して、外のまぶしい光にさらしたとき when the Japanese expressions…are taken outside and exposed to the bright light there ▪ はじめて自覚できる、というか、はじめて自覚を強いられるのではないだろうか isn't it only then that one can become aware of that, or rather, is forced to become aware of it?

32 ぼく自身は、最近 I myself recently ▪ アメリカの新聞記者から by an American newspaper reporter ▪「あなたのアイデンティティーはけっきょく何ですか」と聞かれたことがある was asked, "What, after all, is your identity?" ▪ 聞いた人はジャーナリストだから since it was a journalist asking ▪ おそらくは、「最終的に、あなたの帰属する文化はアメリカなのか、日本なのか」という意味だったのだろう probably the meaning was "In the final analysis, do you belong to American culture or Japanese culture?"

33 ぼくは少し考えて after thinking a little ▪「ジャパニーズ・ライター」と答えてしまった I answered "Japanese writer" ▪ 日本の作家、日本語の作家、あるいは日本文学の作家 [that would be] a writer of Japan, a writer of Japanese, or a writer of Japanese literature

語の作家、あるいは日本文学の作家。

今思うと、そう答えたとき、ぼくはアメリカの常識に合わせすぎていたのかもしれない

と反省をしている。

もっと素直に答えればよかった。

Maybe a bungakusha と。

34 今思うと thinking about it now ■ そう答えたとき when I answered that way ■ ぼくはアメリカの常識に合わせすぎていたのかもしれないと反省をしている I wonder if I wasn't fitting myself too much to American assumptions

35 もっと素直に答えればよかった I should have answered straight out: